PHR® and
Professional in Human Resources
Resources

Complete Practice Tests

Sandra M. Reed, SPHR

SYBEX®
A Wiley Brand

Senior Acquisitions Editor: Kenyon Brown
Development Editor: Kelly Talbot
Senior Production Editor: Christine O'Connor
Technical Editor: Karin M. Hill
Copy Editor: Kim Wimpsett
Content Enablement and Operations Manager: Pete Gaughan
Production Manager: Kathleen Wisor
Executive Editor: Jim Minatel
Book Designers: Judy Fung and Bill Gibson
Proofreader: Louise Watson, Word One New York
Indexer: Jack Lewis
Project Coordinator, Cover: Brent Savage
Cover Designer: Wiley
Cover Image: Getty Images Inc. / Jeremy Woodhouse

ISBN: 978-1-111-942680-6
ISBN: 978-1-111-942689-9 (ebk.)
ISBN: 978-1-111-942671-4 (ebk.)

Manufactured in the United States of America

This one is for you.

Acknowledgments

I used to think that the creative process was quite romantic in many ways. After all, as inhabitants of a quirky world made up of inspired leaps and profound discoveries, writers, I thought, must guard their process closely. I could not have been more wrong! Taking a concept from idea to delivery requires the (sometimes) herculean efforts of many talented individuals, the least of which is the author. To the editors Kenyon Brown, Kelly Talbot, Kim Wimpsett, Karin Hill, Pete Gaughan, and the countless other hands that touched this text, I give my utmost respect and gratitude. Their thoughtful guidance and professionalism carried this book through many iterations, contributing to what I believe is the best version of this material to date!

To my clients, I am equally indebted, for it is in their people-and-process-centric laboratories that I am able to explore so many of the critical HR systems and behavioral science practices that inform the basis of the PHR and SPHR exams.

I would also like to acknowledge the consummate professionals at the Human Resource Certification Institute. Their dedication of purpose to the field of HR is clearly embedded in their quest for excellence, and I feel privileged to help bring the HRBoK to life through applied practice.

Finally, Ralph Waldo Emerson noted, "In my walks, every man I meet is my superior in some way, and in that I learn from him." This could not be more true of my family, friends, mentors, clients, colleagues, employees, coaches, and students, who daily show me yet another perspective of the important work of our lives. I am fortunate to know each of you.

About the Author

Sandra M. Reed, SPHR, has more than 20 years of experience in the field of human resources. With a bachelor's degree in I-O psychology and her graduate work in organizational leadership in progress, she has led the work of many professionals in the development of the Human Resource Body of Knowledge. This culminated in the bringing together of HR thought leaders of today to share their insights and technical proficiencies in HRCI's *A Guide to the Human Resource Body of Knowledge (HRBoK)*, Second Edition, published in 2017.

Sandra is a certified practitioner of the MBTI Personality Assessment and an endorsed trainer of the Leadership Training for Managers (LTM) program with Dale Carnegie. Additionally, she leads a team of human resource professionals for a manufacturing company in the Central Valley of California, where she is also an active member of the local HR community.

Find her on the Web at http://epochresources.com.

About the Technical Editor

Karin M. Hill, MBA, SPHR, SHRM-SCP, acquired extensive experience managing human resources and organizational development departments. Her HR experience—from entry level to executive—was gained while working for international companies, an outplacement/career development/team-building consulting business, and major Midwest health systems in St. Louis and Kansas.

She earned her BA in journalism and government from Southern Illinois University at Edwardsville and her MBA from St. Louis University. Hill is currently on the continuing education adjunct faculty at Midlands Technical College, providing facilitation in the leadership and employee development areas. She also serves as a human resources and organizational development consultant for small businesses in the Columbia, South Carolina, area. She holds several national training certifications as well as the SPHR and SHRM-SCP certifications.

Currently, Hill consults with and provides leadership, employee, and customer service training for multiple organizations, including manufacturing and service industries, healthcare and related health services, insurance companies, educational institutions, and government entities and agencies at the city, county, and state levels.

Contents at a Glance

Contents

Contents

Professional in Human Resources (PHR)

Chapter

1

PHR Practice Area 1: Business Management

THE PHR EXAM CONTENT FROM THE BUSINESS MANAGEMENT FUNCTIONAL AREA COVERED IN THIS CHAPTER FOCUSES ON "USING INFORMATION ABOUT THE ORGANIZATION AND BUSINESS ENVIRONMENT TO REINFORCE EXPECTATIONS, INFLUENCE DECISION-MAKING, AND AVOID RISK." IT CONSISTS OF THE FOLLOWING RESPONSIBILITIES:

✓ 01   Interpret and apply information related to general business environment and industry best practices

✓ 02   Reinforce the organization's core values, ethical and behavioral expectations through modeling, communication, and coaching

✓ 03   Understand the role of cross-functional stakeholders in the organization and establish relationships to influence decision-making

✓ 04   Recommend and implement best practices to mitigate risk (for example: lawsuits, internal/external threats)

✓ 05   Determine the significance of data for recommending organizational strategies (for example: attrition rates, diversity in hiring, time to hire, time to fill, ROI, success of training)

IN ADDITION TO THE RESPONSIBILITIES LISTED ABOVE, AN INDIVIDUAL TAKING THE PHR EXAM SHOULD HAVE WORKING KNOWLEDGE OF THE FOLLOWING, USUALLY DERIVED THROUGH PRACTICAL EXPERIENCE:

✓ 01   Vision, mission, values, and structure of the organization

✓ 02   Legislative and regulatory knowledge and procedures

✓ 03   Corporate governance procedures and compliance

✓ 04   Employee communications

✓ 05   Ethical and professional standards

✓ 06   Business elements of an organization (for example: other functions and departments, products, competition, customers, technology, demographics, culture, processes, safety and security)

✓ 07   Existing HRIS, reporting tools, and other systems for effective data reporting and analysis

✓ 08   Change management theory, methods, and application

✓ 09   Risk management

✓ 10   Qualitative and quantitative methods and tools for analytics

✓ 11   Dealing with situations that are uncertain, unclear, or chaotic

1. Which of the following is not one of the four elements of the acronym VUCA?
   A. Visionary
   B. Unemployed
   C. Clarity
   D. All of the above

2. Which option is the correct term describing the near-term activities involved in transferring the product or service from the business to the customer?
   A. Sales
   B. Marketing
   C. Placement
   D. Both A and B

3. Managing payroll and recruiting for open positions are examples of which human resource role?
   A. Strategic
   B. Operational
   C. Administrative
   D. Employee relations

4. A conduct statement is most likely to be found in which corporate document?
   A. Employee handbook
   B. Ethics policy
   C. Injury and Illness Prevention Plan (IIPP)
   D. All of the above

5. Which of the following tools would HR most likely recommend to an employer who wants to tailor an employee wellness program to the needs of the workforce?
   A. Workers' comp aggregate report
   B. Utilization reports
   C. Employment trends
   D. Workforce analytics

6. Reengineering, corporate restructuring, and workforce expansion are all examples of what type of management strategy?
   A. Change
   B. Authoritarian
   C. Risk
   D. Transformational

7. The employer you work for is looking to open a large paint facility in a neighboring state. It will be the second location, with corporate headquarters continuing to be home base. Which change management structural intervention will HR most likely need to address?

   A. Reengineering

   B. Corporate restructuring

   C. Workforce reduction

   D. Workforce expansion

8. Which metric should you use to communicate to an executive team the expenses associated with recruiting and selection?

   A. Cost per hire

   B. Time to hire

   C. Replacement cost

   D. Accession rate

9. A supervisor complained to HR that one of his employees is often tardy. When asked about it, the employee said that he thought being on time wasn't really that important, as his supervisor seemed to come and go as he pleased. The supervisor himself is a nonexempt employee with a regular schedule. What should HR recommend as a first step?

   A. Discipline the employee for violating the attendance policy.

   B. Discipline both the employee and the supervisor for violating the attendance policy.

   C. Coach the supervisor on modeling appropriate workplace behaviors and communicating proper standards.

   D. Provide the employee and supervisor with the company's standards of conduct.

10. How do employee handbooks contribute to an organization's risk management plan?

    A. Employee handbooks are required by law.

    B. Employee handbooks help protect the organization from potential risk.

    C. Employee handbooks act as an insurance policy by identifying procedures and checklists.

    D. Employee handbooks are the only way to defend against unlawful discrimination claims.

11. Why is it important for HR professionals to keep up to date on employment litigation statistics?

    A. It is the first step toward compliance with labor laws.

    B. These statistics provide insight into updated labor laws in response to cultural or technological trends.

    C. Doing so helps to predict unemployment trends.

    D. These statistics help to predict areas of vulnerability and recommend risk management strategies.

12. Which of the following usually present the most risk of a discrimination charge being filed with the Equal Employment Opportunity Commission?

   A. Retaliation, race, disability

   B. Race, age, disability

   C. Sex, race, age

   D. Race, ethnicity, national origin

13. What is the purpose of a legislative committee?

   A. To unify members of the U.S. Congress either for or against a specific bill

   B. To sponsor a bill, agreeing to seek support of its passage

   C. To study a bill and determine the likelihood that the bill will be able to pass a vote in the full body of Congress

   D. To make changes to a bill prior to its forwarding to the full body for a vote

14. An activity in which anybody can participate to influence laws and regulations is known as which of the following?

   A. Lobbying

   B. Administrative law

   C. Corporate governance

   D. Social responsibility

15. A code of conduct is to _____ as an ethical statement is to organizational standards of behavior.

   A. Employee professionalism

   B. Policies

   C. Work rules

   D. Employee standards of behavior

16. An assembly-line configuration and standard operating procedures for taking a sales call are examples of which of the following organizational functions?

   A. Scheduling

   B. Production layout

   C. Capacity

   D. Facility location

17. Considering inputs such as available material and labor is an activity of which organizational function?

   A. Capacity

   B. Production layout

   C. Scheduling

   D. Facility location

18. The evolution from pagers to cellular phones is an example of which of the following forces in the external business environment?

   A. Availability of skilled workers in the labor force

   B. Legal and regulatory activity

   C. The economic environment

   D. Technology developments driving industry change

19. In which of the following ways does the finance department contribute to the achievement of HR outcomes?

   A. A financial analyst can provide information related to incentives for customers to buy.

   B. A financial analyst can provide models to predict the number of employees needed at different production levels.

   C. A financial analyst can aid in tracking real-time inventory related to sales.

   D. The finance department can process employee payroll.

20. Forecasting is most likely to be used when a company is doing which of the following activities?

   A. Conducting a feasibility study

   B. Creating an annual budget

   C. Completing an environmental scan

   D. Developing a training matrix

21. The company for which you work has partners who have agreed to share responsibility for managing the business on a day-to-day basis. This is an example of which of the following business structures?

   A. Limited liability partnership

   B. Joint venture

   C. General partnership

   D. Corporation

22. Under what conditions would employees be most receptive to organizational change?

   A. If they understand the benefits of the changes to their own working conditions

   B. If they receive a pay increase as the result of the change

   C. If the organizational change does not directly affect their own jobs

   D. Employees are never initially receptive to change.

23. Fill in the blank: Technological challenges are to project management as _____ challenges are to change management.

   A. Financial

   B. Human

   C. Risk

   D. Environmental

24. During the strategic planning session, the organizational leaders of a custom cabinet shop identified that there were serious quality defects in the wood being sourced from an outside vendor. Additionally, these flaws were contributing to the reason existing product packaging was no longer adequate to properly prepare the product for freight transport. This company has identified problems in which business function?

    A. Shipping and receiving

    B. Inventory

    C. Supply chain

    D. Purchasing

25. A company objective is to help managers perform through a series of 90-day goals. The goals will be set by the executive team, and managers will be expected to report weekly progress via email. Which of the following internal relationships should HR cultivate to help the company achieve this strategic objective?

    A. Twice-a-month meetings with the managers to identify and support any workforce changes that will need to occur to achieve the goals

    B. Weekly planning sessions with the executive team to address any obstacles that hinder goal achievement

    C. Bi-weekly meetings with the CFO to advocate for the financial resources management needs to achieve the goals

    D. Weekly meetings with the HR generalists to get updated on their own progress toward department goals

26. Which of the following is an example of a human capital measurement?

    A. Employee attitudes

    B. Employee capabilities

    C. Productivity

    D. All of the above

27. A values statement does *not* need to include which of the following?

    A. Standards of behavior

    B. Ethical components

    C. Action items

    D. A definition of what is important to the company

28. A painting company has decided to organize its services by industrial and residential. It plans to hire division directors to form key account teams in both sales and marketing but keep operations as its own division. This is an example of which strategy?

    A. Divisional

    B. Regional market

    C. Organizational development

    D. Business unit

29. Inventory, employees, and accounts receivable are all examples of what?

- **A.** Assets
- **B.** Liabilities
- **C.** Capital
- **D.** Competitive advantage

30. Which number is the mode in the following sequence: 1334555?

- **A.** 1
- **B.** 3.7
- **C.** 5
- **D.** 26

31. One of the corporate values of your company is the concept of "Ohana" that is centered around behaviors such as transparency and trust. Which of the following conditions would you expect to find at this organization?

- **A.** Rules prohibiting disclosures of pay rates
- **B.** Encouragement to challenge the status quo
- **C.** Generous family leave policies
- **D.** Practices that encourage diversity

32. The large company that you work for has decided that addressing the leadership needs of their organization is necessary to advance their growth objectives. Which of the following should be your first priority?

- **A.** Hiring strong leaders
- **B.** Replacing poor leaders
- **C.** Evaluating current leaders
- **D.** Identifying future leaders

33. Which of the following is the most likely reason that some organizational leaders struggle with ethical decision-making?

- **A.** Most leaders have personalities that make them inclined to test boundaries.
- **B.** Ethics do not lead to measurable outcomes.
- **C.** Laws are not consistent from country to country or state to state.
- **D.** Not everyone shares the same set of values.

34. A startup company is focused on innovation, driven by its research and development efforts. The skillsets necessary for its workforce do not currently exist in the available labor market. Which of the following strategies should you recommend?

A. Offer paid internships to high school students in the communities where you operate.

B. Pay above market value for your research and development team.

C. Invest in training and development for your management staff.

D. Encourage a creative, nontraditional workplace culture.

35. The executive team at a major retailer has decided that it must close 68 stores nationwide, with an anticipated loss of more than 10,000 jobs. Which of the following external partnerships would have the biggest impact on the laid-off workers?

A. County unemployment offices

B. State and local political leadership

C. Local staffing agencies

D. Local universities and/or training centers

36. Who is hiring, what price points are selling, and what are the current trends and cultural factors are questions answered by a scan of which of the following?

A. Industry practices and developments

B. Economic environment

C. The general business environment

D. The legal and regulatory environment

37. HR provided the strategic planning committee with a report showing the unemployment rate at the state and county levels and the availability of labor by skillset. The committee is most likely preparing for which of the following planning activities?

A. A training needs assessment

B. Strategic workforce planning

C. A strategic compensation review

D. The launch of a diversity management team

38. Which of the following is a major characteristic of evidence-based management?

A. Conducting a training needs assessment

B. Launching a diversity management team

C. Completing a strategic compensation review

D. Making decisions using scientific evidence

39. Which evidence would you use to make a decision about how many employees a company may need during peak season?

   A. Scientific evidence

   B. Experiential evidence

   C. Industry evidence

   D. Strategic evidence

40. In developing the exam content outline, a major exam administrator identifies subject-matter experts to review the existing exam content and anonymously make suggestions for changes. A facilitator gathers the feedback and then sends out proposed changes to each member for revisions and comments. The facilitator repeats this process round after round until a consensus is reached. This company is employing which of the following decision-making methods?

   A. Evidence-based management

   B. SME processing

   C. Delphi technique

   D. Nominal group process

41. Which of the following is *most* likely to increase employee commitment to change?

   A. Increasing employee trust in management

   B. Increasing associated pay levels with new responsibilities and tasks

   C. Terminating employees who have bad attitudes toward the change

   D. Adding technological components that increase employee skills

42. Purchasing employment practice liability insurance (EPLI) is what type of risk management technique?

   A. Avoid

   B. Transfer

   C. Mitigate

   D. Accept

43. HR is most likely to serve in what type of role related to an employer's use of workforce analytics?

   A. Administrative

   B. Technical

   C. Legal

   D. Advisory

44. For what purpose is a churn model most likely to be used?

    A. To understand why benefit costs continue to increase

    B. To predict which way employees may vote for (or against) union representation

    C. To identify the root cause of turnover

    D. To improve overall employee services

45. Suppliers, employees, and local community groups are all examples of which of the following?

    A. Communities of interest

    B. Protected whistleblowers

    C. Company shareholders

    D. Company stakeholders

46. A code of ethics, accounting rules, and sustainability guidelines are all examples of what type of company behavior?

    A. Legal compliance

    B. Ethical management practices

    C. Corporate governance

    D. Diversity management

47. Which of the following technological tools would best help HR manage résumés, training documents, and service awards?

    A. A human resource information system (HRIS)

    B. An applicant tracking system (ATS)

    C. Workforce analytics

    D. Cloud computing

48. The collective knowledge, skills, and abilities of an organization's employees based upon which an employer may compete is best known as which of the following?

    A. Core competencies

    B. Strategic workforce planning

    C. Human capital

    D. Head count

49. Your favorite news outlet just announced that interest rates will be going up in the next calendar quarter. This is an example of which of the following?

    A. A leading economic indicator

    B. A key performance indicator

    C. An element of the consumer price index

    D. An effect on the labor rate

50. You have tasked a department with coming up with a proposed schedule for the holiday season. You are asking them in effect to form which of the following?

   A. An autonomous review

   B. An evidenced-based decision

   C. A team review

   D. A group consensus

Chapter

2

PHR Practice Area 2: Talent Planning & Acquisition

THE PHR EXAM CONTENT FROM THE
TALENT PLANNING & ACQUISITION
FUNCTIONAL AREA COVERED IN THIS
CHAPTER IS FOCUSED ON "IDENTIFYING,
ATTRACTING, AND EMPLOYING TALENT
WHILE FOLLOWING ALL FEDERAL LAWS
RELATED TO THE HIRING PROCESS."
THE EXAM CONTENT CONSISTS OF THE
FOLLOWING RESPONSIBILITIES:

✓ 01   Understand federal laws and organizational policies
to adhere to legal and ethical requirements in hiring (for
example: Title VII, nepotism, disparate impact, FLSA,
independent contractors)

✓ 02   Develop and implement sourcing methods and techniques (for example: employee referrals, diversity groups,
social media)

✓ 03   Execute the talent acquisition lifecycle (for example:
interviews, extending offers, background checks,
negotiation).

IN ADDITION TO THE RESPONSIBILITIES LISTED ABOVE, AN INDIVIDUAL TAKING THE PHR EXAM SHOULD HAVE WORKING KNOWLEDGE OF THE FOLLOWING, USUALLY DERIVED THROUGH PRACTICAL EXPERIENCE:

✓ 12 Applicable federal laws and regulations related to talent planning and acquisition activities

✓ 13 Planning concepts and terms (for example: succession planning, forecasting)

✓ 14 Current market situation and talent pool availability

✓ 15 Staffing alternatives (for example: outsourcing, temporary employment)

✓ 16 Interviewing and selection techniques, concepts, and terms

✓ 17 Applicant tracking systems and/or methods

✓ 18 Impact of total rewards on recruitment and retention

✓ 19 Candidate/employee testing processes and procedures

✓ 20 Verbal and written offers/contract techniques

✓ 21 New hire employee orientation processes and procedures

✓ 22 Internal workforce assessments (for example: skills testing, workforce demographics, analysis)

✓ 23 Transition techniques for corporate restructuring, mergers and acquisitions, due diligence processes, offshoring, and divestitures

✓ 24 Metrics to assess past and future staffing effectiveness (for example: cost per hire, selection ratios, adverse impact)

1. A supervisor interviewed an applicant for an open position and rated the applicant high because she displayed so much more energy and confidence than all of the other candidates. This is an example of which type of interviewer bias?

    A. Stereotyping

    B. First impression

    C. Similar to me

    D. Contrast

2. A supervisor interviewed an applicant for an open position and rated the applicant low because he had a bad feeling about the applicant's ability to last in the job. This is an example of which type of interviewer bias?

    A. Stereotyping

    B. Gut feeling

    C. Discrimination

    D. Contrast

3. Which of the following rater error occurs when the interviewer knows how a candidate scored on a pre-employment test and rates the candidate high or low based on this information?

    A. Knowledge of predictor

    B. First impression

    C. Similar to me

    D. Contrast

4. During an interview, it was disclosed that the applicant was convicted of driving under the influence six years ago. The position for which the candidate is applying is a retail sales clerk and does not require driving. The supervisor of the department does not want to hire the applicant because of the DUI conviction. Which of the following statements is false?

    A. The applicant was correct in disclosing the conviction on the application.

    B. The conviction should not be considered as it is not job-related.

    C. The supervisor is guilty of the negative emphasis form of interviewer bias.

    D. The supervisor makes the correct decision not to hire.

5. A national airline company refuses to hire a 66-year-old applicant for a captain's position because the FAA has a rule that captains cannot be older than 65. Which of the following statements is true?

    A. The airline is guilty of unlawful discrimination.

    B. The applicant has a right to sue under the EEOC.

    C. The airline is correct because the protected-class characteristic, age, is a bona fide occupational qualification (BFOQ).

    D. The determination of the legality of the airline's decision varies state by state.

6. Which of the following statements is true regarding bona fide occupational qualifications?

    A. There are no conditions under which age may be considered a bona fide occupational qualification.

    B. Indian reservations may give preference to Native American applicants.

    C. Religious organizations may not give preference to members of that religion in hiring.

    D. An employer may refuse to hire an applicant based on their race because of perceived customer preferences.

7. Discriminatory recruiting, compensation, and access to training are examples of which of the following?

    A. Selection efforts

    B. Prohibited behaviors under the Civil Rights Act of 1991

    C. Protected-class characteristics

    D. Unlawful employment actions

8. Which of the following was not originally identified for protection under Title VII of the Civil Rights Act of 1964?

    A. Sexual orientation

    B. Family status

    C. Age

    D. All of the above

9. "To promote employment of older persons based on their ability rather than age" is the preamble to which of the following labor laws?

    A. Title VII of the Civil Rights Act

    B. The Age Discrimination in Employment Act (ADEA)

    C. The Older Workers Benefits Protection Act (OWBPA)

    D. The Americans with Disabilities Act

10. The Age Discrimination in Employment Act prohibits discrimination against individuals over the age of what?

    A. 35

    B. 40

    C. 55

    D. 63

11. The ADA defines a disability as a physical or _____ impairment that causes substantial limitation of one or more major life activities.

    A. Essential

    B. Life

    C. Mental

    D. Protected

12. The Americans with Disabilities Act applies to employers with how many employees?

   A. 15

   B. 25

   C. 50

   D. More than 50

13. The ADA Amendments Act of 2008 included language that allows protection for individuals who can demonstrate that they have been the subject of prohibited activities under the ADA, whether or not they actually have some type of disability. This is the concept of which of the following?

   A. Assumed to be disabled

   B. Factually disabled

   C. Mentally disabled

   D. Regarded as being disabled

14. The ADA Amendments Act of 2008 defined *disability*. It included which of the following?

   A. A physical or mental impairment that substantially limits one or more major life activities

   B. A record of impairment

   C. An individual regarded as being impaired

   D. All of the above

15. Under the ADA Amendments Act of 2008, caring for oneself, performing manual tasks, eating, sleeping, and functions of the endocrine and immune systems are which of the following?

   A. Examples of mitigating measures

   B. Types of reverse discrimination claims

   C. Examples of the definition of disability

   D. Examples of major life activities

16. Which of the following agencies is tasked with regulating compliance with the ADA?

   A. Office of Federal Contract Compliance

   B. Equal Employment Opportunity Commission

   C. Department of Labor

   D. Fair Employment and Housing Commission

17. Which of the following acts codified the concepts of "business necessity" and "job-relatedness" with regard to determining whether discrimination has occurred?

   A. Title VII of the Civil Rights Act of 1964

   B. The Age Discrimination in Employment Act

   C. The Americans with Disabilities Act

   D. The Civil Rights Act of 1991

18. Under the Civil Rights Act of 1991, the maximum allowable damage award for employers with between 101 and 200 employees is which of the following?

    A. $50,000

    B. $100,000

    C. $200,000

    D. $300,000

19. Which of the following acts prohibits employers from unlawfully discriminating against employees and their families related to genetic information?

    A. Uniformed Services Employment and Reemployment Rights Act (USERRA)

    B. Genetic Information Nondiscrimination Act of 2008 (GINA)

    C. Title VII, Civil Rights Act

    D. Family and Medical Leave Act (FMLA)

20. Executive orders become law after how many days?

    A. 15

    B. 30

    C. 180

    D. 365

21. Which executive order prohibits employment discrimination on the basis of race, creed, color, and national origin?

    A. EO 11246, 1965

    B. EO 11375, 1967

    C. EO 11478, 1969

    D. EO 13152, 2000

22. Which executive order prohibits employment discrimination on the basis of sex (gender)?

    A. EO 11246, 1965

    B. EO 11375, 1967

    C. EO 11478, 1969

    D. EO 13152, 2000

23. Which executive order prohibits employment discrimination on the basis of parental status?

    A. EO 11246, 1965

    B. EO 11375, 1967

    C. EO 11478, 1969

    D. EO 13152, 2000

24. Hispanic or Latino, White, Black, Native Hawaiian, Asian, American Indian, and two or more races are the definitions of which of the following?

   A. Protected-class groups

   B. Original race/ethnicity categories on the EEO 1 report

   C. Revised race/ethnicity categories on the EEO 1 report

   D. Classification of laborers/helpers on the EEO 1 report

25. Placement goals, identification of problem areas, and periodic internal audits are all components of which of the following type of plan?

   A. Human capital management

   B. Affirmative action

   C. Knowledge management

   D. Recruiting strategy

26. The goal of which of the following workforce planning objectives is to realign operational processes in a way that adds value to the customer?

   A. Restructuring

   B. Mergers

   C. Reengineering

   D. Acquisitions

27. Which of the following processes provide the foundation for identifying the knowledge, skills, and abilities needed to achieve specific results in an organization?

   A. Needs assessment

   B. Corporate restructuring

   C. Reengineering

   D. Job analysis

28. Organizations have three options for locating the qualified talent necessary to achieve organizational objectives. They include internal transfers or promotions, external hires, and what else?

   A. Job bidding

   B. Alternative staffing methods

   C. The Internet

   D. Previous applicants

29. Which of the following statements is true regarding professional employer organizations (PEOs)?

   A. The employer eliminates all risks associated with employees, such as workers' compensation insurance and unemployment.

   B. A company transfers the functions of a department to a PEO that specializes in that particular function, such as payroll processing.

C. A PEO is made up of nontraditional workers, such as part-time and seasonal.

D. The PEO becomes the employer of record.

30. Of the following choices, which best describes the factors for determining whether an individual is an employee or an independent contractor?

A. Who trains the individual

B. Degree of control

C. Reimbursed expenses

D. The existence of a written contract

31. A staffing needs analysis seeks to identify which of the following?

A. Which employees are ready for promotion

B. What knowledge, skills, and abilities (KSAs) will be necessary in the future

C. What knowledge, skills, and abilities (KSAs) are currently available internally

D. All of the above

32. "Those individuals who are not currently looking for work" describes which of the following?

A. Active candidates

B. Passive candidates

C. External recruits

D. None of the above

33. Which of the following is the best answer for why HR must work with line managers to fill open positions?

A. To manage the expectations of the line manager

B. To ensure that the job specifications are accurately presented

C. To take into account the hiring preferences of a particular department

D. To seek input on the best sources for recruiting qualified candidates

34. What are the two methods used to publicize current openings throughout an organization?

A. Employee referrals and job posting

B. Employee referrals and bona fide seniority systems

C. Job bidding and job posting

D. Job transfers and promotions

35. School alumni websites, videos, and virtual interviews are all examples of which of the following HR activities?

A. Social media/online recruiting

B. Search engine optimization (SEO)

    C. Corporate branding efforts

    D. Personal networks

36. The compilation of employment selection procedures defined by various agencies, such as the EEOC, OFCCP, and court cases, resulted in which of the following guidelines?

    A. Pre-employment testing

    B. Amendments to Title VII of the Civil Rights Act

    C. Selection guidelines

    D. Uniform Guidelines on Employee Selection Procedures (UGESPs)

37. In an audit, HR discovers that a high school diploma requirement results in a hire rate of 19 percent males and 13 percent females in their southern branches. This is an example of which of the following?

    A. Unlawful discrimination

    B. Reflection of the applicant pool

    C. Adverse impact

    D. A violation of Title VII

38. When the most important aspects of a job are assigned heavier emphasis than the less essential on an application, which selection tool is most likely being used?

    A. Unlawful application

    B. Job-specific application

    C. Short-form application

    D. Weighted application

39. Which of the following is the best answer to why employment interviews are important?

    A. They provide supervisors with the opportunity to determine how well a candidate will fit in with their peers.

    B. They provide an opportunity to rate candidates on their overall ability to perform the required duties of the job.

    C. They provide visual cues to help determine whether the candidate will meet customer preferences.

    D. They give the candidate the opportunity to find out more about the position.

40. A bank wants to determine an applicant's honesty when acting on the job. Which of the following tests would be the best predictor of this characteristic?

    A. Aptitude test

    B. Cognitive ability test

    C. Physical assessment

    D. Integrity test

41. In an interview, an applicant is given a work sample test to assess their ability to lift more than 50 pounds on a continuous basis. This is an example of which of the following type of pre-employment tests?

    A. Aptitude test

    B. Cognitive ability test

    C. Physical assessment

    D. Integrity test

42. Which of the following court cases determined that pre-employment tests that were found to be discriminatory in effect, though not in intent, and were thereby unlawful?

    A. *Albemarle Paper v. Moody*

    B. *Washington v. Davis*

    C. *Griggs v. Duke Power*

    D. None of the above

43. Which of the following measures determines whether a test produces consistent results over time?

    A. Reliability

    B. Validity

    C. Nondiscriminatory practices

    D. The UGESPs

44. A pre-employment test was designed to predict the interpersonal skills of sales candidates. After three months in use, it was determined that employees who scored high on this test were in fact better salespeople than those who scored lower. This test can be said to be what?

    A. Reliable

    B. Valid

    C. Nondiscriminatory

    D. Useful

45. If an employer wants to find out whether an employee is re-hireable, they should conduct which of the following?

    A. An interview

    B. An employment reference check

    C. An integrity test

    D. A personal reference

46. If an employer knowingly hires an employee who had been previously convicted for violent behavior and that employee goes on to commit a violent act against a co-worker, the employer may be guilty of which of the following?

   A. Willful violation under OSHA

   B. Shortsighted hiring practices

   C. Negligent hiring

   D. None of the above. Employers cannot be held responsible for the personal acts of their employees.

47. Which of the following negates the concept of employment at will?

   A. Employee handbooks

   B. Employment contracts

   C. Offer letters

   D. Pre-employment tests

48. Form I-9, Employment Eligibility Verification, must be completed within how many days of the employee's first day of work for wages?

   A. 1

   B. 3

   C. 15

   D. 30

49. An employee claimed on a popular review site that her employer discriminated against her based on her sexual orientation. She subsequently was fired for performance issues, which she denied. Which of the following statements is true?

   A. The employee was a victim of constructive discharge.

   B. The employee may have a claim of unlawful retaliation.

   C. The employee was discriminated against for concerted protected activity.

   D. The employee was unlikely to have been a victim of discrimination.

50. Anonymous online comments disparaging a company, posted by a current employee, that are not intended to be read by co-workers—such as on review sites—may not be which of the following?

   A. Protected under the National Labor Relations Act (NLRA)

   B. Used by the employer to make performance-related decisions

   C. Used by the employer to retaliate against a protected-class individual

   D. All of the above

51. What is the primary purpose of the interactive process under the Americans with Disabilities Act (ADA)?

    A. To protect the rights of an injured worker

    B. To protect the employer from a claim of unlawful discrimination under the EEOC

    C. To keep the lines of communication open between a disabled worker and their employer

    D. All of the above

52. An employer decided to reassign an employee to a position other than his original job to reasonably accommodate his disability. The position met the restrictions from the employee's physician, and there was a current vacancy. Which of the following statements is true?

    A. The employer violated the employee's rights under the Americans with Disabilities Act.

    B. The employer violated the employee's rights under the Rehabilitation Act.

    C. The employer should send a letter to the employee notifying him that they are seeking to reassign him.

    D. The employer must pay the employee the same amount as he was making in his original position.

53. An individual has applied for a receptionist position at your place of business. During the background process, it was discovered that she had a nonviolent, drug-related conviction. How should HR proceed with the screening?

    A. If she is otherwise qualified, she should be hired.

    B. If the position is not one of authority, she should be considered as any other applicant would.

    C. The company should consider how much time has passed since the conviction.

    D. Because of risk, the employer should not hire the candidate.

54. When should the employer begin a background screen on an individual?

    A. After a conditional offer of employment has been made

    B. When the applicant has authorized the background screen by signing the application

    C. After the employee has completed their first day of work for wages

    D. After the applicant has successfully completed an interview with the supervisor

55. What is the primary purpose of validating pre-employment tests?

    A. To effectively manage employer risk

    B. To aid in the recruitment process

    C. To comply with the Americans with Disabilities Act

    D. To ensure the tests accurately measure job requirements

56. A workforce plan is *most* likely to address which of the following?

   A. The company's business objectives

   B. Orientation and onboarding processes

   C. Job analysis requirements

   D. An employer's staffing needs

57. Which of the following operational HR activities has impact upon all other HR competencies?

   A. Wage surveys

   B. Job analysis

   C. Pre-employment test validation

   D. Compliance with various labor laws

58. Your HR director has asked you to identify the percentage of time spent on each task within a job and scale the tasks based on how important they are to successful performance on the job. Your boss is most likely asking you to do what?

   A. Determine whether the position is exempt.

   B. Complete the job description.

   C. Identify the essential functions.

   D. Gather data to create pre-employment tests.

59. The primary difference between job posting and job bidding is which of the following?

   A. A job posting is an external activity, whereas job bidding occurs internally.

   B. Job posting occurs when a job is open, whereas job bidding may occur before the position is available.

   C. Job posting is an administrative HR activity, whereas job bidding is an operational HR activity.

   D. There are no differences between these two.

60. Helping a new employee learn the formal and informal rules of the organization is the main focus of which HR activity?

   A. Orientation

   B. Acclimation

   C. Assimilation

   D. Onboarding

61. Which of the following best describes the type of applicants an employer will find when using college as a recruiting source?

   A. Highly intelligent applicants

   B. Very diverse applicants

   C. Local applicants

   D. All of the above

62. Which strategy should you recommend to your HR leader if you are getting too many unqualified candidates applying for open positions?

    A. Rewriting the job descriptions

    B. Posting the salary range

    C. Using prescreening questions

    D. Finding a different recruiting source

63. A cognitive ability test is most likely screening for which of the following?

    A. Intelligence

    B. Physical aptitude

    C. Personality profile

    D. Job skills

64. An aptitude test is most likely to predict which of the following employee competencies?

    A. General intelligence

    B. Overall job performance

    C. Ability to learn a new skill

    D. Employee attitude

65. A pre-employment personality profile is likely to identify which of the following individual characteristics?

    A. Conscientiousness

    B. Motivators

    C. Extroversion or introversion

    D. All of the above

66. There is currently a skills shortage in industries such as nursing and technology. Graduate rates are projected to be low for these highly skilled jobs throughout the 2020s. This data is most likely provided by which of the following reports?

    A. Third-party vendor reports

    B. Federal and state data reports

    C. HR demographic reports

    D. Reports by educational institutions

67. Given the projected skills gap in science, technology, engineering, and math (STEM) talent, which of the following strategies should you recommend for an employer that is dependent on these highly skilled workers?

    A. Participate in community partnerships for long-term planning.

    B. Invest in in-house apprenticeship programs.

    C. Hire students out of high school.

    D. Change the business strategy to be less dependent on STEM skills.

68. Which of the following tools will help HR best assess the skillsets of the current workforce?

    A. Audit of employee applications

    B. Job shadowing

    C. Supervisor observations

    D. Skills inventory

69. The employment brand is best defined by which of the following?

    A. The employer identity

    B. How happy employees are

    C. The company culture

    D. The company logo

70. Knowing the company brand is helpful for HR so that they may conduct which of the following HR activities?

    A. Recruitment

    B. Employee development

    C. Culture training

    D. All of the above

71. Google has a reputation for having a creative, innovative, and leadership-driven environment for their employees to work within. This is the best example of which of the following?

    A. The company brand

    B. The company strategy

    C. The company mission

    D. The company values

72. What is the greatest risk to employers that want to use offer letters for potential hires?

    A. Complying with labor law

    B. Inconsistent use from position to position

    C. Inadvertently creating an employment contract

    D. Complying with wage theft prevention laws

73. The primary difference between an offer letter and an employment contract is which of the following?

    A. An offer letter will define exemption status.

    B. An employment contract will include reasons an employee may be discharged.

    C. An offer letter must be signed by the employee.

    D. An employment contract will describe employee benefits.

74. You have been tasked with hiring an IT specialist for your company, with a pay range between $35 and $55 per hour. The applicant who is most qualified requested a minimum pay rate of $65 per hour but is willing to negotiate. You have permission to come back with an offer of $50 per hour, mainly because your boss doesn't think he would take less. This is an example of what type of negotiation bias?

   A. Anchoring bias

   B. Escalation-of-commitment bias

   C. The halo effect

   D. Competitiveness bias

75. Which of the following recruitment sources would be most likely to help you attract passive candidates?

   A. Social media

   B. Employee referrals

   C. Billboards

   D. Ads on online job boards

76. Which of the following data sets should be included when calculating cost per hire?

   A. Advertising and marketing fees

   B. Costs for background checks

   C. Recruiter wages

   D. All of the above

77. The metamorphosis stage of employee socialization is characterized by which of the following?

   A. The employee participates in a formal orientation to the company work rules and mores.

   B. The employee has internalized the culture and is comfortable with their job.

   C. The employee is able to review a realistic job preview prior to starting work.

   D. The employee works with a mentor to learn about the unwritten rules of the organization.

78. Which of the following is an HR best practice for employees wanting to job share?

   A. Documenting the reasons for the alternative work schedule

   B. Offering the job-sharing options to any employee who wants it

   C. Creating a memo of understanding between two job-sharing workers

   D. Managing risk by not offering job sharing as a staffing option

79. With the continued aging of the workforce population, which alternative staffing arrangement may most benefit an employer?

   A. Using a contingent workforce

   B. Engaging in a reduction in force (RIF)

   C. Laying off older workers first

   D. Offering phased retirement programs

80. Business strategy, the skillsets of the current workforce, and labor market demographics are all factors used to complete which HR activity?

   A. Creating a demand analysis

   B. Forecasting

   C. Making a business case

   D. Calculating turnover

81. The manager of HR has asked that you research ways in which to acclimate new hires to the workplace beyond training them for their jobs. She recommends introducing them to the CEO, having a welcome luncheon, and checking in with them each week for the first 30 days. Which HR activity is your manager describing?

   A. New-hire engagement

   B. New-hire acclimatization

   C. New-hire orientation

   D. New-hire onboarding

82. In what way can employee onboarding influence employee retention?

   A. The process can help new hires understand what is expected of them.

   B. Onboarding provides support to new hires so they feel like they can succeed.

   C. Onboarding will help build employee loyalty.

   D. All of the above.

83. Which of the following conditions is most likely to have the greatest impact on employee retention?

   A. Base pay

   B. Relationship with supervisors

   C. Enjoyable work

   D. Nice co-workers

84. Which of the following conditions is an obstacle to effective diversity recruiting?

   A. Bias

   B. Stereotyping

   C. Heuristics

   D. All of the above

85. One study found that when recruiters searched for candidates on social media platforms such as LinkedIn, they were more likely to look at male profiles than female profiles. This is an example of which of the following?

    A. Unlawful discrimination

    B. Misogyny

    C. Bias

    D. All of the above

86. Asking candidates to provide their social media passwords during the recruitment process is best represented by which of the following statements?

    A. May violate state and federal law

    B. Is an unreasonable request because social media is mostly used for personal purposes

    C. May be required in certain industries

    D. Is appropriate for executive-level hires

87. The Federal Aviation Administration (FAA) has set the age limit for pilots at 65. This is an example of which of the following?

    A. A federal exemption to the ADEA

    B. A bona fide occupational qualification

    C. A discriminatory practice

    D. A union hiring clause

88. It has been 48 hours since the employee you hired has begun work, and he still has not provided you with proof of identity. Which course of action should you take?

    A. Terminate the employee and tell him he may reapply when he has the proper documentation.

    B. Wait for the employee's first pay period to be complete to follow up.

    C. Meet with the employee to remind him of the requirements and review document options.

    D. Nothing, as it has not yet been 72 hours as required by IRCA.

89. Which of the following employers may be required to have a written affirmative action plan?

    A. An employer with 200 or more employees

    B. An employer with federal contracts in excess of $50,000

    C. Federal contractors with at least 50 employees and $50,000 in federal contracts

    D. All employers subject to the requirements of the Equal Employment Opportunity Commission

90. Which of the following elements of affirmative action programs is prohibited by law?

    A. Hiring quotas

    B. Discriminating against veterans

    C. Requiring self-identification

    D. All of the above

91. Which of the following should be HR's priority when building a record retention program for their employer?

    A. Controlling the storage costs of high-volume files

    B. Improving efficiency and office appearance

    C. Ensuring that paper and digital files may be easily accessed on demand

    D. Properly securing confidential employee information

92. Your HR manager has tasked you with cleaning up the HR files and coming up with a process to handle records that may be destroyed. Which factor is the most important for you to consider?

    A. Any pending litigation that may involve the records, even if the retention requirements have expired

    B. Comparing the cost and security of a third-party vendor versus an in-house destruction effort

    C. The different laws governing digital versus paper file destruction

    D. The tasks that a large project such as this will take you away from

93. The R&D department has had a hard time keeping qualified hires in the engineering role; in fact, the last two hires were both terminated because they could not perform the essential tasks of the job. The manager has asked you to reopen the job ad and get him interviews by the end of the week. Which course of action should you take?

    A. Reopen the job and start immediately recruiting

    B. Conduct meetings with current staff to find out what the job actually entails

    C. Request to conduct a thorough job analysis to identify the true needs

    D. Call the former employees and complete a more thorough exit interview

94. An employee is injured while at work and has been sent to the company's occupational clinic for evaluation. Which of the following documents should you send over to the clinic?

    A. The job description with essential functions

    B. Authorization for treatment form from the employee

    C. A copy of your post-injury drug screen policy

    D. The employee's medical file

95. The VP of HR has tasked the HR department with completing job analysis for all company positions at your 500+ employee facility. With more than 25 different job classifications and limited resources, which job analysis approach would be best?

    A. Questionnaire

    B. Observation

    C. Interview

    D. Supervisor surveys

96. For jobs that are considered exempt from overtime regulations, which of the following is the most important to include in the job description?

    A. The physical requirements of the job

    B. The use of the employee's own tools or equipment

    C. The duties that support the exemption status

    D. All essential functions of the job

97. As part of an HR technology strategy, your HR manager has decided to computerize employee skills inventories. Which of the following approaches should you recommend?

    A. Sitting one on one with employees to update their skills profiles

    B. Utilizing a self-service feature to have employees update their own records

    C. Hiring a temporary employee to input the data from employee applications

    D. Asking the supervisors to collect the data and report it to HR

98. Under which condition would it be most beneficial to consider former employees to fill open positions?

    A. If the employee left for personal reasons, such as to go back to school

    B. If another employee provides a good reference for the former employee

    C. If filling the position is urgent and the former employee is available

    D. If it is a short-term vacancy so you can evaluate the former employee's performance

99. Car rentals, per diem expenses, and temporary home-finding assistance are all characteristics of which HR activity?

    A. Building a travel policy

    B. Classifying employee expenses

    C. Identifying qualified reimbursements

    D. Employee relocation

100. Conducting a general Internet search using key words plus AND, OR, and NOT when recruiting is known as what type of search?

    A. Social media

    B. Google

    C. Workforce analytics

    D. Boolean

101. The company you work for hires 4,000 new employees per year, onboarding 150 people through boot camps every two weeks at their corporate headquarters. A survey of employee engagement on the last day of a boot camp shows a high level of employee engagement. Ninety days later, however, employee engagement levels for the same group are reduced. What strategy should you recommend to your employer?

   A. Work with management to find ways to expand onboarding activities into the employees' first 90 days.

   B. Lengthen the number of days employees must attend boot camp.

   C. Ask senior HR leadership for more resources to expand training and culture content.

   D. Improve recruiting efforts to find employees who are a better fit for their jobs.

102. What is the primary relationship between affirmative action programs and diversity initiatives?

   A. Diversity initiatives may be court-ordered to remedy past discrimination using affirmative action quotas.

   B. Affirmative action is aimed at increasing diversity in the workplace.

   C. Both affirmative action and diversity initiatives are governed by the EEOC.

   D. Affirmative action and diversity are the same thing.

103. As the new HR generalist, you have been tasked with creating a record retention schedule for all employee files. Which data should you source first to guide your recommendations?

   A. The types of records currently being stored

   B. Labor laws that have record-keeping requirements

   C. Who is currently managing records storage

   D. The number of employees at the company

104. The company you work for has a practice of hiring employees who are still in high school to fill summer jobs. Which of the following actions is necessary for HR to take?

   A. Advise the employer of work-hour restrictions for minors.

   B. Check state and federal laws regarding any permit requirements for employing minors.

   C. Research internship pay requirements.

   D. Advise the employer against this practice because of wage, hour, and safety risks.

105. When designing employee onboarding programs, which of the following must be included?

   A. Which employees will be included

   B. How often the employees will be onboarded

   C. The learning styles of each employee

   D. How the program will be measured

106. Which of the following terms best describes the practice of due diligence?

    A. Compliance

    B. Investigation

    C. Assistance

    D. Fiduciary

107. What is a primary reason for one company to merge with another company?

    A. Increasing profitability

    B. Eliminating a competitor

    C. Avoiding market redundancies

    D. All of the above

108. To accurately conduct a labor market trend analysis, HR would need information from which of the following agencies?

    A. The Department of Labor (DOL)

    B. The Department of Industrial Relations (DIR)

    C. The Equal Employment Opportunity Commission (EEOC)

    D. All of the above

109. An employee is requesting to get off work two hours early every Friday while he attends his Alcoholics Anonymous meetings for the next three months. At that time, there will be a weekend meeting closer to his home that he will begin to attend. The employer he works for has 19 employees, and accommodating this request would require that other workers be trained in his regular closing responsibilities that are considered essential. How should the employer respond?

    A. The employer should accommodate this request, as it is short term and protected under the ADA.

    B. The employer should accommodate this request because the company would otherwise lose this employee and have to replace him.

    C. The employer does not have to accommodate this request, as it may cause undue hardship on other workers.

    D. The employer does not have to accommodate the request, as it is not large enough to be subject to the ADA requirements.

110. Which of the following is an example of a knowledge requirement from a job description for a receptionist?

    A. Managing files and records in accordance with company procedures

    B. Having a typing speed of 65 words per minute

    C. Greeting customers in a professional manner

    D. Effectively dealing with angry customers over the phone

111. According to the DOL, an HR generalist will regularly be called upon to give an employee their full attention when the employee is speaking. This is an example of which of the following?

   A. Knowledge of employee service principles

   B. Critical thinking skills

   C. Professional abilities

   D. Active listening skills

112. The labor market should be analyzed by _____ current and future staffing needs against market data.

   A. Balancing

   B. Considering

   C. Comparing

   D. Dissecting

113. What is the primary purpose of assessing the internal skillsets of current employees?

   A. To create the company's strategic plan

   B. To predict future workforce needs

   C. To create a workforce plan

   D. To tie compensation to employee performance

114. The use of digital badges in employee onboarding helps the employer accomplish which of the following HR objectives?

   A. Drive new-hire engagement

   B. Identify who has and has not completed training

   C. Establish a benchmark knowledge base for new hires

   D. All of the above

115. Which of the following information is *most* critical for HR to have when negotiating salaries during job offers?

   A. Market rates

   B. Health benefits offerings

   C. Time-off options

   D. Executive pay rates

116. Which of the following is a direct cost of employee turnover?

   A. Delays in production because of lost productivity

   B. Accrued time off owed to the exiting employee

   C. Loss of workplace diversity

   D. Lost clients

117. All of the statements regarding employee record-keeping are true except which of the following?

    A. Some records apply only to private employers, and some records apply only to federal contractors/subcontractors.

    B. Some record requirements are dependent on specific industries.

    C. Retention periods may vary from law to law.

    D. State requirements may not exceed federal requirements.

Chapter 3

PHR Exam: Learning and Development

THE PHR EXAM CONTENT FROM THE LEARNING AND DEVELOPMENT FUNCTIONAL AREA COVERED IN THIS CHAPTER FOCUSES ON "CONTRIBUTING TO THE ORGANIZATION'S LEARNING AND DEVELOPMENT ACTIVITIES BY IMPLEMENTING AND EVALUATING PROGRAMS, PROVIDING INTERNAL CONSULTATION, AND PROVIDING DATA." EXAM CONTENT CONSISTS OF THE FOLLOWING RESPONSIBILITIES:

- ✓ 01 Provide consultation to managers and employees on professional growth and development opportunities

- ✓ 02 Implement and evaluate career development and training programs (for example: career pathing, management training, mentorship)

- ✓ 03 Contribute to succession planning discussions with management by providing relevant data

IN ADDITION TO THE RESPONSIBILITIES LISTED ABOVE, AN INDIVIDUAL TAKING THE PHR EXAM SHOULD HAVE WORKING KNOWLEDGE OF THE FOLLOWING, USUALLY DERIVED THROUGH PRACTICAL EXPERIENCE:

- ✓ 25 Applicable federal laws and regulations related to learning and development activities

- ✓ 26 Learning and development theories and applications

✓ 27 Training program facilitation, techniques, and delivery

✓ 28 Adult learning processes

✓ 29 Instructional design principles and processes (for example: needs analysis, process flow mapping)

✓ 30 Techniques to assess training program effectiveness, including use of applicable metrics

✓ 31 Organizational development (OD) methods, motivation methods, and problem-solving techniques

✓ 32 Task/process analysis

✓ 33 Coaching and mentoring techniques

✓ 34 Employee retention concepts and applications

✓ 35 Techniques to encourage creativity and innovation

1. Talent management encompasses which of the following HR activities?

    A. Employee development

    B. Training

    C. Business management and strategy

    D. All of the above

2. Which of the following statements is true regarding the Copyright Act of 1976?

    A. Original work patents belong to the individual who authored the work, regardless of who paid for its development.

    B. The employer that hires an employee to create original work as part of their normal job duties is the owner of the copyright.

    C. Copyrights protect original work for 30 years.

    D. Employers must obtain permission from employees to use their work for training.

3. The author of an original work has been deceased for more than 80 years. Under which of the following exceptions may their work be used without permission?

    A. Public domain

    B. Work for hire

    C. Fair use doctrine

    D. U.S. Patent Act

4. Which of the following types of patents protect new, original, and ornamental designs of manufacturing items for 14 years?

    A. Utility patents

    B. Creative patents

    C. Plant patents

    D. Design patents

5. Which of the following types of patents protect the invention of new and useful processes and machines?

    A. Utility patents

    B. Creative patents

    C. Plant patents

    D. Design patents

6. A systematic method of examining an organization's technology, processes, structure, and human resources, and then developing action strategies to achieve business results, is known as which of the following processes?

    A. Human resource development

    B. Organization development

    C. Organizational interventions

    D. Individual interventions

7. The company that you work for has decided to implement a new inventory management system that affects all departments. Which of the following management strategies should HR recommend?

   A. Learning organization

   B. Lean systems

   C. TQM

   D. Change management

8. Unfreezing, moving, and then refreezing are the three stages for change according to which of the following theories?

   A. Change process theory

   B. Theory X

   C. Motivation/Hygiene theory

   D. Hierarchy of needs

9. A survey was sent out to all training participants asking them to rate various training elements. This information will be used to inform new iterations of the training material. This activity belongs in which stage of the ADDIE training model?

   A. Assessment

   B. Design

   C. Develop

   D. Evaluate

10. Using the information from question 9, which stage of Kirkpatrick's training evaluation model are post-training surveys asking about the trainer's knowledge of the training material?

    A. Level 1, reaction

    B. Level 2, learning

    C. Level 3, behavior

    D. Level 4, results

11. Of the following disciplines described by Peter Senge, which one relates to a high level of expertise in an individual's chosen field?

    A. Systems thinking

    B. Mental models

    C. Personal mastery

    D. Team learning

12. Of the following disciplines described by Peter Senge, which one refers to the deep-seated beliefs that drive employee and organizational behavior?

    A. Systems thinking

    B. Mental models

    C. Personal mastery

    D. Team learning

13. Total Quality Management (TQM) is a technostructural intervention that focuses company-wide efforts on which of the following?

    A. The ability of a process to generate revenue

    B. Waste management

    C. Employee needs

    D. Customer needs

14. Dr. Kaoru Ishikawa developed which of the following TQM tools?

    A. Checksheets

    B. Histograms

    C. Pareto charts

    D. All of the above

15. If a company wants to identify the root cause of most of the issues driving turnover and then represent that data using the 80/20 rule, which of the following TQM tools should HR recommend?

    A. Checksheets

    B. Histograms

    C. Pareto charts

    D. Stratification

16. Visually representing the consequences of specific actions can best be represented using which of the following TQM tools?

    A. Cause-and-effect diagram

    B. Histograms

    C. Pareto charts

    D. Stratification

17. Which of the following technostructural intervention strategies uses Define, Measure, Analyze, Improve, and Control (DMAIC) in the analysis quality improvements?

    A. Total Quality Management

    B. Six Sigma

    C. Juran Trilogy

    D. Learning interventions

18. Broadly defined jobs in flat hierarchies are characteristics of which of the following types of organizations?

    A. Learning

    B. High involvement

    C. High functioning

    D. Competitive

19. Which of the following is an example of a human process intervention?

   A. Discipline

   B. Team building

   C. Rewards

   D. Job design

20. The company that you work for has had difficulty finding and retaining qualified individuals for its marketing department. After conducting an analysis, it has been determined that the department lacks leadership and accountability for outcomes. Which of the following human resource development interventions should HR recommend?

   A. Redesign the jobs to increase employee satisfaction.

   B. Develop a leadership evaluation and development program.

   C. Develop a diversity program to ensure that employees feel like they belong.

   D. Create an incentive program that is directly tied to performance.

21. Teaching the accounting staff how to use new accounting software is an example of which of the following talent management activities?

   A. Skills training

   B. Job enlargement

   C. Supervisory training

   D. Development

22. Performance management, progressive discipline, and conflict management are all examples of which of the following talent management activities?

   A. Skills training

   B. Job enlargement

   C. Supervisory training

   D. Feedback

23. An experienced individual who acts as a teacher, guide, counselor, and facilitator providing personalized feedback to an employee in a business context is known as which of the following?

   A. Supervisor

   B. Trainer

   C. Manager

   D. Mentor

24. A mentor is to career development as a coach is to _____ development.

   A. Job

   B. Emotional

   C. Skill

   D. Cultural

25. Which of the following sources for coaching is useful when desired outcomes are the responsibilities of a shared workgroup?

    A. Executive coaching

    B. Peer-to-peer coaching

    C. Mentor program

    D. Facilitation

26. Coaching that combines self-paced learning with email and telephone support is called what?

    A. E-coaching

    B. Personal coaching

    C. Virtual coaching

    D. Video coaching

27. A program that seeks out employees demonstrating management skills is also known as which of the following?

    A. Training program

    B. Diversity program

    C. Coaching program

    D. Leadership program

28. Which of the following types of training involves processes performed in a single job category?

    A. Individual-level training

    B. Task-level training

    C. Organizational-level training

    D. Systems-based training

29. Which of the following types of training focuses on preparing for future needs?

    A. Individual-level training

    B. Task-level training

    C. Organizational-level training

    D. Systems-based training

30. The three types of employee training programs are organizational, task, and what?

    A. Strategic

    B. Individual

    C. Safety

    D. Developmental

31. A training needs analysis seeks to identify which of the following?

    A. Finding a way to pay for the training

    B. The level of executive commitment to the training

    C. The long-term needs of the organization

    D. The type of training necessary to solve a problem

32. At which stage of training needs assessment are all possible means of filling a performance gap considered?

    A. Gathering data

    B. Proposing solutions

    C. Estimating budget

    D. Identifying goals

33. Which of the following type of learning curve is characterized by a slow start in learning that increases as the learner masters different aspects of the process or task?

    A. An S-shaped learning curve

    B. A positively accelerating learning curve

    C. A plateau learning curve

    D. A negatively accelerating learning curve

34. A management trainer prefers to use PowerPoint presentations and graphs to communicate training content to participants. She is most likely relying on what preferred learning style?

    A. Tactile

    B. Kinesthetic

    C. Visual

    D. Auditory

35. A participant in training prefers to take notes on his mobile device. He brings a Bluetooth keyboard and pecks away at the typewriter during training sessions. The typing is most likely engaging which of his preferred learning styles?

    A. Tactile

    B. Visual

    C. Auditory

    D. Chunking

36. A training participant tends to stand up in the back of the room periodically and needs to get up and down fairly frequently. This trainee most likely prefers which learning style?

    A. Tactile

    B. Visual

    C. Auditory

    D. None of the above

37. Under which of the following conditions may employers *not* pay an employee wages for attending training?

A. If the training is truly voluntary

B. If the training is not related to the employee's job

C. If attendance is outside of the employee's working hours

D. If all of the above conditions are met

38. Which of the following has been shown to improve creativity and innovation on the job?

A. Creating flexible work schedules

B. Increasing diversity on work teams

C. Having supervisors in place who are creative

D. Cultural initiatives allowing free play, such as ping pong

39. A highly productive employee has recently been promoted to a supervisory position and is struggling with the new responsibilities. Which of the following talent management strategies should HR recommend to help the employee in their new position?

A. Interpersonal skills training

B. Time management training

C. Team-building training

D. Supervisory training

40. Skill variety, task identity, and task significance are all examples of which of the following talent management strategies?

A. Autonomy

B. Job enlargement

C. Job design

D. Job enrichment

41. It is understood that employees make a decision to stay with or leave an organization within the first three weeks of employment. Which of the following onboarding techniques will most likely result in reducing the stress that comes from not knowing what to expect on the job?

A. Communicating how the job aligns with company strategy

B. Engaging the employee in on-the-job training activities

C. Creating a connection with the new hire

D. Providing performance feedback after the first 90 days

42. Which of the following can actually inhibit the development of creative ideas?

A. Lack of project management skills

B. Lack of flexibility within a bureaucratic structure

C. Lack of expertise

D. All of the above

43. Of the following options, which would be *best* for HR to recommend if they want to increase workforce collaboration between headquartered and telecommuting workers?

A. Team-building activities

B. Technological solutions

C. Call back all telecommuting workers

D. Bootcamp-style training events

44. Which of the following is a main advantage of e-learning platforms over the traditional classroom setting?

A. Ease of use and implementation

B. Increased retention of information

C. Time savings

D. Availability of custom content options

45. Learning a new job by watching the incumbent perform the task is what type of on-the-job training?

A. Job enrichment

B. Job enlargement

C. Job rotation

D. Job shadowing

46. Ben is an operations manager at a large dog food plant in Arkansas. He is working with a junior-level employee who is teaching him the mechanics of the company's new software operating system. This is the best example of which of the following talent management techniques?

A. Mentoring

B. Coaching

C. Development

D. Reverse mentoring

47. An unexpected outcome from harassment prevention campaigns such as #metoo in the area of learning and development is which of the following?

A. An increase in harassment charges filed with the EEOC

B. A decrease in the number of men willing to become mentors to female employees

C. State-by-state changes to required harassment prevention education programs

D. The need for diversity management programs for organizations of all sizes

48. A company's electronic communications policy should include guidelines for which of the following?

A. Copyright use

B. Spamming

C. Confidentiality

D. All of the above

49. Which of the following will best help an employer make an informed decision about how to address gaps in employee competencies?

   A. Employee interviews

   B. Training needs assessment

   C. Job analysis

   D. Supervisor surveys

50. The company you work for needs to deliver warehouse and driver training but is concerned that the classroom environment will not be the most effective form of delivery. Additionally, none of these employees has company computers or email addresses, so e-learning is not a viable option. Which of the following strategies should you recommend?

   A. Bootcamp

   B. Training

   C. Micro-learning

   D. After-hours training

51. Many of the employees at the IT company you help to manage have no interest in moving into a supervisory role. Additionally, because the company is small, there are not enough management positions for employees to move into, even if they desired it. However, in exit interviews you have discovered that many employees are leaving because of the lack of a clear career path within your organization. Which of the following would be an effective solution to the retention problem?

   A. Offer more training programs.

   B. Tie skill development to higher pay levels.

   C. Design dual career ladders.

   D. Pay longevity bonuses.

52. The time it takes for a person to understand and retain information is known as which of the following?

   A. Learning agility

   B. Learning pace

   C. Learning style

   D. Learning motivation

53. Lisa is an accounts payable clerk at the large car dealership for which you are the HR manager. She has been identified as a high-potential employee based on her positive attitude and ability to learn new things quickly. The leadership team has asked you to establish stretch goals for her over the coming year to expand her knowledge and competencies in business finance. Which of the following is the best example of a stretch goal for Lisa?

   A. Ask her to create an annual calendar to track recurring payments.

   B. Work with her to improve her data entry accuracy by 15 percent.

   C. Schedule her to job shadow the salespeople to better understand the selling process.

   D. Task her with researching and recommending a new sales commission structure tied to business growth targets.

54. Using the example in the previous question regarding Lisa the AP clerk, which of the following best represents the *relevant* part of a SMART goal?

   A. The goal is tied to a company need.

   B. The goal must be completed within the annual rating period.

   C. The goal is both clear and understandable.

   D. The goal is challenging.

55. The activity of coaching is best represented in which of the following scenarios?

   A. A manager directs an employee's efforts every day.

   B. An employee meets one on one with a manager to discuss ways to improve his interpersonal skills.

   C. An employee attends formal classroom training to improve communication skills.

   D. All of the above.

56. In implementing an executive coaching program, which of the following activities should HR complete first?

   A. Creating a 360-degree feedback survey regarding the executive

   B. Designing an evaluative system to measure effectiveness

   C. Tying the coaching activities to the company mission or strategy

   D. Deciding how the coaching sessions will be delivered

57. Mentoring is a type of _____ designed to maximize executive and organizational performance.

   A. Perk

   B. Training

   C. Management activity

   D. Partnership

58. The sales manager at the company for which you work tends to have an increasingly laid-back approach to managing her salespeople. This has come up as part of the need to coach and develop her skillsets to make her a more effective leader. What type of leadership style is she practicing?

   A. Transactional

   B. Transformational

   C. Laissez-faire

   D. Authoritarian

59. Which of the following elements of a leadership development program would be most likely to motivate a person with a transactional leadership style?

   A. A bonus upon completion of the program

   B. More autonomy in managing their staff upon completion of the program

   C. The ability to mentor a high-potential employee upon completion of the program

   D. All of the above

60. You have been tasked with creating training for the accounting department at the large CPA firm for which you work. Which of the following would be a copyright infringement if you used it in your training presentation?

   A. A quotation from a blog found on LinkedIn

   B. A photocopy from the Generally Accepted Accounting Principles (GAAPs)

   C. A Dilbert cartoon parody of a typical accountant

   D. Real scenarios from your accounting department

61. As the instructional designer for the financial services company you work for, you have been tasked with gathering data to define the training needs of your financial advisors. What is the best way for you to source this information?

   A. A review of employee benefits utilization

   B. A review of customer portfolio performance for each advisor

   C. An employee survey asking them what type of training they need

   D. A 360-degree feedback survey

62. For many of the employees at the manufacturing company you work for, Spanish is their native language and English is their second. While they are eager to participate in training sessions, you are concerned that they are not actually understanding the content. Which of the following approaches would best help manage this training participant need?

   A. Hire a translator for the training sessions.

   B. Host voluntary English language training after hours.

   C. Design the training to be delivered in both English and Spanish.

   D. Continue to only offer the sessions in English.

63. The healthcare facility you work for is facing a leadership shortage within the next five years as a wave of managers proceed through a phased retirement program. The executive team is concerned because the healthcare industry is already facing a shortage of qualified talent. What should HR recommend?

   A. Increasing employee compensation to be more competitive

   B. Lobbying the government for more healthcare visas

   C. Beginning to engage in continuous recruitment activities for these positions

   D. Building a succession plan using self- and supervisor assessments of the current workforce

64. Of the following, which should come first for a company wanting to design an effective training program?

   A. Getting budgetary approval for training sessions

   B. Completing a job task analysis

   C. Designing training evaluation

   D. Establishing the learning outcomes

65. A warehouse employee came to you, the HR manager, and disclosed that she has dyslexia. She is scheduled to attend training that week and is worried that she will not be able to keep up with the written work. What should your response be?

    A. Ask her what training format would work better and seek to accommodate her request.

    B. Excuse her from the training altogether.

    C. Remind her that training is part of her job duties and she needs to pass to help her keep up with the job requirements.

    D. Tell her not to worry about it because the training is really more of a formality.

66. The last focus group your employer conducted was facilitated by the department manager. Which of the following reasons is the most likely to have made it fail?

    A. The group likely did not have executive support.

    B. The employees were uncomfortable sharing their true opinion with their manager.

    C. The manager was probably not a skilled facilitator.

    D. The focus group lacked a purpose statement.

67. Which training room configuration is most conducive to a successful employee focus group?

    A. Classroom

    B. Chevron

    C. U-shaped

    D. Theater

68. An organization has decided to adopt an employee mentorship program as part of the culture initiative it is rolling out this year. Which of the following should be given the greatest priority in pairing mentors and mentees?

    A. The mentee should believe that the mentor is genuinely interested in their success.

    B. The company has committed an adequate budget for the program.

    C. The mentor should have volunteered for the role.

    D. The mentor should be formally trained.

69. Coaching is to transactional as mentoring is to what?

    A. Transformational

    B. Psychological

    C. Authoritarian

    D. Country club

70. Hiring an external coach may be beneficial to which of the following people?

    A. An employee who expresses an interest in growing in her position

    B. An executive having difficulty generating accountability in his team

    C. Any employee who is experiencing poor job fit

    D. All of the above can benefit from an external coach.

71. If a career plan focuses on the individual employee, then who or what does career management focus on?

    A. Also the individual

    B. On the organization

    C. On the business strategy

    D. On the teams

72. A successful executive coaching program will result in all of the following except what?

    A. A focus on learning to produce results

    B. The development of improved communication skills

    C. The identification of strengths and weaknesses

    D. The development of new business growth strategies

73. What is one limitation of a high-potential employee fast-track program?

    A. The expense in the design of these types of programs

    B. The risk of newly developed employees leaving the organization

    C. The potential low morale of employees not selected

    D. The lack of a true measurable

74. Which of the following statements is true regarding replacement planning?

    A. Replacement planning always requires a significant investment in employee training.

    B. Replacement planning is usually focused on the candidate with the most development potential.

    C. Replacement planning spans a longer-term outlook.

    D. Replacement planning is generally completed for a short-term period.

75. Which of the following tools is most likely to be used to identify an employee's development potential?

    A. Replacement plan

    B. Performance improvement plan

    C. Succession plan

    D. Workforce plan

76. Redesigning the workflow of a manufacturing assembly line is an example of what type of organizational intervention?

    A. Technological intervention

    B. Human resource intervention

    C. Process flow mapping

    D. Structural

77. Which of the following key words *best* describes the nature of an organizational development intervention?

- **A.** Planned
- **B.** Project-based
- **C.** Company-wide
- **D.** Employee-driven

78. Which of the following is almost always a byproduct of an OD intervention?

- **A.** Employee turnover
- **B.** Leadership development
- **C.** Change management
- **D.** Re-training efforts

79. Why is succession planning most often focused on filling leadership-level and above jobs?

- **A.** Older workers tend to leave the workforce more often, and they hold the most leadership positions.
- **B.** The value of these jobs is higher than that of individual contributors.
- **C.** These positions are the most important within an organization.
- **D.** These positions are most difficult to fill.

80. In terms of importance, which of the following positions should you create a succession plan for first?

- **A.** Leadership roles
- **B.** Critical roles
- **C.** Individual contributor roles
- **D.** Line management

Chapter

4

PHR Practice Area 4: Total Rewards

THE PHR EXAM CONTENT FROM THE TOTAL REWARDS FUNCTIONAL AREA COVERED IN THIS CHAPTER FOCUSES ON "IMPLEMENTING, PROMOTING, AND MANAGING COMPENSATION AND BENEFIT PROGRAMS IN COMPLIANCE WITH FEDERAL LAWS." EXAM CONTENT CONSISTS OF THE FOLLOWING RESPONSIBILITIES:

✓ 01   Manage compensation-related information and support payroll issue resolution

✓ 02   Implement and promote awareness of non-cash rewards (for example: paid volunteer time, tuition assistance, workplace amenities, and employee recognition programs)

✓ 03   Implement benefit programs (for example: health plan, retirement plan, employee assistance plan, other insurance)

✓ 04   Administer federally compliant compensation and benefit programs

IN ADDITION TO THE RESPONSIBILITIES LISTED ABOVE, AN INDIVIDUAL TAKING THE PHR EXAM SHOULD HAVE WORKING KNOWLEDGE OF THE FOLLOWING, USUALLY DERIVED THROUGH PRACTICAL EXPERIENCE:

✓ 36   Applicable federal laws and regulations related to total rewards

✓ 37   Compensation policies, processes, and analysis

1. What are the two main types of compensation?

    A. Base pay and incentives

    B. Static and variable

    C. Monetary and nonmonetary

    D. Mandatory and voluntary

2. Direct compensation is to wages as indirect compensation is to what?

    A. Intrinsic

    B. Fringe benefits

    C. Variable pay

    D. Pay for performance

3. An employee in your company has complained that the compensation data used to establish his pay rate is out of date. This is an example of which of the following?

    A. Distributive justice

    B. Pay openness

    C. External market conditions

    D. Procedural justice

4. Discouraging employees from talking about their pay rate or annual bonuses is an example of a low degree of _____.

    A. Tolerance

    B. Pay openness

    C. Privacy

    D. Procedural justice

5. Organizations that believe employee inputs should be closely tied to their compensation have which type of compensation philosophy?

    A. Rewards

    B. Performance-based

    C. Entitlement

    D. Equitable

6. Which of the following is used to determine how the organizational financial resources may be best used to attract, retain, and motivate the organization's human resources?

    A. Change-management strategies

    B. Compensation strategies

    C. Compensation philosophy

    D. Performance-based philosophy

7. The SEC requires public companies to disclose compensation fully for the top _____ executives.

   A. Two

   B. Three

   C. Five

   D. Seven

8. Confidence or trust and the highest standard of care are the definition of which of the following terms?

   A. Fiduciary responsibility

   B. Ethics

   C. Integrity

   D. Conflict of interest

9. External factors affecting compensation decisions include all but which of the following?

   A. Economic factors

   B. Labor market

   C. The importance of jobs relative to each other

   D. Supply and demand

10. Which of the following acts established the federal minimum wage?

    A. Portal to Portal Act

    B. Rehabilitation Act

    C. Equal Pay Act

    D. Fair Labor Standards Act

11. Enterprise coverage under the FLSA applies to businesses employing at least two employees with at least how much in annual sales?

    A. $150,000

    B. $300,000

    C. $500,000

    D. $1,000,000

12. To which of the following business types does the FLSA not apply?

    A. Railway workers

    B. Airline captains

    C. Private employers doing business with the government

    D. Both A and B

13. In the exemption requirement of the FLSA, what is the employee most likely exempt from?

    A. Age requirements

    B. Record-keeping requirements

    C. Minimum wage

    D. Payment of overtime

14. Determining the job responsibilities of a position for the purpose of defining exemption status under the FLSA is known as which of the following?

    A. An exemption test

    B. Criterion validity

    C. A duties test

    D. Job evaluation

15. The federal hourly minimum wage is currently set at what amount?

    A. $6.25

    B. $7.25

    C. $7.50

    D. $8.00

16. Which of the following is true of compensatory time off?

    A. Public employers may compensate employees with comp time instead of overtime payments.

    B. Both private and public employers may compensate employees with comp time instead of overtime pay.

    C. Neither private nor public employers may utilize comp time instead of overtime payments.

    D. All of the above are false.

17. Which of the following examples is compensable as waiting time under the FLSA?

    A. An employee waiting to clock in for work

    B. A receptionist reading a book while waiting for the phone to ring

    C. An employee on call who cannot be more than 15 minutes away from home

    D. An employee driving to an alternate work site outside of their normal commute

18. Short breaks lasting less than how many minutes are considered compensable time under the FLSA?

    A. 5

    B. 10

    C. 20

    D. 35

19. Which of the following provisions protect employers who unintentionally violate the exemption status of employees through improper payroll deductions?

   A. Safe harbor

   B. Due diligence

   C. Good faith

   D. Affirmative defense

20. A member of management who regularly directs the work of others would be classified according to which of the following FLSA exemptions?

   A. Management

   B. Executive

   C. Administrative

   D. Professional

21. An employee hired as a research scientist may be classified according to which of the following FLSA exemptions?

   A. Management

   B. Executive

   C. Administrative

   D. Professional

22. An employee is offered a job at $52,000 per year. This is a form of which type of compensation?

   A. Indirect

   B. Performance-based

   C. Base pay

   D. Perks

23. An employee promotion is classified as which type of compensation?

   A. Variable pay

   B. Incentives

   C. Bonus

   D. Performance-based

24. Employees on the second shift are paid $0.50 more per hour. This is known as which of the following?

   A. Hazard pay

   B. Bonuses

   C. Pay differential

   D. Geographic pay

25. When an employee is called in to work and there is no work available, which of the following is true?

    A. There is never an obligation to pay the employee.

    B. The employer may be required to pay the employee for a minimum number of hours.

    C. The employer is guilty of an unlawful practice.

    D. The employer is required to allow the employee to complete the scheduled shift.

26. Wages are to base pay as incentives are to what?

    A. Bonuses

    B. Indirect compensation

    C. Variable pay

    D. Performance

27. If an employer wants to reward perfect attendance, which of the following variable pay programs would be the most effective?

    A. Doubling the amount of unused days at the end of the year available for the employee to take in the future

    B. Using attendance as one criterion for determining pay increases

    C. Handing out perfect attendance certificates at a company event

    D. Cashing out the unused days as a holiday bonus

28. Plans that reward employees based on cost savings are known as which of the following?

    A. Improshare

    B. A Scanlon plan

    C. Gainsharing

    D. ESOPs

29. A percentage of a sales employee's compensation is at risk, depending on the individual's ability to sell the company's products or services. This is commonly referred to as which of the following?

    A. Gainsharing

    B. Profit sharing

    C. Commissions

    D. Base pay

30. If an employee receives a lump-sum payment at the end of a company's fiscal year, they are more than likely receiving which of the following?

    A. Commission pay

    B. A bonus

    C. A pay increase

    D. A special incentive

31. Determining the relative worth of jobs within an organization is also known as which of the following?

   A. Wage surveys

   B. Comparisons

   C. Internal equity

   D. Job evaluation

32. As part of the job evaluation process, supervisors are asked to place the jobs in their department in order of importance. Which job evaluation method is being used?

   A. Rating

   B. Ranking

   C. Classification

   D. Job pricing

33. Which of the following is considered a source to use to complete a salary survey?

   A. Employee surveys

   B. Government surveys

   C. Outsourced vendors

   D. All of the above

34. When new employees are hired at a higher rate of pay than that of the incumbent, what is said to have occurred?

   A. Inequitable treatment

   B. An unlawful act

   C. Wage compression

   D. Red circling

35. Which of the following statements is true about employee benefits programs?

   A. There are two types of benefits: voluntary and involuntary.

   B. Health benefits are mandated by state laws.

   C. Employers are required to have retirement plan options for employees.

   D. Workers' compensation is a voluntary benefit.

36. Employers are obligated to provide 12 weeks of unpaid leave for eligible employees in covered organizations for the purposes of caring for a serious illness of themselves or a family member under which of the following labor laws?

   A. Portal to Portal Act

   B. Americans with Disabilities Act

   C. Fair Labor Standards Act

   D. Family Medical Leave Act

37. Which of the following statements regarding the FMLA are true? (Choose all that apply.)
    A. The FMLA applies to all public schools and agencies, regardless of their size.
    B. The FMLA applies to private employers with 50 or more employees.
    C. Eligible employees must have worked a minimum of 1,000 hours in the previous 12 months.
    D. Both A and B.

38. Which of the following acts did the Consolidated Omnibus Budget Reconciliation Act (COBRA) amend?
    A. Fair Labor Standards Act
    B. Family Medical Leave Act
    C. Americans with Disabilities Act
    D. Employee Retirement Income Security Act (ERISA)

39. In many organizations, compensation is the _____ operating expense.
    A. Most important
    B. Most difficult
    C. Largest
    D. Smallest

40. "To attract and retain the best qualified workers while ensuring industry-competitive wages and family-friendly benefits" is an example of which of the following?
    A. A corporate mission statement
    B. A compensation philosophy
    C. A company value
    D. All of the above

41. Which of the following is an internal condition that affects an organization's compensation philosophy?
    A. Willingness to pay
    B. Market conditions
    C. What the competition is paying
    D. All of the above

42. It was brought to the attention of the HR director that the employees out on the production line were not being paid overtime because their supervisor was requiring them to put only 40 hours per week on their timecards, even though they often worked beyond that. Which of the following labor laws was being violated?
    A. Pay Equity Act
    B. Fair Labor Standards Act
    C. Equal Employment Opportunity Act
    D. Portal to Portal Act

43. Which of the following acts excludes normal commute time as compensable?

    A. The Portal-to-Portal Act

    B. The Fair Labor Standards Act

    C. The Equal Pay Act

    D. The Davis-Bacon Act

44. The executive team has decided that all employees should receive a discretionary bonus at the end of the fiscal year, the amount to be determined by years of service. This is an example of which of the following?

    A. Individual incentive

    B. Scanlon plan

    C. Group incentive

    D. Improshare

45. Which of the following are examples of compensable factors that are defined during the job evaluation process?

    A. Education

    B. Skills

    C. Experience

    D. All of the above

46. Which of the following is not one of the three factors used to evaluate jobs according to the Hay system?

    A. Experience required

    B. Knowledge

    C. Problem-solving

    D. Accountability

47. Your company regularly engages in a pay increase process that relies on external survey data to calculate raises. It is employing which of the following types of increase?

    A. Merit increases

    B. Annual reviews

    C. Performance-based increases

    D. Cost-of-living increases

48. There are two basic types of employee benefit programs. What are they?

    A. Direct, indirect

    B. Intrinsic, extrinsic

    C. Tangible, intangible

    D. Legally mandated, voluntary

49. What do Social Security, workers' compensation, and unemployment insurance have in common?

    A. They all have wage replacement benefits for qualifying employees.

    B. Employers must offer all three to employees.

    C. Taxes to support these programs are paid by both the employer and the employee.

    D. Both A and B.

50. Maritime Services Inc. is a growing employer with 42 full-time employees and 5 part-time workers. One of the workers has just called in to his manager, informing her that he broke his leg and will need to take off the next two weeks for surgery and recovery. Which of the following labor laws applies?

    A. FMLA

    B. ADA

    C. Workers' compensation

    D. None of the above

51. Which of the following statements is false regarding the Family Medical Leave Act?

    A. An employer may require medical certification to verify leave requests.

    B. An employer is required to use Department of Labor forms for notifying employees of their eligibility, rights, and responsibilities.

    C. Eligible employees must have worked for an employer who is subject to the FMLA for at least 12 months.

    D. Workers within a 75-mile radius must be counted in the 50-employee determination.

52. The employer for whom you work has just rolled out a retirement plan in which all qualified employees will receive 1 percent of their average salary for the last five years of employment for every year of service with the employer. This is known as which type of retirement plan?

    A. Defined contribution

    B. Defined benefit

    C. 401(k)

    D. Simplified Employee Pension

53. If an employer that offers a retirement benefit to their employees fails to provide a summary plan description, they are more than likely violating which of the following laws?

    A. Employee Retirement Income Security Act

    B. Consolidated Omnibus Budget Reconciliation Act

    C. Health Insurance Portability and Accountability Act

    D. Family Medical Leave Act

54. If an employee must complete five years of service to own the employer contributions to their retirement plan, the company has which of the following in place?

    A. An immediate vesting schedule

    B. A cliff vesting schedule

    C. A retention vesting schedule

    D. A graded vesting schedule

55. ERISA requires that employers fund the accrued obligations of a retirement plan on which basis?

    A. Annual

    B. Bi-annual

    C. Quarterly

    D. Monthly

56. Which of the following labor law amendments requires employers to offer an employee a waiver of their rights to sue under the ADEA?

    A. Unemployment Compensation Amendment

    B. Omnibus Budget Reconciliation Act

    C. Older Workers Benefit Protection Act

    D. Pension Protection Act

57. Employers may charge COBRA participants what maximum of the group premium for continuation of coverage?

    A. 25 percent

    B. 52 percent

    C. 75 percent

    D. 102 percent

58. Which of the following is false about the Health Insurance Portability and Accountability Act?

    A. HIPAA prohibits discrimination in insurance for individuals with a disability.

    B. HIPPAA places limits on health insurance restrictions for preexisting conditions.

    C. HIPAA allows employers to require plan participants to pass a physical examination prior to enrolling.

    D. Flexible spending accounts have a partial exemption from the requirements of HIPAA.

59. A group health plan may not use a waiting period that exceeds how many days?

    A. 30

    B. 60

    C. 90

    D. 120

60. What was the main focus of the Pension Protection Act of 2006?

  A. To address excessive executive compensation

  B. To mandate that employers offer retirement plans

  C. To require employers to fully fund their pension plans

  D. All of the above

61. Of the following conditions, which is the *best* reason a company should outsource payroll?

  A. When payroll is processed by an HR department of one person

  B. When the company's cash flow is tight

  C. If the company decides to allow voluntary deductions

  D. When new payroll regulations are passed

62. Which of the following is an example of a voluntary deduction?

  A. Wage garnishment

  B. Federal income tax

  C. 401(k) contribution

  D. Social Security payment

63. What would be the main advantage for a small company to use a payroll outsourcing vendor?

  A. Transfer of risk if a payroll error is made

  B. Subject-matter expertise in payroll-related regulations

  C. Cost savings

  D. All of the above

64. Which of the following represents an HR function that provides the *least* benefit to an employer and thus may be an argument for outsourcing?

  A. COBRA administration

  B. Payroll

  C. Employee recognition

  D. Recruiting

65. If outsourced, what types of COBRA administration activities should HR be sure the vendor will manage?

  A. Eligibility tracking

  B. COBRA notices

  C. Monitoring coverage periods

  D. All of the above

66. As the new HR manager, you have conducted a benefits survey/needs assessment. The findings showed that employee utilization is high, but the costs have grown an average of 18 percent over the past three years alone. What should you recommend to management?

    A. Eliminate the most expensive benefit.

    B. Begin to research new brokers.

    C. Increase cost sharing for premiums and deductions.

    D. Explore all strategies to contain the cost.

67. The new part-time receptionist you hired has come to you with a question regarding her enrollment in the health insurance plan. She is having difficulty understanding why she is not eligible to enroll in the company health insurance plan until November 1 if her first day of work was September 7. Her sister-in-law (who happens to be in HR at the state) told her that the company must allow her to enroll after 30 calendar days of work. Which of the following statements is *true*?

    A. The company does not have to comply with the 30-day rule because she is a part-time employee.

    B. The law allows for a waiting period of 30 business days, not calendar days.

    C. The law allows for a 90-day waiting period, not 30 days.

    D. The company is out of compliance with Affordable Care Act regulations.

68. Which of the following *must* be counted in the 90-day waiting period calculation under the Affordable Care Act?

    A. Weekends

    B. Holidays

    C. Calendar days

    D. All of the above

69. The employees at your place of business seem to dread benefits open enrollment. You conducted a focus group and found that a common complaint was that the employees had to fill out their addresses multiple times on benefits paperwork. Your employer is no more satisfied—the executive team found that lost productivity because of the administrative meetings made the open enrollment period a time of lost revenue. Which of the following solution should you recommend for open enrollment?

    A. Create employee self-service portals.

    B. Request that the broker come in to hold meetings.

    C. Hire a temporary administrative worker to complete redundancies.

    D. Conduct training for employees on how to complete the paperwork more efficiently.

70. Which of the following key features should be *most* important for a small-employer HR department to look for when shopping for employee self-service systems?

    A. The least expensive option for your employer size

    B. Minimal technical knowledge required to manage once live

    C. Integration capabilities with existing systems

    D. Intuitive site designs

71. Which of the following data sources would be the *most* effective if HR needed to gather market-based competitive pay rates?

   A. State unemployment offices

   B. The Department of Labor

   C. Industry surveys

   D. Websites such as `salary.com`

72. Which of the following pairs *best* represents the primary purpose of employer pay practices?

   A. Fair and balanced

   B. Lawful and generous

   C. Needs-based and legal

   D. Competitive and equitable

73. Ben begins working 25 hours per week for Company Z on January 3 and is considered part-time for purposes of the company's group health insurance. Company Z sponsors a group health plan that provides coverage to employees after they have completed a cumulative 1,200 hours of service. What is the approximate *latest* date Ben may be eligible for company health insurance under the plan?

   A. February 15

   B. April 1

   C. August 1

   D. December 15

74. Of the following factors, which is the *most* important for HR to consider when preparing for benefits open enrollment?

   A. The needs of the employees

   B. The availability of technology

   C. The percentage of increase to benefits programs

   D. The company's compensation philosophy

75. Which of the following strategies may help engage employees in the benefits open enrollment process?

   A. Communicating information early and often

   B. Holding raffle drawings every day for employees who have turned in their paperwork

   C. Following up with employees who have not signed up to encourage them to do so

   D. All of the above

76. Which of the following options is the *least* effective in communicating changes to employee health benefits plans?

   A. Face-to-face sessions

   B. Going to remote work sites to answer questions

   C. Group meetings

   D. Asking a broker to come in to explain changes

77. Many employers are beginning to recognize the need to offer extended bereavement leave for the loss of an employee's loved one. Of the following options, which benefit would *best* serve both the employer and the grieving employee?

   A. Offering unlimited paid time off

   B. Giving employees at least three days off for bereavement

   C. Encouraging an employee who needs more time off to get a doctor's note so the employee can be placed on job-protected leave

   D. Clearly defining the leave policy in the employee handbook

78. An employee at your organization emailed a benefits spreadsheet to his spouse so she could help him format the data. Which of the following risks did this action cause?

   A. Privacy breach

   B. Negligence

   C. Identity theft

   D. All of the above

79. What is the primary data used to calculate the monthly retirement benefits from Social Security?

   A. Current pay rate

   B. Time spent in the workforce

   C. Average earnings

   D. All of the above

80. When an employee or spouse has health insurance coverage under multiple plans, the employee's primary insurance company will most likely engage in which practice?

   A. Coordination of benefits

   B. Balance billing

   C. Gatekeeping

   D. Carve-outs

81. What is the primary purpose of a health insurance purchasing cooperative?

   A. To reduce the overall costs of healthcare

   B. To help small businesses comply with the Affordable Care Act

   C. To provide self-funded companies with stop-loss coverage

   D. To provide smaller organizations with the bargaining power of larger organizations when purchasing health plans

82. You are the leave specialist for a 100-employee hospital in Chicago. On Tuesday, an employee came to you to let you know that she is three months pregnant. She would like to know what her paid leave options are for when she takes time off. Which of the following would be the first place she may receive wage replacement?

    A. Social Security benefits

    B. The Family Medical Leave Act (FMLA)

    C. Personal sick time

    D. Paid Family Leave (PFL)

83. Which of the following individuals would be said to have fiduciary responsibility over an employer's group health plan?

    A. The company board of directors

    B. The human resource manager

    C. The plan administrator

    D. All of the above

84. According to the Fair Labor Standards Act, how long must payroll records be kept?

    A. One year

    B. Three years

    C. Five years

    D. Seven years

85. How long is the statute of limitations for filing a claim under the Fair Pay Act with the Equal Employment Opportunity Commission?

    A. One year from the time the discriminatory act occurred

    B. One year following employee separation

    C. Two years from the time the discriminatory paycheck was received

    D. 180 days from the last pay period

Chapter

5

PHR Exam: Employee and Labor Relations

THE PHR EXAM CONTENT FROM THE EMPLOYEE AND LABOR RELATIONS FUNCTIONAL AREA COVERED IN THIS CHAPTER IS FOCUSED ON CANDIDATE ABILITY TO "MANAGE, MONITOR, AND/ OR PROMOTE LEGALLY COMPLIANT PROGRAMS AND POLICIES THAT IMPACT THE EMPLOYEE EXPERIENCE THROUGHOUT THE EMPLOYEE LIFECYCLE." CONTENT RELATED TO THIS FUNCTIONAL AREA CONSISTS OF THE FOLLOWING RESPONSIBILITIES:

✓ 01 Analyze functional effectiveness at each stage of the employee lifecycle (for example: hiring, onboarding, development, retention, exit process, alumni program) and identify alternate approaches as needed

✓ 02 Collect, analyze, summarize, and communicate employee engagement data

✓ 03 Understand organizational culture, theories, and practices; identify opportunities and make recommendations

✓ 04 Understand and apply knowledge of programs, federal laws, and regulations to promote outreach, diversity, and inclusion (for example: affirmative action, employee resource groups, community outreach, corporate responsibility)

✓ 05 Implement and support workplace programs relative to health, safety, security, and privacy following federal laws and regulations (for example: OSHA, workers' compensation, emergency response, workplace violence, substance abuse, legal postings)

✓ 06 Promote organizational policies and procedures (for example: employee handbook, SOPs, time and attendance, expenses)

✓ 07 Manage complaints or concerns involving employment practices, behavior, or working conditions, and escalate by providing information to appropriate stakeholders

✓ 08 Promote techniques and tools for facilitating positive employee and labor relations with knowledge of applicable federal laws affecting union and nonunion workplaces (for example: dispute/conflict resolution, anti-discrimination policies, sexual harassment)

✓ 09 Support and consult with management in performance management process (for example: employee reviews, promotions, recognition programs)

✓ 10 Support performance activities (for example: coaching, performance improvement plans, involuntary separations) and employment activities (for example: job eliminations, reductions in force) by managing corresponding legal risks

IN ADDITION TO THE RESPONSIBILITIES LISTED ABOVE, AN INDIVIDUAL TAKING THE PHR EXAM SHOULD HAVE WORKING KNOWLEDGE OF THE FOLLOWING, USUALLY DERIVED THROUGH PRACTICAL EXPERIENCE:

✓ 44 General employee relations activities and analysis (for example, conducting investigations, researching grievances, working conditions, reports, etc.)

✓ 45 Applicable federal laws and procedures affecting employment, labor relations, safety, and security

✓ 46 Human relations, culture and values concepts, and applications to employees and organizations

✓ 47 Review and analysis process for assessing employee attitudes, opinions, and satisfaction

1. The concept that either party may terminate the employment relationship at any time, and for any reason, is known as which of the following common law doctrines?

    A. Respondeat superior

    B. Constructive discharge

    C. Employment at will

    D. Duty of good faith and fair dealing

2. An employee was in a vehicle accident while on duty for her employer. The employer is liable for all costs associated with the accident. This is in accordance with which of the following common law doctrines?

    A. Defamation

    B. Respondeat superior

    C. Duty of good faith and fair dealing

    D. Promissory estoppel

3. It has come to the attention of HR that a supervisor reassigned an employee from the day shift to the night shift because the supervisor wanted the employee to quit. This would be a case of which of the following?

    A. Constructive discharge

    B. Discipline

    C. Termination

    D. Fraudulent misrepresentation

4. If a supervisor demands that an employee go out on a date with him or else he will not give her a raise, he is most likely engaged in which of the following types of harassment?

    A. Hostile work environment

    B. Quid pro quo

    C. Constructive discharge

    D. None. It is OK to ask an employee out for a date.

5. A vendor was accused of making sexually crude remarks and jokes to the purchasing manager of an organization. The purchasing manager's employer investigated and found that, while offensive, the vendor's behavior did not result in any tangible psychological injury and promptly requested that the vendor assign a new representative to service their account. If the purchasing manager were to file suit nevertheless, the employer would most likely justify their response under which of the following court cases?

    A. *Harris v. Forklift Systems*

    B. *Faragher v. City of Boca Raton*

    C. *Meritor Savings Bank v. Vinson*

    D. *Oncale v. Sundowner Offshore Services*

6. A military reservist who has been working for your organization for the last three years is called to active duty. Which of the following must you, as the employer, grant to this employee?

    A. Retirement vesting must continue to accrue as though there was no break in employment.

    B. The employee must be reinstated in a position that he would have earned had he remained on the job.

    C. The employer must continue to pay the employee his regular wages during the military absence.

    D. Both A and B.

7. General job duties, separation terms, and compensation/benefits are generally spelled out in which of the following documents?

    A. Employee handbook

    B. Job descriptions

    C. Employment contract

    D. Offer letter

8. Why are employee relations and involvement strategies important?

    A. Effective employee relations begin with employee input on decisions that affect them.

    B. Labor law compliance is impossible to achieve without employee input.

    C. Alignment of employee behavior with organizational strategy is completely dependent on employees choosing to be involved.

    D. All of the above.

9. Organizational climate is *what* people experience at work, whereas organizational _____ is the factor that influences (most of the answers are singular) *why* they feel the way they do.

    A. Commitment

    B. Motivation

    C. Culture

    D. Satisfiers

10. If an employer wants to increase retention by improving employee work-life balance, which of the following tools could they choose from?

    A. Compressed workweeks

    B. Job sharing

    C. Flextime

    D. All of the above

11. Which of the following would be the best choice for an employer who needs to communicate to employees that unlawful harassment is prohibited?

   A. Policy

   B. Procedure

   C. Rule

   D. Reference guide

12. Employers with effective employee relations systems in place work to _____ employee discipline.

   A. Support

   B. Prevent

   C. Implement

   D. Defend

13. If an employer wants to avoid costly litigation in defending future claims of wrongful discipline or wrongful termination, which of the following dispute resolution efforts should HR recommend?

   A. Voluntary arbitration

   B. Mediation

   C. A peer review panel

   D. Compulsory arbitration

14. Which of the following is one of the disadvantages of mediation as an alternative dispute resolution method?

   A. Mediation can be too complex.

   B. Mediation can be expensive.

   C. Mediators must be impartial.

   D. Mediation is not binding.

15. Which of the following acts allowed employers to use court-ordered injunctions to break strikes?

   A. The Clayton Act

   B. The Norris-LaGuardia Act

   C. The Sherman Antitrust Act

   D. The National Labor Relations Act

16. As a result of the violence used by employers to prevent union organizing, which of the following acts was passed?

   A. Norris-LaGuardia Act

   B. Clayton Act

   C. The National Labor Relations Act

   D. Sherman Antitrust Act

17. The Taft-Hartley Act was established as the result of which of the following?

    A. The election of a Republican majority to Congress

    B. Employer complaints about union abuses

    C. To respond to the imbalance of power between unions and employers

    D. All of the above

18. A supervisor at the company for which you work told an employee that the company would move their operations to Mexico if an organizing attempt were successful. This is an example of which of the following?

    A. An unfair labor practice

    B. Intimidating behavior

    C. Featherbedding

    D. A fact, allowable under the NLRA

19. Which of the following agencies is tasked with oversight of union organizing activities?

    A. National Labor Relations Board

    B. Department of Labor

    C. National Labor Relations Committee

    D. Equal Employment Opportunity Commission

20. A union is attempting to obtain authorization cards from a bargaining unit that will be made up of 50 employees. How many signatures must they have to petition the NLRB for an election?

    A. 5

    B. 10

    C. 15

    D. 25

21. Under what conditions may temporary workers be included in a bargaining unit?

    A. If they are joint employers

    B. If they receive authorization from the NLRB

    C. If a community of interest exists between the regular workers and temporary workers

    D. None—temporary workers are excluded from bargaining units.

22. During collective bargaining, the employer refuses to increase retirement contributions if the union demands a flat percentage increase to wages during the period covered by the collective bargaining agreement (CBA). This is known as which type of bargaining?

    A. Principled bargaining

    B. Integrative bargaining

    C. Positional bargaining

    D. An unfair labor practice

23. During collective bargaining, the employer agrees to give employees additional paid holi-days, and the union agrees to reduce the demand for increased shift premiums. This is an example of which of the following types of bargaining?

    A. Principled bargaining

    B. Integrative bargaining

    C. Positional bargaining

    D. An unfair labor practice

24. Which of the following statements is true about a collective bargaining agreement?

    A. A CBA requires that all employees of that organization join the union.

    B. A CBA still allows for "at-will" employment.

    C. A CBA is a binding employment contract.

    D. A CBA includes the management personnel of the bargaining unit.

25. Why may a lack of perceived fairness in the distribution of pay lead employees to vote in a union?

    A. Unions generally regulate pay as part of the negotiating process.

    B. Unions offer leadership opportunities as shop stewards and union officers within an existing structure.

    C. Employees may feel that they need a voice because they are not being heard.

    D. Both A and C.

26. The executive team at your place of work has communicated that they want HR to help them change the organizational culture to one of transparency and trust. Which of the following positive employee relations strategies should you recommend *first*?

    A. Publish the company financials so employees can see how the business is doing.

    B. Implement employee feedback mechanisms to identify major barriers to transparency.

    C. Create task forces to implement positive employee relations strategies related to transparency and trust.

    D. Discipline or terminate supervisors who are not trusted by the workforce.

27. Which of the following business impact measures can identify employee satisfaction?

    A. An HR audit

    B. Timeliness of performance reviews

    C. Absenteeism reports

    D. Number of open positions

28. Measuring the number and type of charges filed with the EEOC to make recommenda-tions to employers is which of the following types of HR metrics?

    A. Operational excellence

    B. Tactical accountability

C. An HR audit

D. All of the above

29. An employer may terminate an employee with or without cause. This is known as which of the following common law doctrines?

   A. Respondeat superior

   B. Constructive discharge

   C. Employment at will

   D. Statutory exceptions

30. If an employer terminates an employee to avoid paying the employee an earned sales commission, the employer has violated which of the following exceptions to employment at will?

   A. Contract exception

   B. Duty of good faith and fair dealing

   C. Promissory estoppel

   D. None of the above

31. Which of the following exceptions to employment at will prevents an employer from enticing a prospective employee with the promise of a reward and then failing to deliver it?

   A. Promissory estoppel

   B. Duty of good faith and fair dealing

   C. Contract exceptions

   D. Employment contracts

32. "Let the master answer" is the meaning of which of the following employment doctrines?

   A. Promissory estoppel

   B. Respondeat superior

   C. Defamation

   D. Vicarious liability

33. A supervisor at a manufacturing plant has a personality conflict with one of her subordinates, who otherwise performs very well in the position. The supervisor begins a campaign to discredit the employee, changing her shift, deriding her in meetings, and gossiping behind her back. The employee quits because she just can't take it anymore. What may the supervisor be guilty of?

   A. Constructive discharge

   B. Sexual harassment

   C. Unfair treatment

   D. Nothing, because her employment was at will

34. Vulgar jokes, offensive calendars, and inappropriate touching could all be examples of which of the following?

  A. Unlawful practices

  B. Sexual harassment

  C. Quid pro quo harassment

  D. All of the above

35. The Supreme Court determined that there does not have to be a "tangible employment action" taken against an employee for there to be a legitimate claim of harassment under which of the following court cases?

  A. *Harris v. Forklift Systems*

  B. *Oncale v. Sundowner*

  C. *Faragher v. City of Boca Raton*

  D. *Meritor Savings Bank v. Vinson*

36. The Glass Ceiling Act identified three barriers that prevent women and minorities from advancing to senior-level positions. They are societal barriers, internal structural barriers, and what?

  A. Governmental barriers

  B. Labor market barriers

  C. Family barriers

  D. Educational barriers

37. Employees returning to work from military leaves of more than 30 days but fewer than _____ days may not be discharged without cause for six months after the date of re-employment under USERRA.

  A. 90

  B. 122

  C. 181

  D. 366

38. If an employee is performing well in her current position but does not want to move to the next level, which of the following employee involvement strategies may work best to maximize her talent?

  A. Creating a work team that she leads

  B. Creating a task force to identify the key strengths and weaknesses of the department

  C. Delegating authority of a relevant process to her

  D. None. She should be allowed to remain functioning at her current level.

39. Which of the following methods of communication is the means by which most employees obtain information?

    A. Word of mouth

    B. Company newsletters

    C. Brown-bag lunches

    D. Staff meetings

40. Cecelia, a customer service representative, was recently asked questions by her manager's manager about the level of her company and job satisfaction. This is an example of which of the following methods for gaining employee feedback?

    A. Discipline session

    B. Skip-level interview

    C. Open door policy application

    D. Employee survey

41. Without this, an employer will have a difficult time initiating positive employee relations' strategies.

    A. A culture of mutual respect and fair treatment

    B. Job descriptions

    C. Performance-based pay

    D. All of the above

42. Of the following, which is the most important aspect of employee recognition programs?

    A. That they are self-funded

    B. That they are properly designed to support desired outcomes

    C. That they clearly communicate the ever-changing "measures of success" to align with goals

    D. That they reflect the diversity of the workgroup

43. If an organization changes an employee's schedule from 8:00 to 5:00 to 8:30 to 5:30 to allow him to get his kids to school every day, they are employing which of the following positive employee relations strategies?

    A. Compressed workweek

    B. Flex time

    C. Job sharing

    D. Telecommuting

44. A customer service representative uses a list of the item numbers of most frequently ordered items to aid her customers in placing their orders. This list would be called which of the following?

    A. A standard operating procedure

    B. A procedure

    C. Work instructions

    D. A reference guide

45. Employee handbooks are designed for which of the following purposes?

   A. To manage employee risk

   B. To aid employers in compliance with labor laws

   C. To maintain an employer's status as "at will"

   D. To manage organizational risks and communicate expectations effectively

46. The goal of any performance improvement system should be which of the following?

   A. To avoid legal action

   B. To balance the needs of the employer with the needs of the employee

   C. To document grievance procedures

   D. To guide management decision-making

47. Arbitration, mediation, and constructive conflict are all examples of which of the following?

   A. Alternative dispute resolution methods

   B. Collective bargaining agreements

   C. Labor law compliance

   D. Disciplinary actions

48. An employee disagreed with his supervisor about the performance improvement plan (PIP) to which he was required to commit. HR brought him before a committee of co-workers and managers to discuss the details of his performance and render a decision related to the fairness of the PIP. Which ADR method did the employer use?

   A. Bargaining

   B. A peer review panel

   C. Constructive confrontation

   D. Ombudsmanship

49. An effective absenteeism policy addresses which of the following?

   A. The attendance expectations for the employer

   B. The allowable number of days for non–FMLA-related absences

   C. How absences are counted

   D. All of the above

50. In which of the following situations should HR proceed directly to termination of an employee?

   A. In the absence of a progressive discipline policy

   B. When the employee exceeds the maximum number of missed days identified in the handbook

   C. If the employee engages in an egregious act, such as violence against another employee

   D. If the employee fails to provide medical certification for missed days in accordance with policy

51. What is the usual reason employers take disciplinary action against an employee?

    A. To punish the individual

    B. To motivate the individual

    C. To train the individual

    D. To manage the performance of the individual

52. Which of the following court cases established that union employees have a right to representation at meetings where discipline may occur?

    A. The National Labor Relations Act

    B. *Davis v. O'Melveny & Myers*

    C. *NLRB v. J. Weingarten, Inc.*

    D. *Pharakhone v. Nissan North America, Inc.*

53. Of the following policies, which should HR recommend for all employers?

    A. A description of benefits

    B. An at-will statement

    C. Family Medical Leave Act rights

    D. They are all equally important.

54. The marketing department staff are at odds with each other on the correct course of action to take on a new project. From the perspective of employee involvement, which course should HR recommend?

    A. Defer to the decision of the supervisor.

    B. Appoint a project leader.

    C. Hold a brainstorming session to gain clarity.

    D. Discipline the employee causing the most trouble.

55. Summer BBQs, employee recognition dinners, and diversity programs all help to foster which of the following?

    A. An inclusive workforce

    B. Employee job satisfaction

    C. A positive culture

    D. Employee retention

56. Which of the following is a best practice from a risk management perspective when forming employee-management committees?

    A. Minimize committee involvement on issues related to wages and working conditions.

    B. Avoid having these committees dominated by management.

    C. Consult with a labor attorney regarding potential committee unfair labor practices.

    D. All of the above

57. Providing an employee the opportunity to respond to performance-related issues without terminating them under the at-will common law doctrine is an example of which of the following?

    A. Due process

    B. Duty of good faith and fair dealing

    C. An employee right

    D. Legal compliance

58. The commercial driver members of the union go on strike to protest a bargaining impasse related to their base pay. What type of strike is this?

    A. A lawful strike

    B. An economic strike

    C. A hot cargo agreement

    D. Both A and B

59. If an employer terminates an employee for participating in union organizing activities, they have engaged in which of the following?

    A. An unfair labor practice

    B. An unlawful act

    C. Discrimination

    D. All of the above

60. If a union pushes a work rule guaranteeing a set number of employees on a job as part of the collective bargaining process, regardless of the job size, they may be engaged in which of the following unfair labor practices?

    A. Failure to bargain in good faith

    B. Featherbedding

    C. Prohibited strike

    D. coercion

61. Small groups of employees have been having quiet conversations in the hall, and at the latest staff meeting, another employee from the same department began to deride the company's wages and benefits as being "a joke." Of the following scenarios, which is most likely occurring?

    A. Featherbedding

    B. Union authorization

    C. Union organizing

    D. Nothing, because disgruntled employees will always exist.

62. Which of the following organizing activities may result in a voluntary recognition of a union?

    A. A demand for recognition letter

    B. A neutrality agreement

C. A card-check election

D. All of the above

63. Of the following, which is the most effective method unions may use to campaign for organizing?

   A. Meetings

   B. The Internet

   C. Inside organizing

   D. Picketing

64. What is an Excelsior list?

   A. A list of unfair labor practices

   B. A list of rules the employer must follow at a representation election

   C. A list of trade unions in the United States

   D. A list containing the names and addresses of all employees in a bargaining unit

65. Union shops, agency shops, and closed shops are all examples of which of the following?

   A. Union security clauses

   B. Trade unions

   C. Conditions of employment

   D. Mandatory bargaining subjects

66. What is the ultimate measure of the success of a company's employee relations strategies?

   A. The return on investment of these activities

   B. The satisfaction level of employees

   C. The turnover rates

   D. The absenteeism rates

67. Which of the following analysis tools can best measure the more subjective criteria of employee satisfaction?

   A. Turnover rates

   B. Absenteeism trends

   C. Supervisory reviews

   D. Employee surveys

68. Which of the following is an example of a tactical accountability measure?

   A. Number of claims filed with the EEOC

   B. Employee surveys

   C. Performance reviews

   D. Employee stress levels

69. Multiple unions are competing with each other for the right to represent a single bargaining unit. Which of the following are they competing for?

   A. Exclusive jurisdiction

   B. Weingarten rights

   C. Choice of law representation

   D. Duty of good faith and fair dealing

70. What is the primary purpose of the Workers Adjustment and Retraining Notification (WARN) Act?

   A. Employers must fund retraining efforts for displaced workers.

   B. Employers must allow employees to vote on any alternative work schedule.

   C. Employers must offer job placement assistance for displaced workers.

   D. Employers must notify employees of a mass layoff.

71. Which of the following was the primary consequence for unions as the result of the Sherman Anti-Trust Act?

   A. The act included strikes and boycotts in the definition of unlawful trade restrictions.

   B. The act exempted unions from the strike-breaking penalties established under the Clayton Act.

   C. It increased the types of unfair labor practice charges.

   D. The act increased the amount of fines for unions engaged in unlawful trades.

72. Which of the following established that temporary employees may be included in a company's bargaining unit?

   A. Weingarten

   B. Sturgis

   C. La Guardia

   D. Payne

73. Workplace training programs and inspections conducted by the unions are most likely the result of which of the following union management approaches?

   A. Collective bargaining

   B. Safety initiatives

   C. Co-employment

   D. Joint management

74. Workplace monitoring systems seek first to accomplish which organizational objective?

   A. Catch employees who are violating company policies

   B. Protect the company and customers from unauthorized access or data theft

   C. Create proof and documentation to defend a potential charge of negligence

   D. Manage risks in high hazard environments

75. Employee rights are most often offset by what?

   A. Obligations

   B. Statutory protection

   C. Responsibilities

   D. Freedoms

76. What is a challenge to using a handbook to communicate policies to employees?

   A. Readability

   B. Downward communication

   C. Employee perception

   D. Relevance

77. What is an HR best practice for distributing the employee handbook?

   A. Using the company intranet for easy access

   B. Holding new-hire orientations to review the handbook policies and obtain signatures

   C. Making an honest attempt to ensure employees read and understand the policies

   D. Asking the supervisors to review the handbook with employees any time changes are made

78. The primary purpose of an HR audit in risk management is to accomplish which of the following?

   A. Analyze a department budget

   B. Evaluate a department mission

   C. Identify organizational risks

   D. Align organizational goals

79. Of the following options, which is federal legislation that affects the risk management activities of an HR department?

   A. Americans with Disabilities Act

   B. Occupational Safety and Health Act

   C. Civil Rights Act of 1964

   D. All of the above

80. Which of the following acts requires employers to provide employees with a place of work that is "free from recognized hazards that are causing or likely to cause death or serious physical harm"?

   A. Occupational Safety and Health Act

   B. Sarbanes-Oxley Act

   C. Rehabilitation Act

   D. Workers' Compensation Act

81. Which of the following did the Occupational Safety and Health Administration Act of 1970 establish?

    A. National Institute of Occupational Safety and Health (NIOSH)

    B. Occupational Safety and Health Administration (OSHA)

    C. Occupational Safety and Health Review Commission (OSHRC)

    D. All of the above

82. What is the primary purpose of OSHA's injury record-keeping requirements?

    A. To collect data for OSHA and NIOSH to identify emerging hazards and recommend new standards

    B. To have documentation available in the event of an OSH inspection

    C. To calculate relevant penalties based on the type of violation

    D. To reference evidence in the application of enforcement standards

83. Which of the following created safety and health standards for mine workers?

    A. Occupational Safety and Health Administration

    B. Mine Safety and Health Act

    C. Needlestick Safety and Prevention Act

    D. Rehabilitation Act

84. Asbestos and corrosives are examples of which of the following types of environmental health hazards?

    A. Physical

    B. Biological

    C. Chemical

    D. All of the above

85. Which of the following types of assets would need to be evaluated in a security risk assessment?

    A. Information assets

    B. Environmental assets

    C. Cultural assets

    D. Trade secrets

86. The companies that had staff in New York on September 11, 2001, lost power as the result of the terrorist attacks on the World Trade Center. One of the companies was able to activate their emergency response plan, including automated backup of data and employee egress. This is an example of which of the following types of risk management?

    A. Injury and illness prevention

    B. Environmental hazard assessments

    C. Business continuity

    D. Information asset management

87. Training management and having an employee assistance program (EAP) in place are steps taken to minimize which of the following?

    A. Disgruntled employees

    B. Stress in the workplace

    C. Workplace violence

    D. Business disruption

88. If an employee is injured on the job but is still qualified to complete some essential functions, which of the following return-to-work (RTW) strategies should HR recommend?

    A. Modified duty

    B. An independent medical exam

    C. Time off from work

    D. A short-term administrative position

89. Which of the following is the most important consideration for workplace privacy concerns?

    A. Controlling privacy abuses

    B. Balancing employer security needs against employee privacy concerns

    C. Having a workplace privacy policy

    D. Avoiding legal issues

90. Which of the following statements belongs in an electronic media privacy policy?

    A. Emails sent using company equipment are the property of the employer and may be monitored or reviewed at any time.

    B. The employer reserves the right to terminate the employee at any time and for any reason, including for electronic media abuse.

    C. The employer prohibits the use of company cell phones for personal calls.

    D. All of the above.

91. Of the following plans, which describes the best way for the organization to evacuate company personnel and on-site visitors in the event of a natural disaster?

    A. Continuity of operations plan

    B. Disaster recovery plan

    C. Emergency response plan

    D. Critical incident plan

92. If an employer wants to prevent fraud by having an impartial review of an injured worker's ability to return to work, they should use which of the following?

    A. An occupational clinic

    B. An independent medical exam

    C. The employee's personal physician

    D. The emergency room

93. An effective substance abuse policy in the workplace has which of the following components?

    A. A plan for random drug tests

    B. A description of the return-to-work process

    C. A succession plan, should an employee separation occur

    D. Top management support of a substance abuse program

94. Which of the following risk classifications are threaded throughout all HR activities?

    A. Legal compliance

    B. Employee safety

    C. Financial mismanagement

    D. All of the above

95. If an employer receives a complaint about sexual harassment from an employee, which of the following risk assessment tools should they employ?

    A. HR audit

    B. Workplace investigation

    C. Legal compliance review

    D. Discrimination audit

96. A male supervisor chose a male candidate over a female candidate because he was worried about the potential loss of productivity the woman may have because of childcare issues. Which of the following types of unlawful discrimination did the supervisor commit?

    A. Work-life discrimination

    B. Caregiver discrimination

    C. Disparate treatment

    D. All of the above

97. If a federal contractor with more than $100,000 in contracts has an employee who is convicted of a drug-related offense, which of the following actions must they take?

    A. Notify the OFCCP.

    B. Notify the contracting agency of the violation within 10 days of the offense.

    C. Notify the Department of Labor.

    D. None of the above. The employee has a right to privacy.

98. Your employer has asked you to conduct research on the merits of having warehouse employees use back braces in an effort to decrease soft tissue injuries. Which of the following resources would yield this information?

    A. National Institute of Occupational Safety and Health (NIOSH)

    B. Occupational Safety and Health Administration (OSHA)

    C. Center for Disease Control (CDC)

    D. The Department of Labor (DOL)

99. An off-duty employee was on site at his place of work, visiting a co-worker on the co-workers lunch break. The off-duty employee slipped on a spill that had not been properly cleaned up. Which of the following statements is true?

    A. The injury is recordable.

    B. The injury is not recordable.

    C. The injury is both compensable and recordable.

    D. The injury is considered work-related, but the recordability is determined by the type/severity of the injury.

100. An employer discovers a gas leak in the company's break room, and an employee places a call to OSHA to report it. Under which priority is OSHA likely to conduct an inspection?

    A. Imminent danger, first

    B. Catastrophes, second

    C. Employee complaints, third

    D. High hazard, fourth

101. At what stage of an OSHA inspection would the compliance officer review the employer's written safety and health program?

    A. The opening conference

    B. The facility tour

    C. The closing conference

    D. The appeals process

102. Prison guards exposed to tuberculosis are threatened by which of the following types of workplace health hazards?

    A. Environmental hazards

    B. Physical hazards

    C. Biological hazards

    D. Chemical hazards

103. Cecelia, a customer service representative, has been recently complaining about pain and swelling in her wrist. Which of the following steps should HR take first?

    A. Conduct ergonomics training

    B. Evaluate her workstation for potential causes

    C. Offer to send her to the occupational clinic for treatment

    D. Give her a refusal of treatment form

104. An employer has 350 full-time employees working 40 hours a week, 50 weeks per year. Of those, 35 had a soft-tissue injury related to office ergonomics. What is the employer's EIR?

    A. 2.5 percent

    B. 5 percent

    C. 10 percent

    D. 12.5 percent

105. Workers' compensation insurance was originally designed to do what?

  A. Compensate employees for injuries sustained on the job

  B. Set regulations for telecommuting workers

  C. Establish guidelines for dealing with substance abuse in the workplace

  D. Cover the emotional impairment from a work-related injury

106. Which of the following statements is true with regard to leave coordination for an injured worker?

  A. The FLSA will have to be considered when coordinating leaves.

  B. An employee may not be compelled to use any accrued sick time while out with a work-related injury.

  C. FMLA leave may run concurrently with an employee out for a work-related injury.

  D. All of the above are true.

107. What is the primary distinction between modified duty and reasonable accommodation?

  A. Modified duty is typically a short-term solution.

  B. Reasonable accommodation applies only to compliance with the ADA.

  C. Employers are not required by law to offer reasonable accommodation to injured workers.

  D. None. They can be used interchangeably.

108. In what way can an employer's modified duty program dilute the essential functions of the job under the Americans with Disabilities Act?

  A. If the employer modifies a function that is nonessential, they may need to do so for a disabled worker as well.

  B. If the employer removes an essential function in order to accommodate modified duty, the task may not actually be considered essential.

  C. The length of time an employer accommodates a modified duty assignment may set precedent for the long-term accommodation of a disabled individual.

  D. All of the above.

109. Which of the following is the *primary* act that governed the use of child labor in the workplace?

  A. Fair Labor Standards Act (FLSA)

  B. Occupational Safety and Health Act (OSHA)

  C. Railway Labor Act

  D. All of the above

110. An assessment may be conducted to identify which of the following types of risk?

  A. Employee safety and health

  B. Union activity

  C. Labor law compliance

  D. All of the above

111. Why would an audit of an employer's hiring practices be a form of risk management?

    A. The audit could discover disparate pay rates.

    B. The audit may uncover practices that are contrary to a company's recruiting philosophy.

    C. The audit may analyze the proper use of pre-employment tests.

    D. The audit may measure new-hire development practices for consistency.

112. The best way to prepare for an internal workplace investigation is to do which of the following?

    A. Call the labor attorney.

    B. Establish a legally compliant procedure.

    C. Speak with a manager first.

    D. Review current practices for comparison.

113. A retina scan to open doors is a security measure designed using what kind of data?

    A. Scanned

    B. Biological

    C. Passively collected

    D. Biometric

114. The agricultural producer you work for in the southern United States is complaining of the rising temperatures typical of summer. Under what OSHA standard must you address this hazard?

    A. HAZCOMM

    B. Heat illness

    C. General duty

    D. Self-inspections

115. What is the best way to know which safety laws apply to your organization?

    A. Conduct a risk assessment

    B. Join a local HR group

    C. Obtain a bachelor's degree in human resources

    D. Become a certified safety specialist

116. What is the primary reason for conducting a self-inspection?

    A. To keep an OSHA inspector from coming to your place of work

    B. To correct hazards and prevent incidents

    C. To reduce workers' compensation costs

    D. To demonstrate compliance with the law

117. Of the following, which is the *least* effective way to abate a safety hazard related to a piece of machinery?

  A. Limit operation to trained users

  B. Require personal protective equipment (PPE)

  C. Train employees on use and type of hazards

  D. Don't allow machine guards to be removed

118. Of the following jobs, which is *most* likely to cause an ergonomic injury?

  A. Running a bottling line

  B. Working in a loud factory

  C. Operating a jackhammer

  D. Working with chemicals

119. A written injury and illness prevention program is an example of what type of OSHA-defined hazard control?

  A. Engineering

  B. Administrative

  C. PPE

  D. Operational

120. One of your forklift drivers was not paying attention and crushed his ankle between the forklift and a beam. What was the *direct* cause of the injury?

  A. The employee's lack of attention

  B. The placement of the beam

  C. The contact between his ankle and the beam

  D. Lack of training

121. Using the information from the accident described in the previous question, what was the *indirect* cause of this injury?

  A. The employee's lack of attention

  B. The placement of the beam

  C. The contact between his ankle and the beam

  D. Lack of training

122. What is the *first* priority when responding to the scene of a workplace incident?

  A. Identifying and then separating any witnesses

  B. Taking pictures to document the conditions for an investigation

  C. Obtaining medical attention for any injured worker

  D. Securing the area so nobody else gets hurt

123. Which of the following steps should you take to avoid witness contamination after a workplace incident?

    A. Speak to all of them in a group to see what the consensus is.

    B. Separate them as soon as is practicable and interview them separately.

    C. Obtain all of their accounts in writing.

    D. Interview only a few of them and compare their findings to your own impressions.

124. For a written injury and illness prevention plan (IIPP) to be effective, it should contain which of the following elements?

    A. A description of the disciplinary actions that will be taken if an employee gets injured

    B. A detailed summary of the type of benefits available to an injured worker

    C. A map or listing of the closest place to seek medical care, should an employee sustain an injury

    D. A statement of top-level management commitment to employee safety and health

125. Requiring managers to write descriptive comments about employee performance is an example of what type of performance appraisal?

    A. Comparison

    B. Narrative

    C. BARS

    D. Ranking

126. When do employers most often conduct employee performance reviews?

    A. After the employee's first 90 days of work

    B. Quarterly

    C. Annually

    D. All of the above

127. An employee at your place of work was not wearing the required eye goggles and accidentally splashed bleach into his eyes. He went to the occupational clinic for treatment, and the doctor gave him an eye patch that he must wear for three days. He was able to return to work the next day. Is this injury recordable?

    A. Yes, because he did not return to work on the same day.

    B. Yes, because he was prescribed an eye patch.

    C. No, because the treatment was considered first aid only.

    D. No, because the injury may have been his fault.

128. Under which of the following conditions has unlawful discrimination in performance appraisals *not* occurred?

A. The supervisor rates a female employee lower on attendance because she uses her sick leave more often for her children, not herself.

B. The supervisor rates a Muslim employee low on his attendance because he takes more time off than other workers to practice his religion.

C. The supervisor rates an older worker low on technical performance because he asks so many questions about the system.

D. The supervisor is in a relationship with a subordinate and is in a position to rate her performance.

129. Which of the following is an employer best practice when delivering performance feedback?

A. Use specific examples of behavior that covers the entire rating period.

B. Ensure that the employee knows when his personal life is affecting his professional life.

C. Allow co-workers to review the performance feedback prior to delivering the feedback.

D. All of these are best practices.

130. A supervisor is reluctant to give an employee a low rating on his poor attendance, mainly because the employee—when present—is his most productive worker. This is an example of what type of rater bias?

A. Primacy

B. Recency

C. Halo/horn

D. Leniency

Chapter

6

PHR Practice Exam

1. What is the primary difference between leading and lagging economic indicators?

    A. Leading indicators show that the economy will change, whereas lagging indicators show that the economy has already changed.

    B. Lagging indicators show that the economy is behind in the global marketplace, whereas leading indicators show that the economy is ahead of their global counterparts.

    C. Leading indicators show that the economy has grown, whereas lagging indicators demonstrate that the economy is slow.

    D. There is no major distinction between the two.

2. During recruiting, a supervisor told you that she wanted to pay more to an applicant than was advertised. While the salary amount was still within the range for the position, when asked why, the supervisor said that the applicant asked for a higher salary and the supervisor was afraid if she offered less, the applicant would not accept the position. This is the *best* example of what type of bias?

    A. Anchoring

    B. Framing

    C. Overconfidence

    D. Confirmation

3. Your company has decided to offer company-sponsored, outsourced retirement planning to employees as a voluntary benefit. Which data set did the employer *most* likely use to make this decision?

    A. Ethical

    B. Compliance

    C. Demographic

    D. Economic

4. Analyzing the probability of a particular outcome is the primary function of which strategic planning and budgeting tool?

    A. ROI formulas

    B. Quantification

    C. Zero-based budgeting

    D. Forecasting

5. The executive team at your organization meets quarterly to review strategy and generate the goals for each department. This is an example of which goal-setting model?

    A. SMART

    B. Cascading

    C. AGILE

    D. Cultural

6. The online retailer company Zappo's is committed "to provide the best customer service possible." This statement *best* represents which of the following strategic elements?

   A. Vision statement

   B. Values statement

   C. Mission statement

   D. Quality statement

7. Which of the following types of organizational structure is most likely to be without traditional boundaries?

   A. Modular

   B. Functional

   C. Hierarchical

   D. Matrix

8. Which business function is *most* likely responsible for the bottling of wine at a winery?

   A. Sales

   B. Marketing

   C. R&D

   D. Operations

9. Which performance measure should you use to evaluate the financial outcome(s) of an investment?

   A. ROI

   B. Breakeven

   C. Visual confirmation

   D. Surveys

10. James is an IT professional who is transferring from Wisconsin to the Southern California location of the company you work for. This is an example of what type of recruiting source?

    A. Promotion

    B. University

    C. Lateral

    D. Internal

11. "Helping to serve communities affected by a natural disaster" is most likely the purpose of which of the following time-off policies?

    A. Kin care

    B. Volunteer time

    C. Unlimited paid time off

    D. Family leave

12. Which of the following seemingly neutral employment requirements may be found to result in a disparate impact on protected-class groups?

A. Job descriptions

B. High school diploma requirement

C. Pre-employment drug screen

D. Discriminatory hiring practices

13. Which document is considered the primary documentation for all of the data collected through the job analysis process?

A. Job competencies

B. Job description

C. Job specifications

D. Employment tests

14. Which of the following factors may be considered when identifying the essential functions of a job under the Americans with Disabilities Act?

A. Percentage of time spent

B. Importance

C. Frequency

D. All of the above

15. Adding a metal fabrication department is the *best* example of which of the following?

A. Outsourcing

B. Insourcing

C. Intervention

D. Job enlargement

16. Which of the following elements of job design is *least* likely to result in an employee pay increase?

A. Promotion

B. Performance feedback

C. Job enlargement

D. Cross-training

17. Formalizing the tasks, duties, and responsibilities of each job within the organization is a major function of which of the following?

A. Job analysis

B. Job design

C. Handbook development

D. Task analysis

18. The use of judgmental forecasts to anticipate hiring needs is primarily based on which of the following data sets?

    A. Sales estimates

    B. Zero-based

    C. Financial and growth

    D. Historical and current

19. Of the following, which is the *best* strategy for a company seeking to avoid laying off workers in a short-term business downturn?

    A. Retraining

    B. Redeployment

    C. Hiring freezes

    D. RIFs

20. For which scenario should you recommend to your employer that they engage the services of a staffing agency?

    A. For difficult-to-fill positions

    B. When supervisors are very selective about who they hire

    C. For an HR department of one

    D. When the employer wants to reduce the cost of the employee burden

21. Which of the following is a main characteristic of a workforce plan?

    A. Gap analysis

    B. Advertising budget

    C. Risk assessment

    D. Head count

22. The total process of recruiting, integrating, and developing new and current workers is known as which of the following?

    A. Workforce planning

    B. Talent management

    C. HR planning

    D. The selection process

23. Which of the following activities *best* aligns training and development activities with business strategy?

    A. Training customer service reps on new software

    B. Developing employees throughout a clear career path

    C. Training sales employees on how to upsell to achieve growth targets

    D. Training customers on how to use the company's products

24. Conducting a needs assessment designed to address the future skill needs of employees is an attempt to generate which of the following?

   A. An instructional design

   B. Employee development plans

   C. A task analysis

   D. A future budget

25. Which of the following tools would be *most* beneficial if you were conducting a needs assessment to write training content?

   A. A task analysis

   B. A risk assessment

   C. Observation

   D. Focus groups

26. Measuring employees' current skills and comparing them to future skill needs is the purpose of which of the following tools?

   A. Needs assessment

   B. Gap analysis

   C. Task analysis

   D. Training needs assessment

27. An employee's performance is below standard, and you help the manager determine that this is because the employee did not receive the proper training for his job. Which of the following performance management tools should you recommend?

   A. Discipline

   B. Performance improvement plan

   C. Retraining

   D. Termination

28. Which of the following should you reconsider to increase diversity in your company's hiring practices?

   A. The job requirements

   B. Keyword searches

   C. The recruiting source

   D. All of the above

29. Requiring 10 years of experience for a job opening is most likely to discourage which protected-class group from applying for jobs within your organization?

   A. Women

   B. Older workers

   C. Millennials

   D. Veterans

30. Personal satisfaction is an example of which of the following types of motivators?

    A. Material

    B. Intangible

    C. Extrinsic

    D. Intrinsic

31. Stanley is an employee in your insurance office, and he prefers to make his own decisions and measure his own progress. Which of the following from Hackman & Oldham's job characteristics model is he showing a preference for?

    A. Task identity

    B. Task significance

    C. Autonomy

    D. Feedback

32. Which of the following characteristics from Hackman & Oldham's job characteristic model gives employees a sense of ownership in their jobs?

    A. Task identity

    B. Task significance

    C. Skill variety

    D. Feedback

33. According to Frederick Herzberg's Motivator/Hygiene theory, which of the following statements is true?

    A. If high-paying jobs are satisfiers, then low-paying jobs must be dissatisfiers.

    B. Job satisfiers and dissatisfiers are independent of one another.

    C. Correcting dissatisfiers will increase job satisfaction.

    D. Removing satisfiers will increase job dissatisfaction.

34. Employee behavior that is driven by an absence of a reward is an example of which theory of motivation?

    A. Operant conditioning

    B. Motivator/Hygiene

    C. Hierarchy of Needs

    D. Acquired needs

35. The needs of employees, the mode of training delivery, and the logistics of training sessions must all be addressed in which of the following learning & development activities?

    A. Needs assessment

    B. Training intervention

    C. Instructional design

    D. Transfer of learning

36. The ADDIE model is primarily what type of tool?

   A. Instructional design

   B. Project management

   C. Change management

   D. Lean manufacturing

37. What is the primary difference between customized and tailored training content?

   A. Customized training is most often delivered online, whereas tailored training is classroom-based.

   B. Customized training uses an outside expert, whereas tailored training relies on in-house staff.

   C. Customized training is built from scratch, whereas tailored training is modified off-the-shelf.

   D. None, the terms are used interchangeably.

38. Sally is the training manager for the large insurance services firm for which you work. She found an excellent resource for financial services training and realized that if she purchased only a single bundle, she could print out copies of the material for handouts in her larger training sessions, thus avoiding the expensive per-seat fees of the provider. Sally is *most* likely violating which of the following?

   A. Privacy laws

   B. Licensing laws

   C. Copyright laws

   D. Patent laws

39. You have enrolled in a PHR exam preparation program that occurs online. The instructor and other students are live online every Tuesday and Thursday evening from 6:00 p.m. to 8:00 p.m. This is the *best* example of what type of learning?

   A. Distance learning

   B. Asynchronous training

   C. Synchronous training

   D. E-learning

40. You recently joined a company whose training consists of a video database. For example, customer service representatives may access videos that are less than three minutes long, allowing them to learn about company products to assist in helping customers. What type of training does this *best* represent?

   A. E-learning

   B. Video

   C. Micro-learning

   D. Self-directed

41. Once a new hire begins work, he is paired with an experienced employee who shows him how to perform the job while working. This is the *best* example of which of the following?

  A. Mentoring

  B. Job shadowing

  C. On-the-job training

  D. Coaching

42. Air traffic controller trainees go through intense training that is designed to create realistic aircraft conflict and hazardous situations in which they must respond as though it is actually happening. This is most likely what type of training?

  A. Distance

  B. Vestibule

  C. On-the-job

  D. Simulation

43. You have been tasked with designing culture training for a small group of upcoming organizational leaders. The content includes a PowerPoint presentation and exercises designed to communicate the company's position on the value of diversity. Which program delivery method would be best for this type of training?

  A. Simulation

  B. Classroom

  C. Virtual

  D. Socratic seminar

44. The process of setting goals, measuring progress, and providing performance feedback all *best* belong in which of the following systems?

  A. Performance appraisals

  B. Employee development

  C. Talent management

  D. Performance management

45. Which of the following is an important tool for an HR professional who seeks to ensure that the performance appraisal process is fair to employees?

  A. Nondiscriminatory supervisors

  B. Valid instruments

  C. Job description

  D. All of the above

46. In the month of January your company hired 50 workers. Fifteen of them separated within the first 90 days. What is the turnover rate?

    A. 3 percent

    B. 13 percent

    C. 30 percent

    D. 35 percent

47. The supervisor of the accounting team has been tasked with setting 90-day goals for the department. He is supposed to meet with HR every week and provide a status update. This is what type of performance feedback?

    A. Disciplinary

    B. Micro

    C. Progress review

    D. Formal appraisal

48. Which of the following best represents the Likert scale for use in a performance appraisal?

    A. 1, 2, 3, 4, 5

    B. Agree, Neutral, Disagree

    C. Always, Sometimes, Never

    D. All of the above

49. Asking supervisors to rate 25 percent of their employees as "groom for promotion," 50 percent as "stay in current position," and 25 percent as "separate" is what type of evaluation activity?

    A. Forced distribution

    B. Forced ranking

    C. Graphic rating

    D. Management by objective

50. Which of the following statements regarding the Family Medical Leave Act is true?

    A. Employers may deny perfect attendance awards for employees whose leave disqualifies them.

    B. Employers may require the use of all accrued vacation time by eligible employees.

    C. Employers are not allowed to count light-duty assignments against an employee's leave bank.

    D. All of the above.

51. The primary purpose behind the passage of the Family Medical Leave Act was which of the following?

    A. To mandate privacy for health-related employment issues

    B. To allow for the continuation of health benefits should an employee lose their job

    C. To provide wage replacement for employees needing to care for sick family members

    D. To provide job security for employees needing to care for sick family members

52. How many employees must an employer have in order to be considered an "applicable large employer" for purposes of shared responsibility under the Patient Protection and Affordable Care Act (PPACA)?

  A. At least 50 employees within the previous tax quarter

  B. At least 50 full-time employees in the preceding calendar year

  C. At least 100 employees within the previous tax quarter

  D. At least 100 employees within the preceding calendar year.

53. The Equal Pay Act was originally written to protect which of the following groups?

  A. Women

  B. African Americans

  C. The gay and lesbian community

  D. All of the above

54. Willful violators of the Fair Labor Standards Act may face up to how much in fines?

  A. $3,000

  B. $5,000

  C. $10,000

  D. $25,000

55. Which act requires employers to pay nonexempt employees for the time it takes to put on company-required gear?

  A. The Lilly Ledbetter Act

  B. The Equal Pay Act

  C. The Portal to Portal Act

  D. The Fair Pay Act

56. What is the recommended amount of time employers should retain payroll records?

  A. 1 year

  B. 3 years

  C. 5 years

  D. Length of employment, plus 1 year

57. Your nonunion company is rapidly losing valuable personnel to the union company across town. During exit interviews, you discovered it was because the other company was paying an additional $5 per hour yet was not offering any health insurance coverage for families or paid time off. Which of the following strategies should you immediately employ?

  A. Union avoidance

  B. Increase all employee pay

  C. Create hidden paychecks and meet with employees

  D. Reach out to the separated employees and try to get them back

58. What is the term used to describe the additional cost from benefits and taxes that are beyond a employee salaries?

    A. Expenses

    B. Liabilities

    C. Perquisites

    D. Burden

59. Which of the following is most important for HR to consider when making a decision to outsource payroll?

    A. The availability of technology

    B. The nature of joint liability

    C. How mistakes will be corrected

    D. The cost of the service

60. The employer for whom you work makes a 3 percent lump-sum contribution to individual employee retirement plans at the end of each fiscal year. This is which type of plan?

    A. Defined benefit plan

    B. Contributory plan

    C. Deferred compensation plan

    D. Self-employment plan

61. To which of the following retirement plans may both an employer and an employee add funds?

    A. Defined benefit plan

    B. Contributory plan

    C. Deferred compensation plan

    D. Self-employment plan

62. Which of the following is the *best* reason for larger companies such as Salesforce or Netflix to offer unlimited time-off programs to their employees?

    A. To meet the demands of a younger workforce

    B. To improve work-life balance programs

    C. To get in front of future mandatory benefits

    D. To comply with state and local labor laws

63. Which of the following types of insurance is experience-rated?

    A. Workers' compensation

    B. Unemployment insurance

    C. EPLI

    D. All of the above

64. Social security and workers' compensation are the *best* example of which of the following?

    A. Wage replacement benefits

    B. Financial benefits

    C. Mandated benefits

    D. Indirect benefits

65. A properly conducted benefits risk assessment will give priority to which of the following elements?

    A. Employee satisfaction

    B. Labor law compliance

    C. Joint employer liability

    D. Cost of offerings

66. You recently notified the COO that the company's health insurance costs will be increasing by 12 percent in the next year. The vision insurance in particular seems to carry a higher premium cost. Which of the following strategies should you recommend?

    A. Increase the employee burden for the vision insurance.

    B. Absorb the cost of the vision insurance increase.

    C. Conduct a needs assessment to see whether employees really want the vision insurance.

    D. Decrease the value of other benefits to make up for the vision insurance increase.

67. What is the greatest tax advantage for employees when they take advantage of employer benefits offerings?

    A. Their benefits are tax-sheltered.

    B. They do not have to pay tax on the dollar equivalent of benefits unless they use them.

    C. One dollar in benefits is not taxed the same way as $1 in wages.

    D. There are no significant tax advantages for employees.

68. Which of the following is the most strategic reason for an employer to offer benefits?

    A. To differentiate themselves from the competition

    B. To retain skilled workers

    C. To influence legislation regarding healthcare

    D. Both A and B

69. Company housing, health insurance, and pension contributions are all examples of which of the following?

    A. Perquisites

    B. Health insurance

    C. Involuntary benefits

    D. Benefits

70. Bonuses and additional paid time off are forms of what type of compensation?

   A. Direct

   B. Incentives

   C. Negotiated

   D. Enriched

71. In which of the following scenarios may an employer pay less than the federal minimum wage?

   A. If the state in which the employer operates has a lower minimum wage

   B. If there is a signed employment agreement between the employer and the employee

   C. If a union exchanges minimum wage for another wage-based benefit

   D. If the employee is a student enrolled in a vocational program

72. Which of the following is a component of *direct* compensation?

   A. Minimum wage

   B. Piece rate pay

   C. Incentives

   D. Bonuses

73. Which of the following compensation strategies would be beneficial for an HR department of one person?

   A. Supervisor timecard approval

   B. Employee self-service programs

   C. Outsourcing payroll

   D. All of the above

74. Using direct deposit for employee paychecks and open enrollment self-service systems are examples of which of the following HR compensation activities?

   A. Compensation philosophy

   B. Compensation cost control

   C. Responding to younger generation communication preferences

   D. The shrinking value of face-to-face HR

75. Selecting an employee benefits plan based solely on the fact that you would like to continue to see your personal physician represents which of the following?

   A. Immoral behavior

   B. Lack of fiduciary responsibility

   C. An illegal act

   D. A legitimate business practice

76. Under what condition(s) might an employer be obligated to pay above the federal minimum wage?

    A. If the state has established its own minimum wage

    B. If a city has a prevailing wage

    C. If a job is governed by a union bargaining agreement

    D. All of the above

77. The number of employees an employer has on its payroll is called which of the following?

    A. Full-time employees

    B. Full-time equivalents

    C. Employee burden

    D. Head count

78. A supervisor at work changed an employee's work shift and denied him raises, hoping to make him quit, because the supervisor felt he was a threat to a potential relationship with another worker. The employee did indeed quit and then most likely filed which of the following charges with the Equal Employment Opportunity Commission?

    A. Constructive discharge

    B. Quid pro quo harassment

    C. Defamation

    D. All of the above

79. Employers who choose to give robust employment references to former employees based on factual data is most likely protected by which of the following?

    A. Good Samaritan

    B. Qualified privilege

    C. Duty of care

    D. Duty of fairness

80. Lack of procedural justice would indicate that which of the following elements is missing from an employer's pay system?

    A. Lack of internal equity

    B. Pay fairness

    C. Transparency

    D. Lack of external equity

81. Pay that is based on job tasks, duties, and responsibilities is called what?

    A. Pay for performance

    B. Pay compression

    C. Competency-based pay

    D. Pay equity

82. Donnie is a valuable project manager who has been with the company for more than 17 years. He has received five cost-of-living increases over that period of time. Angie is a new project manager whom the company recently hired, and she is being paid about $1 less than Donnie. Which of the following statements is *most* likely true?

    A. Angie is being discriminated against based on gender.

    B. Pay compression has occurred.

    C. Donnie is being paid more because he is a more valuable employee.

    D. Donnie has reached the maximum of his pay range.

83. What is one of the benefits of building pay ranges?

    A. It allows employers to lawfully discriminate between employees.

    B. It provides both internal and external equity when properly built.

    C. Employers may account for educational and other differences in skillsets.

    D. All of the above.

84. The tomato processing food plant for which you work regularly hires seasonal employees. They generally pay minimum wage for these positions, mainly because of an abundance of this skillset in the relevant labor market. However, more than 75 percent of employers in the area are paying more for the same skillset. What compensation strategy has your company adopted?

    A. A minimalist strategy

    B. A lag the market strategy

    C. A market-based pay strategy

    D. Variable pay strategy

85. Which of the following government resources would be *best* to use if you wanted to calculate COLA increases for your staff?

    A. Office of Economic Development wage survey reports

    B. Modeled Wage Estimates

    C. Consumer Price Index

    D. National Earnings reports

86. Under which of the following conditions might Employee A expect to be paid less than Employee B with the same job title?

    A. If Employee A does not perform as well as Employee B

    B. If Employee A has not been on the job as long as Employee B

    C. If Employee A does not have the same amount of responsibility as Employee B

    D. All of the above

87. Which of the following terms is *most* closely related to variable pay?

    A. Performance-based

    B. Total compensation

    C. Perquisites

    D. Entitlements

88. Tools such as base wages, perquisites, and employee benefits are all part of which of the following?

    A. Entitlement-oriented programs

    B. Total rewards programs

    C. Performance-based pay

    D. All of the above

89. How are full-time employees calculated for purposes of compliance with the PPACA's applicable large employer requirements?

    A. A full-time employee is any employee who works at least 30 hours of service each week in a calendar year.

    B. A full-time employee is any employee who works at least 130 hours of service each month in a calendar year.

    C. Any combination of employees, each of whom individually is not a full-time employee but who, in combination, are equivalent to a full-time employee.

    D. All of the above.

90. What is the primary difference between a closed shop and an agency shop?

    A. Closed shops are allowed only in right-to-work states, whereas agency shops are allowed in all states.

    B. Agency shops are allowed only in right-to-work states, whereas closed shops are allowed in all states.

    C. Closed shops are unlawful, whereas agency shops are allowed in non–right-to-work states.

    D. Nothing—the terms are used interchangeably.

91. Overtime, holiday pay, and seniority are all examples of which of the following in the collective bargaining process?

    A. Mandatory subjects

    B. Voluntary subjects

    C. Illegal subjects

    D. Permissive subjects

92. Which of the following is an example of how to *best* use HR during the collective bargaining process?

    A. Finalizing the agreement

    B. Attending union meetings to approve the CBA

    C. Gathering wage data

    D. Coordinating the agreement's ratification

93. Discrimination against a union member is an unfair labor practice that may be committed by which of the following?

    A. The employer

    B. A union steward

    C. A manager

    D. All of the above

94. The term *hot cargo*, when applied to an unfair labor practice, refers to all of the following *except* which example?

    A. Union members refusing to handle product from nonunion shops

    B. Union members refusing to transport product for an employer that has workers on strike

    C. Union members refusing to cross picket lines in support of a lawful strike

    D. Union members refusing to buy products from nonunion shops

95. Which of the following persons is *least* likely to be considered a supervisor for purposes of exclusion in a bargaining unit?

    A. One who assigns work to others

    B. One who makes recommendations to HR about pay increases

    C. One with the authority to hire but not to terminate

    D. One with the title "supervisor" in their job description

96. All commercial truck drivers for a company's multistate locations are forming a bargaining unit to be represented by their union. This is possible because the truck drivers form which of the following?

    A. Quorum

    B. Community of interest

    C. Industry classification

    D. Work group

97. In a card campaign, a union will seek to get above what percentage to demand voluntary recognition by the employer?

    A. 15 percent

    B. 35 percent

    C. 50 percent

    D. 75 percent

98. A group of teachers from across the state have gathered at the capital to protest potential legislation that will affect their industry. The teachers carry large signs and are chanting slogans to communicate their position on the potential law. This is an example of which of the following?

   A. Striking

   B. Picketing

   C. Leafleting

   D. Salting

99. The union sent a qualified person to apply for an opening in your nonunion company with the specific intent to organize your employees. If you refuse to hire this person based solely on their union affiliation, you are afraid you may commit an unlawful act. This is an example of what union-organizing technique?

   A. Bannering

   B. Picketing

   C. Leafleting

   D. Salting

100. Teamsters International has parked a semi truck and trailer out front with large signs attached declaring their intent to organize your people. This is an example of what union-organizing technique?

   A. Bannering

   B. Picketing

   C. Leafleting

   D. Salting

101. Every union member is guaranteed the right to nominate candidates for union office under which of the following acts?

   A. The National Labor Relations Act

   B. The Labor-Management Reporting & Disclosure Act

   C. The Labor Management Relations Act

   D. The Service Contract Act

102. Which act granted employees the right to form a union?

   A. The National Labor Relations Act

   B. The Labor-Management Reporting & Disclosure Act

   C. The Labor Management Relations Act

   D. The Service Contract Act

103. A successful internal investigation by HR of employee wrongdoing will include which of the following activities?

   A. Look for facts that can be corroborated by documentation.

   B. Remain neutral, avoiding forming an opinion until all information is gathered.

   C. Identify environmental causes to a negative situation.

   D. All of the above.

104. Prohibiting any sort of social media posting that mentions an employee's place of work *most* likely violates which of the following?

   A. The Fair Labor Standards Act

   B. The Privacy Act

   C. The National Labor Relations Act

   D. The U.S. Constitution

105. Which of the following forms of alternative dispute resolution is nonbinding?

   A. Judicial arbitration

   B. Mediation

   C. Mini-trials

   D. All of the above

106. Managing a third-party COBRA vendor is part of which human resource activity?

   A. Dealing with employee terminations

   B. Developing a proper hiring procedure

   C. Complying with job validity studies

   D. Adhering to collective bargaining agreement clauses

107. Sixty days' notice to an employee being laid off by an employer with more than 100 employees is a requirement of which of the following labor laws?

   A. WARN

   B. FLSA

   C. ERISA

   D. REA

108. You recently discovered that an employee is working a second job at night for a competitor. This *most* likely violates which of the following policies?

   A. Featherbedding

   B. Moonlighting

   C. Nepotism

   D. Trademark protection

109. Which of the following legal challenges must HR take steps to avoid when writing an employee handbook?

    A. Creating an express contract

    B. Creating an implied contract

    C. Diluting the doctrine of employment at will

    D. All of the above

110. Two employees got into a physical altercation over their rival sports teams while on lunch break. This is most likely a violation of which of the following standards found in an employee handbook?

    A. Unprofessional behavior

    B. Workplace civility rules

    C. Anti-harassment rules

    D. Code of conduct

111. Employee code of conduct, vacation time, and a statement of at-will employment will most likely be found in which of the following documents?

    A. An SOP

    B. An offer letter

    C. An employee handbook

    D. A collective bargaining agreement

112. Company meetings lately have been marked by unprofessional behavior: some employees have been using their mobile devices to send and receive text messages while others are speaking. Which of the following may be necessary to help manage the gap between the communication preferences of different generations at work?

    A. Ban all cell phone use.

    B. Restructure meetings to allow for mobile devices.

    C. Ask all employees to not text during meetings.

    D. Work with IT to eliminate Internet access in conference rooms.

113. Managers have been complaining to you—their HR representative—that employees are increasingly using their mobile devices and accessing social media while on the job. Which of the following interventions should you recommend?

    A. Disciplining employees for violating the company code of conduct

    B. Diversity training

    C. Banning all cell phone and social media use while at work

    D. Interviewing employees to hear what they have to say

114. An official complaint within a union environment is known as which of the following?

   A. Incident

   B. Charge

   C. Grievance

   D. Indictment

115. The manager of one department has informed HR at your small place of work that he is "fine hiring women but only those beyond childbearing age." His reasoning is that complying with the leave requirements does not allow him to meet the company's productivity standards. This is an example of which of the following?

   A. Unlawful discrimination

   B. Sexual harassment

   C. Hostile work environment

   D. Unreasonable production demands

116. A large automaker and the employee union have agreed to allow union members to determine the amount of management bonuses. This is an example of which of the following?

   A. Autonomy

   B. Codetermination

   C. Works councils

   D. Labor-management cooperative strategy

117. A supervisor sexually harassed an employee and is now facing charges in court. The victim also filed charges against the employer, claiming that the employer was responsible for putting the supervisor into a position of authority. Under which doctrine is the victim's claim based?

   A. Employment at will

   B. Respondeat superior

   C. Duty of care

   D. Promissory estoppel

118. Which agency is responsible for the enforcement of the Older Workers Benefit Protection Act?

   A. The Equal Employment Opportunity Commission

   B. The Department of Fair Employment and Housing

   C. The Industrial Labor Commission

   D. The National Labor Relations Board

119. The name on a document an employee presented to you is spelled slightly differently than the way the employee spelled it on Form I-9. What should you do?

   A. Give them 72 hours to resubmit a proper document.

   B. Rescind the conditional offer of employment.

C. Accept the document, provided the explanation is reasonable.

D. Send them to the issuing agency for a correction.

120. The hotel chain for whom you work asked you to be part of a committee to address the variety of issues that resulted from the terrorist attacks on September 11, 2001. This is an example of what type of work group?

A. Self-directed

B. Global team

C. Task force

D. Cooperative

121. Your HR department has created a team of peers who collectively create work schedules, set goals, and hold each other accountable. This is most likely an example of what?

A. A work council

B. A self-directed work team

C. A group initiative

D. A peer-to-peer work group

122. Positive employee relations strategies should first and foremost be aligned to which of the following?

A. Workforce plan

B. Collective bargaining agreement

C. Strategic plan

D. Labor laws

123. When conducting data analysis, you find that turnover in the warehouse has reached an all-time high. This metric should serve as a what?

A. Red flag

B. Attrition rate

C. Call for supervisor intervention

D. Sign of union organizing

124. An employee is struggling with the decision to stay or leave their job. They told their supervisor that they feel like no matter what they do, the CEO will make changes or be dissatisfied. This is an example of a lack of which of the following?

A. Psychological contract

B. Psychological ownership

C. Employment contract

D. Feedback

125. Loyalty, fair treatment, and job security are all examples of which of the following?

    A. Statutory rights

    B. Elements of the psychological contract

    C. Components of a total compensation package

    D. Clauses in an employment contract

126. An unwritten agreement of shared beliefs, perceptions, and informal expectations between the employer and employee is also known as which of the following?

    A. A statutory agreement

    B. An employment contract

    C. The psychological contract

    D. An implied contract

127. Work design, lighting, and other environmental conditions that influence employee performance are fundamental to which category of motivational techniques?

    A. Needs theories

    B. Reward-punishment

    C. Human relations

    D. Scientific management

128. Needs theories of motivation are most often focused on which of the following?

    A. Path to goal

    B. Reward to punishment

    C. Employee satisfiers and dissatisfiers

    D. Individual behavior

129. Under which of the following conditions would an employee focus group be properly utilized?

    A. Conducting a feedback session regarding their shared supervisor

    B. Identifying how satisfied employees are with their compensation packages

    C. Measuring employee reaction to an active union-organizing campaign

    D. Identifying what is most valuable to a particular work group when it comes to career development

130. The HR director at your organization has asked you to schedule meetings between employees and their direct supervisor's boss. This is an effort to measure the organizational climate. What type of activity is the director asking you to coordinate?

    A. 360-degree feedback

    B. Stay interview

    C. Skip-level interview

    D. Employee survey

131. Gathering feedback to inform HR policies, procedures, and rules may be accomplished using which of the following methods?

    A. Exit interviews

    B. Stay interviews

    C. Focus groups

    D. All of the above

132. Using McClelland's theory of motivation, fill in the blank: achievement, affiliation, and power are all needs that are _____ over time?

    A. Learned

    B. Acquired

    C. Dismissed

    D. Met

133. Communication, conflict resolution, and career development are all characteristics of which of the following HR activities?

    A. Management and strategy

    B. Risk management

    C. Human resource planning

    D. Employee relations

134. Why should employers build return-to-work (RTW) programs for employees who are out due to non–work-related injuries and/or disabilities?

    A. It may lower workers' compensation insurance premiums.

    B. It is the ethical course to take.

    C. It is required by the Americans with Disabilities Act.

    D. It can help keep workflow steady.

135. In the last three years, employer A has had one workplace injury totaling $50,000. In the same period of time, employer B had 10 workplace injuries, also totaling $50,000. Which employer would you expect to have a higher workers' compensation experience modifier?

    A. Employer A

    B. Employer B

    C. They will have exactly the same modifier.

    D. It depends on the number of employees.

136. An employer has an ex mod of 1.2. Which of the following statements is true?

    A. The employer will pay an insurance premium that is about 1.2 times the average for their industry.

    B. The employer will pay a lower insurance premium than an employer with a .80 rating.

    C. The employer will pay a higher insurance premium for a period of five years.

    D. The employer will have to purchase state-run workers' compensation insurance.

137. A field employee working to harvest strawberries is complaining of feeling dizzy and cannot seem to quench her thirst. She is exhibiting signs of what sort of workplace illness?

   A. Heat exhaustion

   B. Respiratory

   C. Lung disease

   D. Heat cramps

138. Which of the following is a preventative behavior that employers commit to in a written injury and illness prevention plan (IIPP)?

   A. The employer will conduct regular worksite hazard analysis.

   B. That the IIPP will be part of an overall safety management program.

   C. That the IIPP will rely upon top-level commitment.

   D. The company will focus on education.

139. An employee tested positive for opiates during a post-injury drug screen. When confronted, she became emotional and told you she plans to enter rehabilitation and is no longer using illegal drugs. Which of the following actions can you take?

   A. Terminate her for unlawful drug use

   B. Offer her unpaid leave while in rehab

   C. Replace her while she is out on leave

   D. All of the above

140. Which of the following employer actions would be considered discriminatory?

   A. Terminating an employee who is using methadone as a prescribed treatment for drug abuse

   B. Terminating an employee for using marijuana if they have a medical marijuana card

   C. Terminating an employee for drinking on the job

   D. Terminating an employee for taking a co-worker's prescription antidepressants

141. Which of the following is true regarding an employee who is suffering from alcoholism?

   A. A current user of an illegal substance is specifically excluded from protection under the ADA.

   B. An employer may prohibit the use of alcohol on the job.

   C. A reasonable suspicion test for being under the influence of alcohol while on the job is considered a medical procedure under the ADA.

   D. All of the above.

142. A return-to-work program can be beneficial to which of the following individuals?

   A. An individual with a work-related injury

   B. An individual with a non–work-related injury

   C. A disabled worker

   D. All of the above

143. You have been tasked with developing the company's safety training program. Which of the following should be your *first* step?

    A. Write training content.

    B. Conduct a needs assessment.

    C. Interview employees.

    D. Identify resources.

144. You are the female HR director for a financial institution. It was brought to your attention that the account executives were opening customer accounts that the customers had not requested. When you brought this to the attention of your superiors, they dismissed your concerns and told you to "not worry your pretty little head about it." They eventually fired you, and you believe it is because you continued to bring it to their attention. Under which agency would you *most* likely have a successful claim of unlawful company behavior?

    A. Occupational Safety and Health Administration

    B. Equal Employment Opportunity Administration

    C. Department of Fair Employment and Housing

    D. Department of Industrial Relations

145. Which of the following OSHA tools charges employers with "finding all hazards in the workplace and developing a plan for preventing and controlling those hazards"?

    A. Participation in OSH's voluntary protection program

    B. A safety management plan

    C. A written OSHA compliance program

    D. An injury and illness prevention plan

146. An injury and illness prevention plan is first and foremost which of the following?

    A. A compliance document

    B. An educational tool

    C. A prevention effort

    D. A requirement from workers' compensation insurance carriers

147. Under what conditions should you create a written business continuity plan?

    A. If your company is located in a hurricane-prone location

    B. If your company staffs with international assignees

    C. If your company is at a higher risk for corporate espionage

    D. All of the above

148. During your first 90 days as an HR generalist, OSHA came to conduct a routine worksite audit. You were able to produce only three out of the last five years of OSHA 300 logs. The company was most likely cited for what type of violation?

    A. De Minimis

    B. Other than serious

    C. Willful

    D. Serious

149. At the structural framing company for which you work, you discovered that although workers are required to wear fall protection, they are not tying off to prevent a fall. OSHA issued two serious citations, but the company failed to abate the fall hazards. What type of citation did OSHA issue next?

    A. De Minimis

    B. Criminal

    C. Willful

    D. Negligent

150. Which of the following types of hazards accounts for the highest number of worker deaths in the construction industry?

    A. Falls

    B. Struck by object

    C. Electrocution

    D. Caught "in between"

Senior Professional in Human Resources (SPHR)

PART

II

Chapter

7

SPHR Exam: Leadership & Strategy

THE SPHR EXAM CONTENT FROM THE LEADERSHIP AND STRATEGY FUNCTIONAL AREA COVERED IN THIS CHAPTER FOCUSES ON "LEADING THE HR FUNCTION BY DEVELOPING HR STRATEGY, CONTRIBUTING TO ORGANIZATIONAL STRATEGY, INFLUENCING PEOPLE MANAGEMENT PRACTICES, AND MONITORING RISK." IT INCLUDES THE FOLLOWING RESPONSIBILITIES:

✓ 01 Develop and execute HR plans that are aligned to the organization's strategic plan (for example: HR strategic plans, budgets, business plans, service delivery plans, HRIS, technology)

✓ 02 Evaluate the applicability of federal laws and regulations to organizational strategy (for example: policies, programs, practices, business expansion/reduction)

✓ 03 Analyze and assess organizational practices that impact operations and people management to decide on the best available risk management strategy (for example: avoidance, mitigation, acceptance)

✓ 04 Interpret and use business metrics to assess and drive achievement of strategic goals and objectives (for example: key performance indicators, financial statements, budgets)

✓ 05 Design and evaluate HR data indicators to inform strategic actions within the organization (for example: turnover rates, cost per hire, retention rates)

✓ 06 Evaluate credibility and relevance of external information to make decisions and recommendations (for example: salary data, management trends, published surveys and studies, legal/regulatory analysis)

✓ 07 Contribute to the development of the organizational strategy and planning (for example: vision, mission, values, ethical conduct)

✓ 08 Develop and manage workplace practices that are aligned with the organization's statements of vision, values, and ethics to shape and reinforce organizational culture

✓ 09 Design and manage effective change strategies to align organizational performance with the organization's strategic goals

✓ 10 Establish and manage effective relationships with key stakeholders to influence organizational behavior and outcomes

IN ADDITION TO THE RESPONSIBILITIES LISTED ABOVE, AN INDIVIDUAL TAKING THE SPHR EXAM SHOULD HAVE WORKING KNOWLEDGE OF THE FOLLOWING, USUALLY DERIVED THROUGH PRACTICAL EXPERIENCE:

✓ 01 Vision, mission, and values of an organization and applicable legal and regulatory requirements

✓ 02 Strategic planning process

✓ 03 Management functions, including planning, organizing, directing, and controlling

✓ 04 Corporate governance procedures and compliance

✓ 05 Business elements of an organization (for example: products, competition, customers, technology, demographics, culture, processes, safety and security)

✓ 06 Third-party or vendor selection, contract negotiation, and management, including development of requests for proposals (RFPs)

✓ 07 Project management (for example: goals, timetables, deliverables, and procedures)

✓ 08 Technology to support HR activities

✓ 09 Budgeting, accounting, and financial concepts (for example: evaluating financial statements, budgets, accounting terms, and cost management)

✓ 10 Techniques and methods for organizational design (for example: outsourcing, shared services, organizational structures)

✓ 11 Methods of gathering data for strategic planning purposes (for example: Strengths, Weaknesses, Opportunities, and Threats [SWOT], and Political, Economic, Social, and Technological [PEST])

✓ 12 Qualitative and quantitative methods and tools used for analysis, interpretation, and decision-making purposes

✓ 13 Change management processes and techniques

✓ 14 Techniques for forecasting, planning, and predicting the impact of HR activities and programs across functional areas

✓ 15 Risk management

✓ 16 How to deal with situations that are uncertain, unclear, or chaotic

1. The implementation of a self-service feature for benefits enrollment on the company's intranet is an example of which of the following?

   A. Cost control

   B. Scheduling

   C. Efficiency

   D. Technology

2. The HR department at the company you work at has asked you to evaluate the compensation and benefits programs to identify variable pay options. Some of the leadership, however, is resisting because of the increased bureaucracy and lack of flexibility. Your company is most likely at which stage in the organization life cycle?

   A. Decline

   B. Maturity

   C. Growth

   D. Startup

3. Decisions that build on employee strengths to meet company goals belong in which of the following HR roles?

   A. Operational

   B. Administrative

   C. Strategic

   D. Global

4. "Where we are now?" and "Where do we want to be?" and "How will we get there?" are all questions answered in which of the following organizational processes?

   A. The ADDIE model

   B. Strategic planning

   C. Training needs assessment

   D. Risk assessment

5. A strategy does which of the following?

   A. Provides preplanning and planning activities to accomplish organizational goals

   B. Provides a specific description of practical steps used to achieve business goals

   C. Describes the direction the business will take and what it will achieve at the corporate and business unit levels

   D. Identifies the strengths and opportunities of a business to its competitive advantage

6. A goal does which of the following?

   A. Provides preplanning and planning activities to accomplish organizational needs

   B. Provides a specific description of practical steps used to achieve business objectives

   C. Describes the direction the business will take and what it will achieve at the corporate and business unit levels

   D. Uses the strengths and opportunities of a business to its competitive advantage

7. An objective does which of the following?

   A. Provides preplanning and planning activities to accomplish organizational needs

   B. Provides a specific description of practical steps used to achieve business goals

   C. Describes the direction the business will take and what it will achieve at the corporate and business unit levels

   D. Uses the strengths and opportunities of a business to its competitive advantage

8. Which of the following stages in the strategic planning process is the commitment of leaders secured?

   A. Preplanning

   B. Environmental scan

   C. Strategy formulation

   D. Strategy evaluation

9. Which of the following stages in the strategic planning process answers the question "Where do we want to be?"

   A. Preplanning

   B. Environmental scan

   C. Strategy formulation

   D. Strategy evaluation

10. Which of the following stages in the strategic planning process answers the question "How do we get there?"

   A. Strategy implementation

   B. Environmental scan

   C. Strategy formulation

   D. Strategy evaluation

11. What is the purpose of an environmental scan?

   A. To collect data for use in formulating strategy

   B. To correct internal weaknesses and external threats

   C. To apply resources toward the development of strengths

   D. To implement strategies based on the legal and regulatory environment

12. Why is the identification of an organization's core competencies so important to its long-term success?

   A. The core competencies will help the company identify its competitive advantage.

   B. The core competencies, when properly managed, may result in increased revenue streams.

   C. Core competency identification will aid in the proper allocation of resources and the making of outsourcing decisions.

   D. All of the above are correct.

13. What should HR recommend if the stated values of an organization identified during the strategy formulation process do not match with existing workforce behaviors?

   A. Recommend an immediate intervention plan.

   B. Recommend that the values statement be rewritten.

   C. Adopt a set of work rules that are written in alignment with the values.

   D. Establish goals that seek to align the values with the behaviors.

14. Which of the following is *not* an example of a short-range goal?

   A. Tactical goals

   B. Action plans

   C. SMART goals

   D. Step-by-step instructions

15. The determination of how many and what kind of resources will be necessary to execute the strategic plan is the definition of which of the following activities?

   A. Cost accounting

   B. Budgeting

   C. Finance

   D. Operations

16. Which of the following is an example of an accrued expense?

   A. Supplies ordered

   B. Commissions owed but not yet paid

   C. Payroll

   D. A bill from a vendor

17. An income statement is often used interchangeably with which of the following terms?

   A. Profit and loss statement

   B. Statement of cash flows

   C. Balance sheet

   D. None of the above

18. Which of the following accounting reports would you request to identify how much the cost of labor was in the month of February?

   A. Income statement

   B. Statement of cash flows

   C. Balance sheet

   D. Audited financial statements

19. Which of the following accounting reports would you request to identify how much cash is available to make payroll this period?

    A. Income statement

    B. Statement of cash flows

    C. Balance sheet

    D. Audited financial statements

20. Which budgeting method would be most appropriate if HR has to make recommendations without the benefit of historical data?

    A. Flat-percentage base

    B. Top down

    C. Zero-based budgeting

    D. Bottom up

21. Making line item changes to the budget in accordance with variances from previous years is known as which of the following budgeting practices?

    A. Zero-based budgeting

    B. Historic budgeting

    C. Variable reporting

    D. Parallel budgeting

22. A benefits utilization review revealed that a company is paying out $3,200 per year per employee for dental insurance, but only $2,400 per year per employee (average) is being paid out in claims. This activity was probably undertaken as the result of which of the following budget development approaches?

    A. Historic information budgeting

    B. Traditional budgeting

    C. Zero-based budgeting

    D. Parallel budgeting

23. Which of the following statements is *not* true about strategy evaluation?

    A. Evaluating a strategy should include evaluating the manager's ability to model behavior that is in alignment with the organization's core values.

    B. Strategy evaluation tells planners whether the organization is on track to achieve strategic goals.

    C. Strategy evaluation may include celebrating successes as the plan is executed.

    D. Strategy evaluation is usually done at the end of the year.

24. The human capital management plan (HCMP) is the HR equivalent of which of the following?

    A. Risk management plan

    B. Strategic plan

    C. Workforce plan

    D. Action plan

25. Which of the following are standard expense items accounted for in an HCMP?

    A. Salaries

    B. Payroll taxes

    C. Travel

    D. All of the above

26. HR tactical goals and action plans are communicated through which of the following strategic tools?

    A. Implementation plan

    B. Human capital management plan

    C. Needs assessment

    D. Objectives

27. HR's attempt to measure the value of the human talent of an organization is known as which of the following?

    A. Strategic management

    B. Resource allocation

    C. Budgeting

    D. Human capital projecting

28. The decision to build or buy the talent necessary to achieve organizational objectives is part of which of the following analyses?

    A. Budgeting

    B. Human capital projecting

    C. Cost-benefit

    D. Return on investment

29. Revenue per employee, units produced per employee, and turnover rate are all examples of which of the following HR metrics?

    A. Balanced scorecard

    B. Business impact

    C. Key performance indicators

    D. Cost-benefit

30. The executive management team is seeking an HR tool that ties financial and customer results to the key internal practices that either supported or hindered positive outcomes. Which of the following tools should you recommend?

   A. Human capital management plan

   B. Cost-benefit analysis

   C. Balanced scorecard

   D. Business impact report

31. Which of the following can be measured using a correlation coefficient?

   A. Absentee rate for new hires

   B. Sales forecasting

   C. Preferred benefits offering

   D. Methods to improve productivity

32. A(n) _____ is to soft costs as _____ is to hard costs.

   A. Quantitative analysis, qualitative analysis

   B. Subjective analysis, objective analysis

   C. Return on investment, cost-benefit analysis

   D. Cost-benefit analysis, return on investment

33. The large merchant services company for which you work has decided that its one-year strategic focus will be to allocate resources to their core competency of selling point-of-service devices and software. Consequently, all other departments must cut their budgets by 10 percent. Which of the following strategies make the most sense for the HR department?

   A. Lay off the compensation specialist

   B. Reduce the training budget

   C. Outsource the benefits function and lay off the benefits specialist

   D. Rewrite the travel expense policy to reduce the per diem rate

34. Ben & Jerry's, the ice cream company, produces a Social and Environmental Assessment Report every year. It highlights the company's efforts toward creating synergy between the corporate mission, vision, values, employees, vendors, franchisees, customers, and communities. This is an example of which of the following strategic efforts?

   A. Corporate responsibility

   B. Strategic alignment with stakeholders

   C. Profitability

   D. Both A and B

35. In a merger or acquisition scenario, HR may be required to provide documents relating to compensation, policies, procedures, and legal compliance. This is in accordance with which of the following processes?

    A. Full disclosure

    B. Risk assessment

    C. Risk mitigation

    D. Due diligence

36. A wine storage manufacturer has decided to sell off the custom cabinet division to focus further on the more profitable cooling unit division. This is an example of which of the following strategies?

    A. Divestiture

    B. Merger

    C. Acquisition

    D. Reduction in force

37. What is the main difference between offshoring and outsourcing?

    A. Offshoring usually results in employee layoffs, whereas outsourcing does not.

    B. Offshoring is a long-term solution, whereas outsourcing is a short-term solution.

    C. Offshoring moves entire production units out of the country, whereas outsourcing moves internal practices to outside organizations regardless of geographic location.

    D. There are no differences—these terms are interchangeable.

38. The ability of an employee to update their own personal data, such as contact information and dependent status changes, is known as which of the following functions of HR technology?

    A. Self-service

    B. Efficiency

    C. Human resource information systems

    D. ATS

39. Shareholders, the board of directors, and management are all included in which of the following terms?

    A. Principal members

    B. Responsible parties

    C. Stakeholders

    D. Employees

40. An obligation to act with the highest regard and in the best interest of the company is known as which of the following?

    A. Integrity

    B. Fiduciary responsibility

    C. Moral code

    D. Legal compliance

41. Section 806 of the Sarbanes-Oxley Act provides all of the following except what?

    A. Broad protection for employees of publicly traded companies who report SEC violations

    B. Broad protection/relief options for employees who suffer an unfavorable employment action as the result of a whistleblower report

    C. Broad protection for employees of private companies that may be engaged in unethical business practices

    D. Broad protection for employees who report violations of federal securities laws

42. Which of the following is not one of Porter's five forces affecting strategic decision-making and planning?

    A. New competitors

    B. Labor force population

    C. Suppliers

    D. Buyers

43. The executive management team has asked you to review the political, economic, social, and technological influences on the relevant labor market to your industry. Which of the following have they asked you for?

    A. A cost-benefit analysis

    B. A human capital management plan

    C. A PEST analysis

    D. A SWOT audit

44. Providing questions to candidates online to allow them to self-screen out of the hiring process if they don't meet the minimum qualifications for the position is a function of which of the following systems?

    A. An applicant tracking system

    B. A hiring management system

    C. Employee self-service

    D. A learning management system

45. Part of your company's strategic initiative is to shift to a paperless system in as many functions as possible, integrating the data across departments. Which of the following HR technology solutions would you recommend to go paperless first?

    A. A qualitative analysis system

    B. A quantitative analysis system

    C. An inventory management system

    D. A learning management system

46. Decreasing expenses by decreasing the size of the workforce is known as which of the following?

    A. A workforce reduction

    B. A reduction in force

    C. Rightsizing

    D. All of the above

47. Simplifying or eliminating unnecessary business practices is the definition of which of the following?

    A. Reengineering

    B. Corporate restructuring

    C. Workforce expansion

    D. Workforce reductions

48. Which of the following is the best strategy to recommend when rapid growth is occurring as the result of increased customer demands over a short period of time?

    A. Reengineering

    B. Corporate restructuring

    C. Workforce expansion

    D. Workforce reductions

49. Communication, goal-setting, and project management skills can all be addressed through which of the following HR functions?

    A. Compensation and benefits

    B. Employee relations

    C. Risk management

    D. Global relations

50. What is the primary purpose of establishing strategic relationships with key individuals in the organization?

    A. To increase interdepartmental communication

    B. To maximize HR credibility

    C. To bring long-range benefits to HR outcomes

    D. To influence organizational decision-making by providing solutions to workforce problems at all levels

51. Determining the number of protected-class groups represented in the management team to assess risk is the objective of which of the following HR activities?

    A. Legal compliance

    B. Needs assessment

    C. HR audit

    D. Data collection

52. As the result of an HR audit you conducted to assess risk in your new HR management position, it is clear that several business practices are out of compliance. Which of the following is your best first step toward managing the risk?

   A. Identify the most obvious abusers, and terminate or demote them to demonstrate a good faith effort toward compliance.

   B. Train all employees and managers about expected standards of behavior.

   C. Rewrite the handbook to mitigate the exposure.

   D. Recommend employment practices liability insurance (EPLI) until an action plan can be defined and executed toward compliance.

53. Which of the following organizations concentrate decision-making authority at higher levels within the organization?

   A. Centralized

   B. Organized

   C. Decentralized

   D. Authoritarian

54. The large healthcare facility for which you work has asked you to evaluate the strategy of outsourcing the recruiting function to a healthcare specialty group. The executive committee has asked you to gather the economic costs to identify the impact on both customers and employees. Which of the following types of analysis would you provide to the executive committee?

   A. Quantitative

   B. Return on investment

   C. Qualitative

   D. Cost benefit

55. The cost of recruiting fees, bill rates, and quality of the workforce are considerations of which of the following functions?

   A. Hiring

   B. Outsourced staffing

   C. Recruiting

   D. Selection

56. Shawn, an executive at a large construction company in New Jersey, has experienced a 23 percent drop in revenue because of the housing crisis. He has asked his executive leadership team to identify staffing cuts of up to 10 percent in all departments to offset some of the revenue loss. Of the following, which action step would be the most critical for the HR director to take?

   A. Lead the executive team members through the development of a workforce plan.

   B. Identify cross-training needs of employees to avoid laying off in one department while hiring in another.

   C. Freeze all hiring until a budget is approved by the executive team.

   D. Begin to research the compliance obligations of the Worker Adjustment Retraining and Notification Act (WARN).

57. In the scenario from the previous question, Shawn is certain the reduction in force is necessary. As CEO, he also knows that he must consider the needs of the workers who will be losing their jobs, as well as the public perception of a mass layoff. How could Shawn be best supported by HR to deliver the message to his workforce?

    A. HR should help Shawn craft the message to employees to avoid any legal pitfalls.

    B. HR should recommend severance packages for all affected workers based on length of service.

    C. HR should provide the CEO with a list of employee resources the company may offer to affected workers, along with the merits of each option.

    D. HR should lead an executive team brainstorming meeting to gather input and ideas from company leaders.

58. A major coffee retailer has an organizational structure that has an HR department, a finance department, an IT department, and a sales/marketing department. This is an example of what type of organizational structure?

    A. Matrix

    B. Divisional

    C. Hybrid

    D. Functional

59. Under what conditions would HR recommend a product-based organizational structure?

    A. When a company's decision-making strategy is to become centralized

    B. When company products or services have a different/unique customer base

    C. When a company strategy is focused on the development of multiple brands

    D. When products or services are manufactured/delivered by multiple work teams

60. The company you work for has recently hired an external agency to come in and review employee personnel files, audit timesheets for meal/rest break compliance, and calculate the retention dates for all Form I-9s. What type of audit is being conducted?

    A. Legal compliance

    B. HR

    C. Risk management

    D. Operational

61. Time Inc. owns multiple magazine titles including *Time*, *Sports Illustrated*, and *People Magazine*. The company unofficially went up for sale in 2017 but decided instead it would only consider selling off single titles. This is an example of what type of business strategy?

    A. Acquisition

    B. Growth

    C. Divestiture

    D. Reengineering

62. International human resource management involves addressing the need of expatriates to be "kept whole" while on an international assignment. Which of the following IHRM activities is most likely to make this happen?

    A. Using a balance sheet approach in designing compensation

    B. Conducting remuneration surveys before selecting an international assignee

    C. Making equity a part of an assignee's total compensation package

    D. Offering fringe benefits as part of an assignee's pay

63. The decision of the New Zealand postal service to start delivering food from KFC restaurants as part of its core service is an example of which of the following business strategies?

    A. Growth

    B. Development

    C. Leveraging

    D. Diversification

64. The labor expense of a large oil producer exceeded 50 percent of operating expenses in the last calendar year. Which of the following is the most likely driver of this cost?

    A. Voluntary benefit offerings

    B. Generous time-off policies

    C. Employee base pay and benefits

    D. Workers' compensation insurance premiums

65. Using the information from the scenario in the previous question, which of the following is the best recommendation you can give to company leadership if they need to reduce expenses?

    A. Stop contributing to state disability insurance programs.

    B. Engage in training and development activities while business is slow.

    C. Eliminate layers of management.

    D. Talk with employees about pay reductions for everyone to avoid layoffs for some.

66. Which of the following is the focus of a human capital management plan (HCMP)?

    A. The development of an employee handbook

    B. The allocation of training and development resources

    C. Addressing discipline and termination procedures

    D. A review of hiring practices

67. An IT service provider wants to develop a strategic plan that incorporates aggressive growth targets aimed at gaining market share over its competitors. Based on your recommendation, which of the following departments should be expanded?

    A. Marketing, R&D, finance

    B. Operations, marketing, sales

    C. Sales, purchasing, operations

    D. Accounting, human resources, quality

68. Specific HR strategies must first and foremost be aligned with which of the following?

    A. The needs of the people

    B. Global integration

    C. Labor law compliance

    D. The company's strategic plan

69. The company you work for has discussed a business strategy that would expand it into Asia. Which of the following actions would you first take to help the company develop this strategic plan?

    A. A discussion of the international compensation strategies of the region

    B. A scan of the environment for both threats and opportunities

    C. A review of company leadership for a qualified expatriate

    D. The development of an advisory board to help them make the decision

70. The nonprofit bone marrow–matching company you work for has established a goal of 10,000 transplants per year; its current rate is 5,000. The CEO is dissatisfied with the company's current measurement tool, telling you that it is "too focused on projects and not focused enough on overall results." Based on his feedback, which measurement tool should you recommend?

    A. Key performance indicators

    B. Critical success factors

    C. A balanced scorecard

    D. A strategic plan

71. Delivered costs, unit costs, and inventory turnover are all examples of what type of supply chain metric?

    A. Value stream mapping

    B. Key performance indicators

    C. A balanced scorecard

    D. Financial reporting

72. Which of the following statements is most likely to strategically align performance standards with leadership expectations?

    A. If this strategy works, we are more likely to see improved attendance.

    B. Not everything that can be measured should be measured.

    C. Companies often measure what is easy, not what is right.

    D. Metrics must be focused to have true impact.

73. Which of the following is a type of forecast completed during the strategic planning process?

    A. A competitor analysis

    B. Scenario building

    C. A SWOT audit

    D. All of the above

74. A major refrigerator manufacturer has decided to expand its operations by offering field repair work on its units. Each department has been tasked with developing objectives to ensure this plan will be successful. As the HR leader, which of the following goals are you most likely to adopt?

    A. To hire and train the initial 12 employees over the next six months

    B. To reduce turnover, allowing department managers to focus on their relevant objectives

    C. To reallocate training resources to account for the new hire training costs

    D. To meet with the department heads to identify their needs

75. As the VP of HR, you are considering the implementation of workforce analytics software that will collect performance data and provide visual interpretations of the information to improve organizational decision-making. Implementation costs, including service fees, are expected to run about $325,000. Which of the following is the most critical information to have to calculate the ROI of the software?

    A. All subsequent years' fees for service

    B. The value received from the software implementation

    C. The cost of attorney fees to update the employer's privacy policy

    D. An estimate of the time it will take for employees to engage with the software

76. A large shipbuilding company in Bangladesh decided to undertake a strategic intervention related to improving the health and safety outcomes of its workers. These included decreased injuries, greater economic security for families, and improved productivity. In deciding to implement this intervention, the company had to weigh these outcomes against the investment in safety training, the building of a new medical clinic to treat minor injuries, and personal protective equipment. Which measurement formula should the company use to help make the decision?

    A. OSH's incident rate

    B. Human economic value add

    C. Cost-benefit analysis

    D. All of the above

77. The talent team at Google commissioned a group of experts to review data on employee backgrounds, capabilities, and performance. The outputs were used to identify the factors that may influence an employee's decision to leave their job and design intervention strategies to improve retention. This is an example of which of the following HR activities?

    A. Data mining

    B. HR metrics

    C. Employment data collection

    D. Workforce analytics

78. Which metric would you recommend to a company that wants to improve profit?

   A. Number of positions filled

   B. Percentage of HR staff in supervisory roles

   C. Employee tenure

   D. Cost per hire

79. The educational institution for which you work has a budgeting process in which executive leadership teams up with the VP of finance to create the annual budget. This is an example of which budgeting approach?

   A. Zero-based

   B. Bottom up

   C. Top down

   D. Parallel

80. Senior management at your place of work has asked you to provide them with staffing projections to include in the annual budget. Which of the following will need to be collected to properly fulfill this request?

   A. Cost of life insurance

   B. Recruitment advertising costs

   C. Attorney fees

   D. Workplace violence prevention and training costs

81. Which of the following has the most significant effect on the likelihood of an employee reporting illegal behavior?

   A. The company having a whistleblower policy that prohibits retaliation

   B. The availability of a confidential 800 number reporting line

   C. The employees having received training in whistleblower protection

   D. The company culture

82. A small construction firm is considering a proposal to outsource one of its HR activities to a third party. The company is subject to prevailing wage orders and job costing as part of its payroll practices. It currently has an assistant to the CEO who is generally in charge of recruiting and selection, along with the maintenance of employee personnel files. In matters of training, they have a matrix that tracks what training is due and when it must be completed. The CEO is in charge of all strategic planning. Which of these tasks would you recommend they outsource?

   A. Payroll

   B. Staffing

   C. Training activities

   D. Strategic planning

83. Which of the following HR practices may inadvertently work against positive organizational outcomes?

    A. Policies

    B. Performance management systems

    C. Compensation practices

    D. All of the above

84. To offset a major shortfall in grant funding over the next three years, the board of directors at the adult literacy agency where you work has asked you to find programs that may be eliminated to reduce costs. Which of the following would you recommend for elimination first?

    A. After-hours language training for students

    B. Company-sponsored daycare

    C. Workers' compensation insurance

    D. Voluntary vision insurance

85. Which of the following is the most likely negative outcome of switching to an HR shared services model?

    A. Loss of face-to-face interaction between HR and employees

    B. Increased liability because of compliance with differing national and state labor laws

    C. Increased threat of data security breaches because of the storage of personnel files at a remote location

    D. Decreased trust of the HR team

86. Which of the following is the most critical pitfall that must be avoided when collecting workforce data?

    A. The depersonalization of the human talent

    B. The collection of data without insight

    C. The implementation and maintenance costs

    D. The threat of employees manipulating the data being collected

87. A major bank moved more than 3,000 of its 25,000 jobs to India, where wages were $20 per hour as opposed to the $50 per hour it would have cost to keep the jobs at company headquarters in the United States. This is an example of which business strategy?

    A. Divestiture

    B. Globalization

    C. Diversification

    D. Offshoring

88. Which of the following conditions best reflect a competitive advantage of U.S. employers?

    A. The United States has the most evolved infrastructure for product transport (air, rail, sea).

    B. The United States has lower costs of doing business, particularly in the Midwest.

    C. The United States has some of the highest-quality colleges and universities in the world.

    D. The labor force participation rate is increasing at a faster rate in the United States than it is in other countries.

89. The large, international retail company for which you are the director of HR found that your HR staff were spending up to 80 percent of their time on administrative work. This included benefits open enrollment, making address changes, and helping employees update their tax deductions. Which of the following strategies would you recommend to reduce the amount of time your staff is spending on these activities?

    A. Hiring an HR assistant

    B. Researching employee self-service technology

    C. Setting up an off-site service center to handle all of the administrative work

    D. Redesigning processes to eliminate redundancies and streamline efficiencies

90. Which of the following should be the first step in the development of a workforce analytics program?

    A. Design a plan to maintain data integrity.

    B. Identify any privacy issues that will need to be addressed.

    C. Create a plan to manage associated risks.

    D. Build a business case to gain executive buy-in.

91. The company you work for has recently acquired a key competitor in its technology market. The company is struggling with incompatible cultures and the loss of key talent from both entities. Which of the following strategies should you recommend?

    A. Revise the company handbook to guide behaviors of the new, blended organization.

    B. Develop new compensation strategies that address the reasons key talent is leaving.

    C. Craft a communication strategy that addresses the needs of both workforces.

    D. Research best practices from other organizations that have managed similar challenges with success.

92. Which of the following merger and acquisition activities is a useful strategy to ensure the retention of key leadership talent?

    A. Conducting confidential interviews with employees as soon as is legally possible

    B. Using outside consultants to administer assessments of key talent

C. Re-recruiting top performers and communicating their new roles as soon as possible

D. All of the above

93. You just found out that the large appliance retailer for which you work is in the early stages of taking bids for a merger. Which of the following is the best way for you to stay informed during the process?

A. Ask the management team to keep you informed of progress.

B. Form a due diligence team made up of key individuals.

C. Meet regularly with the CFO for updates.

D. Wait for direction and an invitation to participate.

94. In early M&A discussions, which of the following should be the top priority of the HR executive?

A. Identifying the compensation disparities between the two organizations

B. Focusing on the factors influencing employee retention

C. Managing the legal issues related to due diligence

D. Addressing employee concerns

95. Which of the following is an example of a human resources SaaS?

A. Applicant tracking software

B. Staffing agencies

C. Harassment reporting hotlines

D. All of the above

96. Which of the following conditions is most likely to increase the success of an outsourced employee wellness program?

A. The quality of the information being presented

B. The level of commitment of the vendor

C. The cost of employee servicing

D. The presence of a company "champion"

97. Online payment processing, applicant tracking, and production scheduling are all examples of what type of computer-based information system?

A. Human resource information system

B. New enterprise software

C. Content management system

D. Supply chain management

98. A large healthcare facility has decided to embark on a company-wide system upgrade to help improve efficiencies and patient outcomes. As the HR leader, you have been tasked with identifying employee concerns and creating response strategies. Your team conducted multiple focus groups and found that most employees were concerned that the new program would be harder to use and not be customized enough to really be different from the current system; in fact, they are struggling to see the point of the change. Based on these findings, which solution should you first recommend to the executive team?

    A. Ask the software vendor to prepare a report that compares the current and proposed system features for each department.

    B. Have the executive team hold off on the system implementation until you can conduct change management training for all staff.

    C. Factor employee training and support resources into the overall cost of system implementation.

    D. Make sure the software development team uses employee representatives to customize the usability of each module.

99. In which organizations would the HR expense to FTE ratio be the lowest?

    A. Organizations with 1 to 25 employees

    B. Organizations with 1 to 100 employees

    C. Organizations with 1 to 250 employees

    D. Organizations with more than 250 employees

100. The IT services company you work for has discovered that almost half of its total expenses are spent on company compensation programs. Which of the following metrics did it most likely use to identify this number?

    A. Salaries as a percentage of operating expense

    B. Utilization review

    C. HR expense factor

    D. Salaries as a percentage of revenue

101. A major online distributor has recently begun its strategic planning session for the upcoming fiscal year. The CFO has proposed an organizational change in which you, the VP of HR, and the departments that you manage begin to report to the finance team instead of serving as an independent department. Which of the following arguments do you think the CFO would find the most persuasive against this structural move?

    A. That there are compelling legal reasons why HR must remain independent

    B. That studies have found no significant bottom-line improvement to having HR report to finance

    C. That a better option would be to have compensation and benefits report to finance, but the functions of people should remain a direct line to the CEO

    D. That a direct line from HR to finance would serve only short-term outcomes

102. The financial institution for which you are the regional HR manager has recently come under fire for potentially unethical business practices by its portfolio managers. The HR team has been tasked with identifying the risky employees and helping to find evidence of any breaches in conduct. Which tools would prove most useful to you in completing this request?

   A. Interviewing all PMs to assess their conduct and asking them to justify/explain any personal trading rules violations

   B. Conducting a deep dive into the trades that resulted in net profits above the threshold set by the compliance department

   C. Working with IT to build an algorithm to search for employees who skipped compliance training and any flagged transactions

   D. Tasking local institution managers with flagging suspected individuals and providing documentation of wrongdoing

103. Why is technology such an important HR competency for 21st century practitioners?

   A. As businesses rely more and more upon technology, so must their human resource departments.

   B. HR must understand what technological tools are being used by competitors.

   C. HR must be the knowledge expert on how to combine technology with people strategies.

   D. All of the above.

104. Skill availability and the age of the workforce are both examples of which of the following strategic planning elements?

   A. Scan of the internal and external environments

   B. Diversity analysis

   C. Preplanning activities

   D. Talent demographics

105. During a workforce planning session, it was identified that many of the sales employees do not have the necessary skills to achieve the company's growth targets. HR must first do what to address this gap?

   A. Design training programs that will transfer the necessary skills.

   B. Design compensation systems to reward employees who demonstrate the desired skills.

   C. Build a business case to gain senior management approval to design programs that will address the skills gap.

   D. Identify nonperformers and create an exit strategy that minimizes risk.

106. Which of the following HR tools serves as a guide for organizational and employee behaviors?

   A. The company handbook

   B. Standard operating procedures (SOPs)

   C. Critical success factors (CSFs)

   D. A code of ethics

107. The term *span of control* is most accurate in which type of organization?

   A. Static companies with clear reporting structures

   B. Collaborative agencies with integrated teams

   C. Businesses using a front-back organizational structure

   D. Business units within the tech industry

108. Which of the following is the most compelling reason an employer would want to create a whistleblower hotline?

   A. To comply with the Occupational Safety and Health Act (OSHA)

   B. To help alert the company to potential wrongdoing

   C. To deal with rogue employees before they become a liability

   D. To improve their EPL insurance premium

109. An ethics policy, fundraising for infrastructure builds, and a whistleblower hotline are all examples of which of the following HR responsibilities?

   A. Corporate citizenship initiatives

   B. Strategic planning initiatives

   C. Corporate governance initiatives

   D. Legal compliance

110. Under which condition would you recommend that your company partner with an NGO?

   A. When the company stakeholders exist across multiple borders

   B. When the country in which you desire to invest lacks infrastructure

   C. When a company's reputation needs to be developed in a particular region

   D. All of the above

111. The Iroquois proverb "In our every deliberation, we must consider the impact of our decisions on the next seven generations" is an example of what type of influence on organizational decision-making?

   A. Sustainable practices

   B. Global ethics policy

   C. Factors of corporate governance

   D. Fiduciary responsibilities

112. The American Psychological Association found that 60 percent of Americans report that work is a significant source of stress, both at work and at home. The financial impact of stressed-out employees is measured in lower productivity, increased absenteeism, poor safety habits, and higher healthcare costs. Based on this, which of the following actions should HR recommend that an employer do to help reduce worker stress?

   A. Adopting policies that guarantee an employee's right to disconnect from work outside of office hours

   B. Adopting well-day leave policies, where employees may "call in well"

   C. Training employees on workplace safety hazards

   D. Offering perks such as on-site massages

113. The phenomenon of "presenteeism" may be best addressed through which HR activity?

   A. Instructing employees to stay home when they are sick

   B. Offering paid sick leave for all workers

   C. Teaching management about the financial impact of presenteeism

   D. All of the above

114. Research suggests that most major decisions by employers have a greater than 50 percent fail rate. Which of the following strategies may HR employ to improve this decision-making metric?

   A. Place greater emphasis on intelligence and experience when hiring/promoting to leadership

   B. Use in-box exercises to measure the quality of management decision-making abilities

   C. Train managers to employ strategies such as "consider the opposite" when making decisions

   D. Focus on generating decision-making trees for complicated processes

115. A major airline experienced a period of negative publicity after two incidents in which passengers were left stranded on the tarmac without food, water, or bathroom access. This is an example of which of the following factors of consumer trust?

   A. Truthfulness

   B. Integrity

   C. Security

   D. Privacy

116. The growth of digital media—information from websites and apps—has had what impact on how organizations compete?

   A. Digital media help to connect like-minded individuals to organize around social causes/volunteering.

   B. Digital media can enhance flexibility for workers and employers.

   C. Digital media services can facilitate educational objectives and employee development activities.

   D. All of the above.

117. One potential negative effect of an increase in digital media services in the workplace includes which of the following?

   A. An increase in bullying or harassing behaviors

   B. An increase in successful union organizing efforts

   C. An increase in mental health disorders

   D. All of the above

118. Which of the following reflects the changing nature of the employment relationship?

   A. Employees expect to be paid higher wages as the economy recovers.

   B. The psychological contract no longer exists.

   C. Technology is changing how (and by whom) work gets done.

   D. Scientific research about the workplace is playing a larger role in organizational design.

119. Narrow spans of control and standardized rules and procedures are most often reflected in which type of business structure?

   A. Authoritarian

   B. Open systems

   C. Scientific

   D. Bureaucratic

120. What is one of the major disadvantages of bureaucratic organizations?

   A. Human relations systems are largely ignored.

   B. Organizational efficiencies are decreased.

   C. An over-reliance on inputs and outputs develops.

   D. Companies lose their ability to manage costs.

121. Open systems theory proposes that _____, throughputs, and outputs are the building blocks of any organizational system.

   A. Energy

   B. Inputs

   C. Effort

   D. Managers

122. In open systems theory, HR departments (or managers) must help their organizations do what?

   A. Measure outputs

   B. Create throughputs

   C. Build workforce budgets

   D. Adapt to feedback

123. The four main functions of management are which of the following?

   A. Strategy, structure, systems, and staff

   B. Analyzing, designing, developing, and implementing

   C. Strategic, Operational, Administrative and Technological

   D. Planning, organizing, directing, and controlling

124. Which of the following is a characteristic of the VUCA business environment?

  A. Globalization

  B. Rapid change

  C. Changes in technology

  D. All of the above

125. In the 21st century HR must be able to plan for and address which of the following demographic conditions?

  A. Uncertain labor law interpretations

  B. Economic volatility

  C. Labor shortages across the globe

  D. All of the above

Chapter

8

SPHR Exam:
Talent Planning &
Acquisition

THE SPHR EXAM CONTENT FROM THE
TALENT PLANNING AND ACQUISITION
FUNCTIONAL AREA COVERED IN THIS
CHAPTER FOCUSES ON "FORECASTING
THE ORGANIZATIONAL TALENT
NEEDS AND DEVELOP STRATEGIES TO
ATTRACT AND ENGAGE NEW TALENT."
CONTENT CONSISTS OF THE FOLLOWING
RESPONSIBILITIES:

✓ 01   Evaluate and forecast organizational needs throughout the business cycle to create or develop workforce
plans (for example: corporate restructuring, workforce
expansion, or reduction)

✓ 02   Develop, monitor, and assess recruitment strategies
to attract desired talent (for example: labor market analysis, compensation strategies, selection process, onboarding, sourcing and branding strategy)

✓ 03   Develop and evaluate strategies for engaging new
employees and managing cultural integrations (for example: new employee acculturation, downsizing, restructuring, mergers and acquisitions, divestitures, global
expansion)

IN ADDITION TO THE RESPONSIBILITIES LISTED ABOVE, AN INDIVIDUAL TAKING THE SPHR EXAM SHOULD HAVE WORKING KNOWLEDGE OF THE FOLLOWING, USUALLY DERIVED THROUGH PRACTICAL EXPERIENCE:

✓ 17 Planning techniques (for example: succession planning, forecasting)

✓ 18 Talent management practices and techniques (for example: selecting and assessing employees)

✓ 19 Recruitment sources and strategies

✓ 20 Staffing alternatives (for example: outsourcing, temporary employment)

✓ 21 Interviewing and selection techniques and strategies

✓ 22 Impact of total rewards on recruitment and retention

✓ 23 Termination approaches and strategies

✓ 24 Employee engagement strategies

✓ 25 Employer marketing and branding techniques

✓ 26 Negotiation skills and techniques

✓ 27 Due diligence processes (for example: mergers and acquisitions, divestitures)

✓ 28 Transition techniques for corporate restructuring, mergers and acquisitions, offshoring, and divestitures

✓ 29 Methods to assess past and future staffing effectiveness (for example: cost per hire, selection ratios, adverse impact)

1. How does the U.S. president pass labor laws without the approval of Congress?

   A. Interpret labor laws

   B. Proclaim executive orders

   C. Rule on court cases

   D. Study case law

2. Which of the following agencies is responsible for enforcing executive orders (EOs) related to unlawful discrimination in companies doing business with the federal government?

   A. Department of Labor

   B. Equal Employment Opportunity Commission

   C. Office of Federal Contract Compliance

   D. All of the above

3. Private employers with 100 or more employees, and federal contractors or subcontractors with 50 or more employees, must submit which of the following reports?

   A. Headquarters report

   B. Consolidated report

   C. EEO-1 report

   D. Diversity report

4. Executive Order 11246 prohibited employment discrimination based on which of the following protected-class characteristics?

   A. Gender, age, religion

   B. Race, color, national origin

   C. Race, ethnicity, age

   D. Race, sex, religion

5. The job group analysis is organized using which of the following categories?

   A. Employee names

   B. Total number of incumbents

   C. Job titles

   D. Salary grade

6. Which of the following scenarios may be the effect of the strategic planning process on workforce goals and objectives?

   A. Reengineering

   B. Merger or acquisition

   C. Outsourcing

   D. All of the above

7. The goal of strategic workforce planning is to ensure that qualified employees are what?

    A. Going to do the work they were hired to do

    B. Effectively managed for successful retention

    C. Properly managed in accordance with federal EEO laws

    D. Available and capable when the organization needs them

8. When a company chooses to outsource existing staff to an outsourcing provider, who becomes the employer of record?

    A. The company and the outsourcing provider become co-employers.

    B. The company

    C. The outsourcing agency

    D. Nobody; they are considered independent contractors.

9. If part of an organization's strategic plan is to increase sales by 15 percent, which of the following workforce planning strategies might HR recommend?

    A. Train and develop the sales staff.

    B. Increase the sales staff.

    C. Evaluate the compensation plans for the sales force.

    D. Review the price structure of the products.

10. Organizations have three options for locating the talent they need to achieve business goals: internal transfers or promotions, external hires, and what?

    A. Alternative staffing methods

    B. Contingent workforce

    C. Temporary employees

    D. Job bidding

11. Which of the following types of alternative staffing methods allows two people with complementary skills to share the duties and responsibilities of a full-time position?

    A. Internships

    B. Part-time workers

    C. Job sharing

    D. Payrolling

12. Teamwork, communication, and customer focus are all examples of which of the following criteria being predicted in an interview?

    A. Job competencies

    B. Abilities

    C. Knowledge

    D. Skills

13. A position has just opened up in the sales department in the organization for which you work. This was the third sales representative to hold the job in as many years, and the exit interviews indicate that the job requirements are unrealistic. Which of the following strategies should you recommend first?

   A. Interview the supervisor of the workgroup

   B. Change recruiting sources

   C. Conduct a thorough job analysis

   D. All of the above

14. Why should job descriptions be signed off on and approved by supervisors?

   A. To hold the supervisor accountable to the outcomes

   B. To verify their accuracy

   C. To ensure that the managers know what is expected of their employees

   D. The employee, not the supervisor, should be the one to sign off on job descriptions.

15. What is the primary purpose of defining the essential job functions?

   A. To collect data for use in formulating workforce planning strategy

   B. To identify gaps in employee desired and actual performance

   C. To comply with equal employment labor laws

   D. To provide the platform for a performance management system

16. Which of the following is not a disadvantage of hiring talent from the external labor market?

   A. Current employees who have been passed over for promotion will likely have lower morale.

   B. It is difficult to predict how the organizational culture will factor into the employee's success.

   C. It is difficult to identify the actual versus stated skillset of the worker.

   D. If there is an urgent need for someone with particular skills, it's usually faster to hire those skills than to provide on-the-job training.

17. Which of the following landmark court cases established that pre-employment requirements, such as having a high school diploma, must not be discriminatory in outcomes regardless of nondiscriminatory intent?

   A. *Automobile Workers v. Johnson Controls, Inc.*

   B. *Washington v. Davis*

   C. *Albemarle Paper v. Moody*

   D. *Griggs v. Duke Power*

18. Which of the following landmark court cases is being violated in the following scenario? An employer relied on a series of pre-employment tests in making selection decisions. As a result, certain protected-class individuals were not hired. These tests had been validated by the subjective ranking of supervisors and couldn't be tied to job-related performance criteria. In addition, they had not been used consistently.

   A. *Automobile Workers v. Johnson Controls, Inc.*

   B. *Washington v. Davis*

   C. *Albemarle Paper v. Moody*

   D. *Griggs v. Duke Power*

19. A pre-employment test was used to predict the success of candidates in making statistical math calculations. Over the course of a year, employees who scored high on this test were rated higher by their supervisors than the employees who did not score as well. This test is most likely what?

   A. Reliable

   B. Valid

   C. Unreliable

   D. Both A and B

20. An employer administered a test to current salespeople to measure their skills related to the specific criteria of their jobs. They administered the test right around the time of annual performance appraisals and had a professional test validation group compare the results. Those who rated highest on their performance reviews were also those who received the highest test scores. The company decides to use the same test to predict the success of future sales hires. This is an example of which validation method?

   A. Construct

   B. Concurrent

   C. Content

   D. Reliability

21. The management team of the Australian division of a multibillion-dollar organization is staffed only with expatriates from the corporate base in New York. This is an example of which type of global staffing strategy?

   A. Ethnocentric

   B. Polycentric

   C. Regiocentric

   D. Geocentric

22. If the multinational company for which you work has instructed your recruiting team to place the best-qualified person in each management position regardless of their country of origin, they are practicing which of the following staffing strategies?

   A. Ethnocentric

   B. Polycentric

   C. Regiocentric

   D. Geocentric

23. If a supervisor complains that it is taking HR too long to find qualified candidates for an open position, which of the following metrics will best define your response?

   A. Cost-benefit

   B. Time-to-hire

   C. Return on investment

   D. Turnover analysis

24. By dividing the average number of total employees for the measurement period by the number of employees who exited the organization, you will identify which of the following?

   A. Replacement rate

   B. Time to hire

   C. Turnover rate

   D. Average tenure

25. Storing legible copies, preventing unauthorized access, creating provisions for backup, and indexing of data are all recommendations for which of the following workforce practices?

   A. Personnel file management

   B. Data integrity

   C. Electronic storage of records

   D. Compliance with labor laws

26. It has been found that a large percentage of the workforce is expected to retire within the next five years. For which of the following strategies should you plan?

   A. Attrition rates

   B. Hiring practices

   C. Succession planning

   D. Outsourcing

27. "Ready for promotion," "develop for future promotion," "satisfactory in current position," and "replace" are all categories that may be reflected on which of the following succession planning tools?

   A. Ranking performance evaluations

   B. Attrition rates

   C. Turnover analysis

   D. Replacement chart

28. School alumni sites, personal networks, and professional Internet networks are all examples of which of the following external recruiting tools?

   A. Union job boards

   B. Social media

   C. Career websites

   D. Virtual reality

29. If you want to reach candidates who are technologically savvy for your IT department, which of the following recruiting sources would be most advisable?

    A. Professional trade shows

    B. University job fairs

    C. Employment agencies

    D. Videos on the company website and on online forums

30. Which of the following guidelines were jointly developed by the EEOC, CSC, OFCCP, and DOJ to assist employers in complying with federal EEO legislation?

    A. Executive orders

    B. Uniform Guidelines on Employee Selection Procedures

    C. Equal Employment Opportunity Fact Sheets

    D. Opinion letters

31. The company for which you work is hiring 100 call center employees. A total of 395 applications were received from female candidates, of which 52 were hired. A total of 255 applications were received from males, of which 48 were hired. What percentage of women were hired, and what percentage of men were hired?

    A. 18 percent, 14 percent

    B. 7.6 percent, 5.30 percent

    C. 14 percent, 20 percent

    D. 13 percent, 19 percent

32. Which of the following is not considered a pre-employment test?

    A. An application

    B. Paper and pencil test

    C. Personality assessment

    D. They are all pre-employment tests.

33. Which of the following "Big Five" personality characteristics is most often correlated with work success when hiring for all positions?

    A. Agreeableness

    B. Conscientiousness

    C. Low neuroticism

    D. Openness

34. An employee claimed on a popular review site that her employer discriminated against her based on her sexual orientation. She subsequently was fired for performance issues, which she denied. Which of the following statements is true?

    A. The employee was a victim of constructive discharge.

    B. The employee may have a claim of unlawful retaliation.

C. The employee was discriminated against for concerted protected activity.

D. The employee was unlikely to have been a victim of discrimination.

35. Anonymous online posts disparaging a company by a current employee that are not intended to be read by co-workers—such as on review sites—may *not* be which of the following?

A. Protected under the National Labor Relations Act (NLRA)

B. Used by the employer to make performance-related decisions

C. Used by the employer to retaliate against a protected-class individual

D. All of the above

36. A supervisor interviewed an applicant for an open position and gave a high rating because the supervisor and the applicant went to the same college. This is an example of which type of interviewer bias?

A. Stereotyping

B. First impression

C. Similar to me

D. Negative emphasis

37. In preparation for the succession planning process at your place of business, you began to analyze jobs and evaluate the existing organizational structure. This is an example of which of the following types of analysis?

A. Workforce

B. Organizational development

C. Business structure

D. Current state

38. The high-tech company for which you work has discovered that 65 percent of its employees are men. It has established a strategic objective to reach out and hire more women in both the short term and the long term. Which of the following strategies would you recommend?

A. Increase the pay rates to attract more qualified workers

B. Recommend an employee daycare center to your management team

C. Partner with schools and other agencies to help remove barriers to girls excelling in STEM domains

D. Establish hiring quotas that give all female applicants priority

39. Which of the following is a benefit of hiring veterans?

A. The company may be eligible for tax credits.

B. Former military workers tend to have strong leadership and problem-solving skills.

C. Former military individuals tend to be underemployed and thus available.

D. All of the above.

40. In succession planning, which of the following comparisons is the best example of a gap analysis?

    A. An employee's current skillset compared to their current job

    B. An employee's current skillset compared to the availability of similar talent in the labor market

    C. An employee's current strengths compared to their current weaknesses

    D. An employee's current role compared with their future interests

41. When considering an internal promotion to an international assignment, which of the following would most likely improve retention?

    A. Provide a realistic job preview.

    B. Offer cross-training.

    C. Provide a senior-level, international job title.

    D. Pay a sign-on bonus.

42. Which of the following would be your best choice to use when making a business case for succession planning?

    A. Succession planning may help offset future leadership vacancies that occur because of attrition.

    B. Succession planning is less expensive than hiring talent from external sources.

    C. Succession planning may reduce turnover for protected-class individuals.

    D. All of the above.

43. Family-related issues remain the primary barrier for the company you work for in terms of hiring for international assignments. Which of the following strategies would best address that obstacle?

    A. Provide a realistic job preview to potential international assignees.

    B. Tie compensation to home country growth and tax burden.

    C. Help potential assignees understand the school system in the international location being considered.

    D. Avoid offering international assignments to female employees, especially in countries with high risk.

44. Which of the following strategies should you recommend for a company that staffs for international assignments?

    A. Send early-career, high-potential employees.

    B. Have a systematic method for selecting international assignees.

    C. Partially base selection decisions on merit.

    D. All of the above

45. You are the HR manager, and the executive team has asked you to review and address the high turnover within a specific business unit. The former HR staff completed a turnover review several years ago, but the problem has persisted. Which of the following methods should you employ?

    A. A wage survey to ensure the employees are being paid competitively

    B. A review of the selection procedures

    C. A 360-degree feedback analysis for the supervisors

    D. All of the above

46. Which of the following is the *least* effective way to communicate an employer brand on the company website?

    A. A Quick Apply button allowing an applicant to access a short-form version of a job application

    B. A Job Alert option so individuals can receive notification of jobs for which they are qualified

    C. A link to video testimonials from current, successful employees

    D. A listing of open jobs within the company that links to the application

47. Of the following choices, which is most important when developing an employer brand?

    A. Matching the organization's external branding look and feel

    B. Defining the value proposition

    C. Creating a professional logo and tagline

    D. Communicating the company values

48. Your employer has asked your HR team to begin the process of building their brand as the "employer of choice." Which of the following questions should you ask your leadership team to help facilitate this objective?

    A. How do the mission, vision, and values influence organizational decision-making with regard to employee programs?

    B. What is most important to employees?

    C. Why are candidates attracted to the company, and what are the priorities for retaining all workers?

    D. What is the organization's strategic direction?

49. Hiring tools such as situational judgment tests, assessment centers, and biodata are collectively known as which of the following?

    A. Assessments

    B. Predictors

    C. Selection battery

    D. Valid predictors

50. What should be the primary purpose of an organization that chooses to use an in-basket test for selection?

  A. That the test has a clear purpose

  B. That the test is not too complicated

  C. That the test is simple to measure

  D. That the test be duplicable among applicants

51. What is the main idea behind an employer's choice to use previous work experience as a job requirement?

  A. It is important to remain consistent with other employers in the same/similar industry

  B. Applicants with similar work experience to the job for which they are applying will have a shorter learning curve

  C. Past performance predicts future performance

  D. All of the above

52. What behavior is the following question trying to predict in an interview: "When you feel strongly about something, what methods do you employ to persuade others to see your point of view?"

  A. Emotional intelligence

  B. Negotiation skills

  C. Interpersonal skills

  D. Customer service skills

53. "Have you ever been arrested?" and "Are you a U.S. citizen?" are two examples of which of the following?

  A. Pre-screening questions

  B. Behavioral interview questions

  C. Stress interview questions

  D. Unlawful interview questions

54. You are tasked with designing a selection battery for general surgeons at the major hospital for which you work. You have decided that the new hire must pass a medical knowledge test, have a minimum of 3.8 GPA from any schools they attended, and receive an above-average first interview score before you will move the candidate forward in the hiring process. This is an example of which selection strategy?

  A. Precision

  B. Distinguishing characteristics

  C. Multiple cutoff

  D. Specificity

55. The degree to which a selection battery is useful and cost efficient is known as its what?

   A. Reliability

   B. Validity

   C. Efficiency

   D. Utility

56. Which of the following is a characteristic of employees who remain after a company makes major layoffs?

   A. Their productivity increases.

   B. Their job attitudes improve.

   C. Their productivity decreases.

   D. There are no changes.

57. Which of the following variables has the most significant impact on whether managers believe layoff decisions were fair?

   A. Belief in procedural justice

   B. Amount of severance packages

   C. Personal control over the decisions

   D. Confidence in other leadership

58. Which of the following is often the first form of training a new employee receives?

   A. Safety

   B. Socialization

   C. Technical

   D. Compliance

59. Which stage of the organizational life cycle is *most* affected by anticipatory socialization activities?

   A. Selection

   B. Onboarding

   C. Training

   D. Performance management

60. Your company uses realistic job previews and onboarding plans to help a new hire understand what is expected and what to expect of their new role. This is an example of an activity at which stage of acculturation?

   A. Anticipatory

   B. Assimilation

   C. Pre-entry

   D. Metamorphosis

61. Jill is a new employee who has recently made a mistake. Instead of accepting responsibility, she complains to HR that she was not trained properly. Jill is most likely engaged in which of the following activities?

    A. Uncivil behavior

    B. Perception management

    C. Denial

    D. Impression management

62. You are the HR director of a large law enforcement agency, and your superiors have asked you to begin viewing applicants' social media accounts as part of the hiring process. Which of the following statements is true?

    A. It is lawful for you to ask for an applicant's social media account password to continue moving forward in the process.

    B. It is reasonable to contact online friends of the applicant as an extension of the reference checking process.

    C. Email addresses may be used in cyber-searches.

    D. All of the above are true.

63. Which of the following staffing strategies would be *most* beneficial for a company seeking to fill difficult-to-fill IT positions?

    A. Employ a continuous recruitment process.

    B. Hire contract workers to fill in until hires are made.

    C. Shift their company's IT services overseas.

    D. Promote employees from within.

64. Which of the following age groups make up the fastest-growing segment of the labor force?

    A. Generation X

    B. Millennials

    C. Generation Z

    D. Baby boomers

65. Implementing diverse recruiting practices has been shown to have significant influence on which of the following outcomes?

    A. Less conflict in the workplace

    B. Higher levels of productivity

    C. Greater creativity on teams

    D. Lower labor costs

66. Fill in the blank: changing the way a job is designed using skill variety, task identity, and other characteristics has been shown to have a _____ effect on employees.

 A. Chilling

 B. Disruptive

 C. Unequal

 D. Motivating

67. The executive directive of a shelter for women and children who have been victims of domestic abuse is most likely to be motivated by which job design characteristic?

 A. Task identity

 B. Task significance

 C. Skill variety

 D. Autonomy

68. During workforce planning, you discovered that your industry is facing a shortfall of the skilled workers necessary to meet the organization's objectives in its five-year strategic plan. Which strategy should you recommend?

 A. Hire contract workers to fill the gap.

 B. Promote and train employees from within.

 C. Adopt a continuous recruitment strategy for critical positions.

 D. Take a multifaceted approach that considers both internal sources and external partnerships.

69. You have been working diligently to help your company finalize an acrimonious acquisition of a major competitor, and in doing so discovered that the soon-to-be-acquired organization has very lax HR systems in place. What should be your first step to address this issue?

 A. Hold training sessions for the acquired employees on your policies, procedures, and work rules.

 B. Analyze elements of both cultures, meeting with the executive team to identify what should stay, go, or be refined.

 C. Adopt the practices that are most legally defensible and less risky while employees adapt.

 D. Nothing, because there will conflict regardless, so it would be best to wait and see where the fires start and begin there.

70. Which of the following is a negotiating technique employed by HR when making job offers?

 A. Anchoring

 B. Primacy

 C. Exploding offers

 D. All of the above

71. Your customer service employees are exhibiting signs of stress and job burnout. When asked what they think the challenges are, they describe frustration at having to be "on" all the time, such as having to be polite to extremely difficult customers. This is an example of what facet of emotions at work?

    A. Emotional labor

    B. Emotional contagion

    C. Emotional intelligence

    D. Emotional burnout

72. When an employee smiles at a co-worker and the co-worker smiles back, this is an example of what characteristic of emotions at work?

    A. Emotional labor

    B. Emotional contagion

    C. Emotional intelligence

    D. Emotional burnout

73. During the redesign of an order entry position, a task was added to "cc the department manager for all orders placed over $500 and for which payment is not immediately received." This is an example of which job design technique?

    A. Vertical loading

    B. Horizontal loading

    C. Autonomy

    D. Task identity

74. A review of any pending employment litigation against a company with the potential to be acquired is an example of what senior-level HR activity?

    A. Due diligence

    B. Fiduciary responsibility

    C. HR audit

    D. Risk assessment

75. The process of ensuring that a company has the right number of employees at the right time to meet strategic goals is the focus of which HR function?

    A. Resource planning

    B. Strategic planning

    C. HR audits

    D. Human resource planning

Chapter

9

SPHR Exam: Learning & Development

THE SPHR EXAM CONTENT FROM THE LEARNING AND DEVELOPMENT FUNCTIONAL AREA COVERED IN THIS CHAPTER DIRECTS CANDIDATES TO DEMONSTRATE THE COMPETENCIES TO "DEVELOP TRAINING, DEVELOPMENT, AND EMPLOYEE RETENTION STRATEGIES." EXAM CONTENT CONSISTS OF THE FOLLOWING RESPONSIBILITIES:

✓ 01   Develop and evaluate training strategies (for example: modes of delivery, timing, content) to increase individual and organizational effectiveness

✓ 02   Analyze business needs to develop a succession plan for key roles (for example: identify talent, outline career progression, coaching and development) to promote business continuity

✓ 03   Develop and evaluate employee retention strategies and practices (for example: assessing talent, developing career paths, managing job movement within the organization)

IN ADDITION TO THE RESPONSIBILITIES LISTED ABOVE, AN INDIVIDUAL TAKING THE SPHR EXAM SHOULD HAVE WORKING KNOWLEDGE OF THE FOLLOWING, USUALLY DERIVED THROUGH PRACTICAL EXPERIENCE:

✓ 30   Training program design and development

✓ 31   Adult learning processes

✓ 32 Training and facilitation techniques

✓ 33 Instructional design principles and processes (for example: needs analysis, content chunking, process flow mapping)

✓ 34 Techniques to assess training program effectiveness, including use of applicable metrics

✓ 35 Career and leadership development theories and applications

✓ 36 Organizational development (OD) methods, motivation methods, and problem-solving techniques

✓ 37 Coaching and mentoring techniques

✓ 38 Effective communication skills and strategies (for example: presentation, collaboration, sensitivity)

✓ 39 Employee retention strategies

✓ 40 Techniques to encourage creativity and innovation

1. When an employee creates original work as part of their regular job duties, to whom do the rights belong?

    A. The employee

    B. The public domain

    C. The employer

    D. The employee and employer share ownership rights.

2. The employer for whom you work is in the process of changing the mission, vision, and values of the company. Which of the following is most likely going to be necessary?

    A. A reduction in force to offset the cost of the planned changes

    B. A series of planned interventions to implement the changes

    C. Consultation with outside legal, accounting, and production experts

    D. All of the above

3. A new process or change to a reporting structure will need to be implemented by people. Therefore, which of the following statements is true?

    A. Most employees dislike change.

    B. Changes often fail because employees are required to implement them prior to being ready to do so.

    C. Employees may be fearful of the unknown.

    D. All of the above.

4. In response to the availability of new technology, Boldwire Ltd. decided to change the way sales orders are processed. Throughout the implementation, management held regular meetings with the sales staff to understand what was working, seek solutions for what was not, and respond accordingly where appropriate. This is an example of which stage in the change process theory?

    A. Unfreezing

    B. Moving

    C. Refreezing

    D. Evaluation

5. A manager believes that if you train millennials, they will simply leave for a better opportunity. This is an example of what type of error?

    A. Halo effect

    B. Horn effect

    C. Bias

    D. Discrimination

6. It was brought to the attention of the HR director that there was only one employee in the department who knew how to process payroll. Of the following management options, which is the most necessary in this scenario?

    A. Change management

    B. Knowledge management

    C. Risk management

    D. Total Quality Management

7. As an HR professional seeking the designation of SPHR from the Human Resource Certification Institute, you are engaging in which of the following disciplines according to Peter Senge?

    A. Systems thinking

    B. Personal mastery

    C. Mental models

    D. Shared vision

8. A SWOT audit indicated that the customer is demanding high-quality construction of the products they are purchasing. As a result, your organization initiates a TQM program that uses a Pareto chart to track causes of quality issues. Which of the following TQM leaders is credited with this approach?

    A. Ishikawa

    B. Deming

    C. Juran

    D. Crosby

9. The executive team has tasked the HR department with figuring out why employees in the IT department are leaving. Which of the following TQM tools would be the easiest way to accomplish this?

    A. Check sheet

    B. Cause-and-effect diagram

    C. Histogram

    D. Pareto chart

10. After conducting a needs assessment, HR has identified that the production department is having a difficult time working together to achieve a goal. Which of the following human process interventions may best address this situation?

    A. Training

    B. Discipline

    C. Change management

    D. Team-building activities

11. A diversity program that blends employees from various backgrounds into cohesive work units is an example of which of the following types of intervention?

    A. Individual

    B. Techno-structural

    C. Human resource management

    D. Risk management

12. The OEM facility you work for has several manufacturing locations across the globe. They recently were awarded a military contract that will require highly skilled workers to be placed strategically at each global location to oversee the building of classified products. Which training needs assessment would *best* assess how HR should proceed?

    A. Individual needs assessment

    B. Organizational needs assessment

    C. Complete needs assessment

    D. Task needs assessment

13. Which of the following diversity strategies has the *least* direct impact on employee retention?

    A. Compensation premiums for bilingual skills

    B. Multilingual training programs

    C. Diversity training for supervisors

    D. Translation services

14. A midsize IT firm is taking on a new customer that will require software and hardware training for 40 technicians who are remote workers within a 30-day timeframe. Which training method would be the most effective?

    A. Virtual

    B. Classroom

    C. On site

    D. Bootcamp

15. If an executive is exhibiting signs of work burnout, which of the following intervention strategies would be most appropriate?

    A. Early retirement

    B. Discipline

    C. Executive coaching

    D. Training

16. If an entire department is struggling with the new phone system, which of the following talent management strategies should HR recommend?

    A. Training

    B. Development

    C. Discipline

    D. Rewards

17. Why is it important to first identify the goals of a training program?
    A. An employer cannot understand the deficiencies without first understanding the goals.
    B. The desired outcome forms the basis for several other steps in the analysis process.
    C. A document review cannot be properly completed unless the goals have been identified.
    D. A training program will not be successful without goals.

18. Sherrie is a customer service rep for your manufacturing organization. She is participating in training for the new customer database software being rolled out company-wide. Sherrie was struggling with the training material until the third day, when she applied the training content from previous sessions with success. This is an example of which of the following learning curves?
    A. Negatively accelerating
    B. Positively accelerating
    C. Plateau
    D. S-shaped

19. It has been determined that multiple facilitators will be retained to deliver training material. Which of the following tools should be created as part of the training design process to ensure the consistent delivery of information?
    A. Leader guide
    B. Manuals
    C. Handouts
    D. Evaluation forms

20. When employees participate in training that is delivered via lecture, which of the following instructional methods is being employed?
    A. Active training
    B. Passive training
    C. Experiential training
    D. Performance-based training

21. When employees participate in training that simulates the conditions under which the employee will be working, they are most likely participating in which of the following instructional methods?
    A. Active training
    B. Passive training
    C. Experiential training
    D. Classroom training

22. Access to standard operating procedures that are available via the company intranet is an example of which of the following types of training delivery?

    A. Classroom

    B. Self-study

    C. Electronic performance support systems

    D. Programmed instruction

23. As a training participant in an SPHR exam preparation class, the instructor has assigned discussion board questions to be answered each week. This is an example of which of the following training delivery methods?

    A. Classroom

    B. Self-study

    C. Programmed instruction

    D. Virtual training

24. A focus group would most likely be used in which of the following training evaluation methods?

    A. Narrative

    B. Summative

    C. Formative

    D. Learning

25. A rating form given to training participants that asks questions about the content, location, instructor, and relevance of the training to their jobs is an example of which of the following training evaluation methods?

    A. Narrative

    B. Summative

    C. Formative

    D. Learning

26. You are the director of training for one of the four largest professional services firms in the world and have been tasked with designing a new training program for entry-level accountants within their first 120 days of employment. The accounting manager disagrees with the content that you believe should be including in the training sessions. What is the best way to resolve the issue?

    A. Defer to senior management's review and comment.

    B. Develop a training needs assessment to identify the points of major conflict.

    C. Defer to the accounting manager's expertise.

    D. Trust your instinct, as you are better positioned to understand the competencies for which the new employees were hired.

27. Which theory of leadership is highly dependent on the relationship with and behaviors of the follower?

    A. LMX theory

    B. Trait-based theory

    C. Behavioral theory

    D. Theory of motivation

28. Which of the following statements regarding culture and leadership is *true*?

    A. Collective cultures may be more accepting of women leaders.

    B. Certain leadership styles are more effective than others in some cultures.

    C. Transactional leadership is the most effective across the globe.

    D. All leadership styles are widely accepted in most countries.

29. The ability to interpret and manage complex feelings is a characteristic of which of the following leadership competencies?

    A. Intelligence quotient (IQ)

    B. Emotional intelligence (EI)

    C. Cognitive processing

    D. Learning

30. Charisma, courage, and integrity are all characteristics of which leadership style?

    A. Authoritarian

    B. Laissez faire

    C. Transactional

    D. Transformational

31. In the situational leadership model, which quadrant explains high-task/high-relationship leadership behaviors?

    A. Directing

    B. Delegating

    C. Supporting

    D. Coaching

32. The more concern for production, the _____ a leader will fall on the Blake-Mouton leadership grid.

    A. Higher

    B. Lower

    C. More central

    D. None of the above

33. A global manufacturer of tomato-based products has recently hired its first female employee for its transportation team. Which of the following programs is most likely going to be necessary to acclimate the new hire to the workgroup?

    A. Harassment training

    B. Diversity initiatives

    C. Reasonable accommodations

    D. Nothing, because this employee should be treated the same as others.

34. The marketing department is in the process of interviewing graphic design candidates for an hourly position that is scheduled from 7:30 a.m. to 4:30 p.m. One applicant appears to be most qualified but cannot start work until 8:00 a.m. because of childcare responsibilities. What should HR recommend?

    A. Make the position exempt from overtime and allow a flexible schedule.

    B. Hire the next qualified candidate.

    C. Change the start time to accommodate the talent.

    D. Increase the pay rate to entice the candidate to accept the job offer.

35. Which of the following talent management processes is critical in the repatriation of overseas employees?

    A. Knowledge management

    B. Risk management

    C. Talent management

    D. Performance management

36. "Increased speed" and "number of rejected items" are examples of which of the following HRD results?

    A. Tactical accountability measures

    B. Cost-benefit analysis

    C. Behavioral measures

    D. Production measures

37. Tactical accountability measures related to learning and development (L&D) efforts include which of the following?

    A. Training cost per employee

    B. Time to hire

    C. Benefits utilization review

    D. Form I-9 compliance

38. Which of the following training methods would effectively deliver training material to global employees?

    A. Virtual training

    B. E-learning

    C. EPSS

    D. All of the above

39. Research suggests that adults learn best when asked to actively engage in the training content. Which of the following active training methods uses a question-and-answer format to facilitate understanding?

    A. Case study

    B. Simulation

    C. Vestibule

    D. Socratic

40. NASA's crew undergoes cloud-based training online prior to being launched into space. The training designers program situations the astronauts are likely to encounter while in space—both day-to-day and extreme emergencies—and the participants are required to practice their responses without ever leaving the training grounds at Johnson Space Center in Houston, Texas. This is most likely what kind of active training method?

    A. Case study

    B. Simulation

    C. Vestibule

    D. Socratic

41. During the holiday season Macy's department stores set up their cash register systems in a large training room at each store. New hires spend a full week learning how to operate the machines prior to being placed on the sales floor. This is the best example of which of the following training methods?

    A. Case study

    B. Simulation

    C. Vestibule

    D. Socratic

42. Socratic seminars are to _____ as facilitation is to moderating.

    A. Lecturing

    B. Training

    C. Presenting

    D. Conferencing

43. The nonprofit for which you work has asked you to attend monthly sessions in which you meet with other nonprofit HR managers to discuss shared challenges and opportunities within your industry. These facilitated sessions focus on helping you become a more effective leader using real-world scenarios and peer feedback. You are most likely attending what type of training?

    A. Networking

    B. Learning circle

    C. College class

    D. Industry association event

44. Employees who are more engaged are also more likely to be more what?

    A. Happy

    B. Productive

    C. Likely to stay

    D. All of the above

45. Which of the following tools should you recommend to an employer who seeks to improve employee engagement?

    A. An increase in compensation

    B. Supervisor training

    C. An investment in engagement analytics

    D. A system for flexible work arrangements

46. The culture of a leading game app developer is widely reported to be characterized by unprofessional leadership outbursts, intensive measurements by management, and threats of hostile work environment lawsuits. Many recruiters are ready to poach talent as soon as employees are able to cash in their stock options. What should HR do to improve the company culture?

    A. Offer coaching to the leadership team.

    B. Rescind the bonus vesting structure to keep key talent.

    C. Increase the employee bonuses.

    D. Offer employee harassment prevention training.

47. You are the director of HR for a global bank based in Australia. The company's current structure is such that talent acquisition and talent management are not managed in the same department. Which of the following arguments could you make for bringing both functions under your leadership?

    A. The candidate experience will drive future performance outcomes, so employee performance begins at the time of hire.

    B. An effective talent strategy requires effective management at both stages—namely, time of hire and performance management—so the functions should be coherent.

    C. Managing diversity initiatives begins by hiring a diverse workgroup.

    D. Most 21st-century applicants want to work for cutting-edge companies.

48. As the VP of HR for a leading technology company, you note through metrics that your conversion rate of applicant to hire remains low. Which of the following strategies would be the most effective to improve your hiring ratio?

   A. Question the accuracy of the conversion rate and dive into the source data.

   B. Train supervisors to be better interviewers and to promote the employer brand.

   C. Build a business case for the executive team that you must start to invest in candidate experience activities.

   D. Conduct a market wage survey to ensure company wage bands are competitive.

49. The company you work for has developed a training program that is delivered through technology. The instructional designers intentionally create scenarios designed to generate an emotional response from the participants. A digital facilitator then helps respondents navigate the feelings of stress so that they are more likely to access that learning when they are in a similar situation "in real life." The company is most likely delivering what kind of training?

   A. Vestibule

   B. Virtual reality

   C. Boot camp

   D. Psychological

50. Which of the following theories of leadership states that effective leaders are the result of a hybrid of individual characteristics and the situations that occur?

   A. Path-goal theories

   B. Behavioral theories

   C. Trait based theories

   D. Contingency theories

51. Studies have found that Japanese businesspeople have expectations of leaders that include discipline, intelligence, and trustworthiness. These traits are known as which of the following?

   A. Leadership prototypes

   B. Leadership characteristics

   C. Leadership styles

   D. Follower needs

52. Which of the following types of organization are most likely to have a need for large, corporate universities?

   A. Highly technical and systematic organizations

   B. Organizations focused on continuous learning

   C. Global organizations

   D. Organizations with more than 500 employees

53. Affective reactions are the opposite of what types of reactions in Donald Kirkpatrick's training evaluation model?

    A. Behavioral

    B. Reactive

    C. Utility

    D. Augmented

54. Helping employees prioritize and achieve performance outcomes is more likely to occur using which of the following development activities?

    A. Tying pay to performance

    B. Building better annual performance appraisal forms

    C. Training managers to be effective coaches

    D. Developing critical success factors for each job

55. Which of the following is an example of the positive benefits of diversity training?

    A. Employees gain greater awareness of the value of diversity within an organization.

    B. Employees tend to treat people better after diversity training.

    C. Diversity training increases organizational citizenship behaviors.

    D. Nontraditional employees are given an advantage.

56. Which of the following employee development activities will help employees build the skills necessary to meet the needs of the customer?

    A. Ask customers to give real-time feedback about their experiences on social media

    B. Reward employees for positive customer interactions

    C. Ask customers to participate in 360-degree feedback efforts

    D. Have employees listen to customer service calls

57. In classroom training sessions, most of the content is transferred through which of the following?

    A. Nonverbal means

    B. Presentation

    C. Active listening

    D. Questions and answers

58. The original equipment manufacturer for which you work recently lost a major customer. The company has directed all departments to engage in and support a cost reduction initiative over the next fiscal year. Part of the cost reduction strategy is the elimination of multiple layers of management and the development of self-directed work teams. Which of the following organizational development initiatives should HR advocate and support?

    A. Training for team managers on how to interpret financial reports

    B. The identification and communication of clear performance targets and expectations

    C. A 360-degree feedback tool for use in teams and across teams

    D. All of the above

59. Which of the following is a major challenge for multinational employers in the area of talent management?

    A. The inability of companies to successfully interpret and apply the data from analytics

    B. The struggle to translate corporate culture across international boundaries

    C. The negative impact automation is having on a company brand

    D. The rise in the contingent/contract workforce

60. The major bank that you work for has decided to allow its tellers to solve customer problems without having to ask for manager approval, up to $100. Tellers will be able to use their own discretion and judgment when refunding service fees, overdraft fees, and other miscellaneous charges depending on the circumstances. This is the best example of which of the following?

    A. Employee involvement

    B. Employee development

    C. Employee trust

    D. Job enlargement

61. To create depth and launch a comprehensive, working employee involvement strategy, which of the following may be necessary?

    A. A reduction of management staff

    B. An increase in employee pay

    C. The creation of self-directed work teams

    D. The gathering of customer feedback

62. Which of the following questions is best for a company that wants to measure the success of employee development activities?

    A. What is the relationship between employee pay increases and productivity?

    B. What percentage of separations are voluntary versus involuntary?

    C. What percentage of promotions come from inside versus outside the company?

    D. What percentage of employees are watching the videos posted on the company intranet?

63. Which of the following strategies can help organziations manage global environmental trends through their performance management system?

    A. Build a region by region competitive strategy

    B. Embed corporate social responsibility initiatives into the talent management system

    C. Create a plan to respond to changing conditions as they emerge

    D. Source local talent to create environmental impact measures

64. Which of the following statements is *true* regarding individual development plans?

    A. They are most often used for underperforming employees.

    B. They are useful only for companies that actually have jobs for employees to grow into.

    C. They should identify employee strengths and weaknesses.

    D. They should be built from 360-degree feedback.

65. Which of the following tools would *best* support a company that wants to create a culture of continuous performance improvement?

   A. After-action review

   B. Quarterly reviews

   C. Real-time digital feedback

   D. Employee suggestion program

66. Why is conflict management so critical to the effective management of organizational change?

   A. Conflict highlights disparate viewpoints so that the most effective solution can be found, often requiring change.

   B. Constructive conflict identifies what kinds of changes need to be made.

   C. Artificial harmony props up the status quo, which results in business stagnation (lack of meaningful change).

   D. All of the above

67. Why is a focus on organizational performance just as important as a focus on individual performance?

   A. Individual performance does not affect organizational performance.

   B. Stakeholders are more interested in organizational performance.

   C. Regulatory compliance is achieved through organizational rather than individual performance.

   D. Organizational performance influences individual performance.

68. Which of the following creates more of an organizational competitive advantage?

   A. Individual talent

   B. High-potential employees

   C. Talent management systems

   D. Leadership pipelines

69. On the Blake-Mouton Leadership grid, which management style is the most desirable?

   A. Team leader

   B. Country club

   C. Middle of the road

   D. Authoritarian

70. At which stage of the ADDIE model would decisions about course content be made?

   A. Needs assessment

   B. Design

   C. Develop

   D. Implement

71. Which of the following statements is true about the employee "grapevine"?

    A. The information that travels the grapevine is most likely destructive to employee morale.

    B. HR should take steps to discourage a grapevine network for communications.

    C. Leaders should pay attention to this information, even if it is unsubstantiated.

    D. All gossip is a negative force for change.

72. Integrated communication—where external and internal communications are fused into one system—reflects which of the following organizational realities?

    A. Individuals with different specialties must be able to share ideas outside of their own departments.

    B. Employees are now stakeholders, and many employees must communicate with people outside of the organization.

    C. Communication may be shared quickly now as the result of social media networks.

    D. Communication must be able to flow freely whether upward, downward, or laterally.

73. Which of the following is a general rule regarding communication within an organization?

    A. Structurally, most communication follows a reliable pattern.

    B. The majority of all communication is done via email.

    C. Nonverbal communication is more important than verbal communication.

    D. Cues should be considered when interpreting messages.

74. Which of the following techniques is characteristic of the nominal group structure in decision-making?

    A. Multivoting

    B. Stepladder

    C. Consensus

    D. Brainstorming

75. Which of the following challenges to group decision-making is characterized by a team whose members relate well to each other?

    A. Suppression of ideas

    B. Group think

    C. Peer pressure

    D. All of the above

76. Organizations in which individuals continually expand their knowledge and adapt to change are known as what types of organizations?

    A. Adaptive

    B. Agile

    C. Learning

    D. Responsive

77. Under what conditions should you design training on a whole task as opposed to modules teaching parts of a task?

    A. If the participants are not located in the same geographic location

    B. If the participants are highly skilled

    C. If the task is highly organized and interdependent

    D. If the task is complex with independent parts

78. You recently hired an HR generalist who will be responsible for training supervisors on the basics of the hiring process. You want to ensure that the new generalist has a firm understanding of the principles prior to asking him to develop content, so the first task you give him is to write standard operating procedures for the selection process. When he is done, he will create a presentation, then conduct a training session for organizational leaders. This is an example of what type of learning?

    A. Passive learning

    B. Active learning

    C. Distributed practice

    D. Massed practice

79. Which of the following HR practices involves both the people and the processes equally?

    A. Organizational behavior theories

    B. Theories of motivation

    C. Human relations theories

    D. Organizational development theories

80. The purpose of a replacement chart is to do which of the following?

    A. Identify which employees within a group will need to be terminated in the coming year

    B. Identify the level of workforce reduction necessary to accomplish strategic direction

    C. Identify potential staff changes and backup candidates

    D. Predict the turnover rate for an organization or department

Chapter

10

SPHR Exam: Total Rewards

THE SPHR EXAM CONTENT FROM THE TOTAL REWARDS FUNCTIONAL AREA COVERED IN THIS CHAPTER FOCUSES ON SENIOR-LEVEL COMPETENCIES THAT "MONITOR THE EFFECTIVENESS OF COMPENSATION AND BENEFIT STRATEGIES FOR ATTRACTING, REWARDING, AND RETAINING TALENT." THE EXAM CONSISTS OF THE FOLLOWING RESPONSIBILITIES:

✓ 01   Analyze and evaluate compensation strategies (for example: philosophy, classification, direct, indirect, incentives, bonuses, equity, executive compensation) that attract, reward, and retain talent

✓ 02   Analyze and evaluate benefit strategies (for example: health, welfare, retirement, recognition programs, work-life balance, wellness) that attract, reward, and retain talent

IN ADDITION TO THE RESPONSIBILITIES LISTED ABOVE, AN INDIVIDUAL TAKING THE SPHR EXAM SHOULD HAVE WORKING KNOWLEDGE OF THE FOLLOWING, USUALLY DERIVED THROUGH PRACTICAL EXPERIENCE:

✓ 41   Compensation strategies and philosophy

✓ 42   Job analysis and evaluation methods

✓ 43   Job pricing and pay structures

✓ 44   External labor markets and economic factors

1. Bill is a salesperson for a midsize winery on the California coast. He knows that if he fails to meet his sales quotas, his commissions will be negatively affected. Bill can be said to have what?

   A. Motivation

   B. Clear line of sight

   C. Intrinsic rewards

   D. An entitlement orientation toward his compensation

2. Boldwire Ltd. has 32 employees and a total rewards package that includes base wages and medical insurance. The company is most likely at which stage of its organizational development?

   A. Infancy

   B. Growth

   C. Maturity

   D. Evolution

3. As an HR director seeking the designation of SPHR from the Human Resource Certification Institute, you are most likely exempt from overtime requirements based on which of the following FLSA categories of exemption?

   A. Creative professional

   B. Management

   C. Administrative

   D. Computer employee

4. A customer service representative is being paid more than her counterparts for doing similar work. Which of the following is most likely true?

   A. Compensation discrimination

   B. Strategic range placement

   C. Wage compression

   D. Comparable worth

5. Why is deferred compensation an attractive component of executive compensation packages?

   A. Qualified plans are not subject to the rules and regulations of ERISA.

   B. Deferred compensation provides tax advantages for both the employer and the recipient.

   C. Deferred compensation is often calculated at a higher rate of earnings because of the risk involved in a promise of payment.

   D. Only the proceeds (gains) of an invested deferred compensation plan are taxed.

6. Stock options, personal travel expenses, and company cars are known as which of the following executive compensation components?

    A. Retirement

    B. Deferred compensation

    C. Perks

    D. Bonuses

7. An employer's compensation philosophy should first and foremost support which of the following?

    A. Legal compliance

    B. Employer needs

    C. Market competitiveness

    D. The strategic direction

8. Which compensation strategy should a high-tech organization adopt if their fundamental business strategy is to hire top talent?

    A. Lead the market

    B. Lag the market

    C. Match the market

    D. Depends on their location

9. Which of the following activities demonstrates strong business acumen in the functional area of compensation and benefits?

    A. Partnering with local resources to understand the market's economy

    B. Researching payroll outsourcing services

    C. Administering a fair and equitable executive compensation program

    D. Creating a legally compliant pay system

10. Which of the following is *not* a type of executive performance-based pay?

    A. Stock options

    B. Profit sharing

    C. Travel expenses

    D. Bonuses

11. Which of the following statements is *true* regarding the ability of corporations to deduct executive compensation from their business taxes?

    A. Companies may deduct only the portion of executive pay that is more than $1 million.

    B. Companies may not deduct any portion of executive compensation.

    C. Executive pay deductions are capped at the first $1 million.

    D. Companies may deduct the performance-based portion of executive pay.

12. An executive expatriate may be able to litigate a wage dispute in their home country provided which of the following exists?

   A. A choice of law clause in their employment contract

   B. The proper employment visa was obtained.

   C. Taxes are filed in the home country.

   D. None of the above

13. Which of the following types of stock options has a time limit on when it may be fully transferred for payment?

   A. Vested stock

   B. Phantom stock

   C. Restricted stock

   D. All of the above

14. Under which of the following circumstances should you recommend to an employer that they purchase *key person* life insurance for their company principals?

   A. When there is only a single owner

   B. For smaller businesses in which an owner or another principal is operationally critical

   C. When their company has more than $100 million in revenue

   D. This is always a wise recommendation.

15. Which of the following statements is *true* of global compensation plans?

   A. Global compensation should be standardized to American laws to ensure equity.

   B. Global compensation should be designed to meet the unique needs of expatriates and host country practices.

   C. Global compensation must comply first with home country and then with host country laws.

   D. There are no significant differences between designing national and multinational pay systems.

16. As an HR executive you are issued stock options to buy 100 shares at the current market price of $10 per share. Two years later, when shares are worth $20, you exercise, paying $10 to purchase another 100 shares. Which of the following statements is true?

   A. Twenty dollars is the strike price.

   B. This is an unlawful stock option, as it is nonqualified.

   C. You will be subject to taxes on the $10 spread.

   D. None of the above.

17. What is the primary purpose of an international compensation strategy that is home-based?

   A. Tax equalization

   B. Expatriate family needs

   C. Standard of living

   D. Business strategy

18. Highly compensated employees under the Fair Labor Standards Act (FLSA) are those who have an annual salary of at least _____.

    A. $75,000

    B. $100,000

    C. $125,000

    D. $175,000

19. Under which of the following stock options does the grantee not have actual equity ownership?

    A. Restricted stock grant

    B. Phantom stock

    C. Unvested stock

    D. All of the above

20. Which metric should you recommend to an employer considering entitlement-oriented options for employee pay increases?

    A. The consumer price index

    B. The current unemployment rate

    C. The current rate of inflation

    D. The housing costs in areas where the company does business

21. Which of the following is an economic factor that affects employee total rewards?

    A. Unemployment rate

    B. Globalization

    C. Cost of living

    D. All of the above

22. Which of the following executive contract clauses would be *best* for a company that wants to keep an executive from leaving in the event of a company takeover?

    A. Golden handcuff

    B. Golden parachute

    C. Equity grants

    D. Key person insurance

23. Factors that significantly influence an international assignee's compensation plan include which of the following?

    A. Work council protections

    B. Tax regulations

    C. Geopolitical hazards

    D. All of the above

24. Which international compensation approach focuses on increasing the likelihood that an expatriate will successfully return to a home country assignment?

    A. Localization

    B. Negotiation

    C. Ad hoc

    D. Balance sheet

25. Which of the following statements is true regarding the relationship between county unemployment rates and employee compensation?

    A. Employers doing business in counties with high unemployment rates should expect to have to pay higher wages.

    B. Employers doing business in counties with low unemployment rates should expect to have to pay higher wages.

    C. Employers doing business in cities with living wage regulations will have to pay higher wages.

    D. The unemployment rate does not affect employee compensation.

26. What is the purpose of using the Efficient Purchaser Index (EPI) as part of an international assignee's compensation plan?

    A. The EPI adjusts for a lower cost of living once the international assignee has acclimated to their host country's economy.

    B. The EPI implies that the assignee will eventually learn to purchase more efficiently after a period of time in the host country.

    C. The EPI is used to offset the learning curve an international assignee will have when purchasing host country goods and services.

    D. All of the above.

27. What is the primary justification for an unpaid internship program under federal law?

    A. The intern may be unpaid only if they are enrolled full time in school.

    B. The internship job responsibilities must be approved by the intern's academic advisor.

    C. The primary beneficiary of the internship must be the intern.

    D. Unpaid internships are unlawful under federal law.

28. Your employer wants you to hire an intern from the local college to replace a worker who has recently quit. This could be a violation of which DOL factor supporting unpaid internships?

    A. The extent to which the internship benefits the intern

    B. The extent to which the internship accommodates the intern's schedule

    C. The extent to which the internship is tied to the intern's course of study

    D. The extent to which the work complements the work of paid employees

29. Hardship premiums are used for which of the following reasons?

    A. If an international assignment will result in lower overall compensation

    B. For locations with less modern or restrictive living conditions

    C. For areas where kidnapping threats are high

    D. For the inconvenience of employee "dislocation" from their home country

30. The job bands within your company are priced by using a standard formula of 85–115 percent of the market midpoint. As your staff recruits for marketing professionals, however, you realize that there will be a need for marketing levels 1 and 2 (junior and senior). Which of the following is the best strategy to avoid pay compression?

    A. Change the titles to be equal.

    B. Expand the band to broaden the spread.

    C. Pay both employees the mid-rate.

    D. Leave the band as is and just pay the junior associate the minimum and the senior associate the maximum.

31. In what way does globalization affect how jobs are priced within organizations?

    A. Globalization may drive down the cost for jobs where there is a surplus of displaced workers.

    B. The increase in the number of approved work visas for work in industries with talent shortages is raising the labor costs.

    C. The rise of the gig economy is driving project-based pay.

    D. All of the above.

32. The Silicon Valley of California is known not only for its high-tech jobs but also for starter home prices that begin at around $800,000. Which economic factor *best* reflects how housing prices affect the way employers must price their jobs?

    A. Globalization

    B. Unemployment rates

    C. Cost of living

    D. Industry conditions

33. What is the primary difference between efficiency wages and empathy wages?

    A. Efficiency wages are based on market conditions, whereas empathy wages are driven by employer altruism.

    B. Efficiency wages are the degree to which jobs are priced according to labor market conditions, whereas empathy wages are the degree to which rewards are discretionary.

    C. Efficiency wages include base pay, whereas empathy wages include discretionary pay.

    D. Efficiency wages are part of an entitlement-oriented philosophy, whereas empathy wages are part of a performance-based pay philosophy.

34. An emerging trend in state laws is the requirement that employers provide employees with a written, good-faith estimate of their schedule at the time of hire. This is also known as what type of law?

  A. Wage and record-keeping

  B. A recall of the De Minimis rule

  C. Predictive scheduling

  D. Off-the-clock standards

35. What is the primary risk of violating the FLSA for a restaurant that has a tip-pooling policy?

  A. Employer violation of the minimum wage standard

  B. Employee violation of tax laws if they falsify their records of earnings

  C. Employer unlawful deduction of credit card processing fees

  D. Employer unlawful deduction of service charges that are not considered tips

36. By 2030, 20 percent of Americans will be 65 years of age or older. Based on this statistic, which of the following benefit leave offerings should employers consider adopting?

  A. Retirement match programs

  B. Paid sick leave

  C. Paid caregiver leave

  D. All of the above

37. Which of the following salary-related information is potentially contributing to pay disparity between men and women?

  A. Hidden paychecks

  B. Pay scale

  C. Desired pay rate

  D. Salary history

38. Of the following pairs, which are most likely to significantly influence the job satisfaction of millennials and baby boomers?

  A. Flexible work schedules and recognition

  B. Portable health insurance and retirement matching

  C. Compensation and recognition

  D. Total rewards and job security

39. Other than to reduce costs, for what other reason should you recommend a defined contribution plan to your employer?

  A. An older workforce that cannot afford the uncertainty of traditional pension plans

  B. A workforce that needs more flexibility in their benefit plans

  C. A workforce that does not place high value on retirement benefits

  D. A younger workforce that expects an employer to fully fund their retirement

40. Based on the changing demographics of the workplace, which type of "other" employee benefit is most likely to improve the retention of highly qualified workers?

    A. Annual bonuses

    B. Retirement plans

    C. Volunteer paid leave

    D. Student loan payoff

41. As the HR director for a private religious hospital experiencing a shortage of qualified workers, which of the following "extra" employee benefits plans should you recommend to your employer?

    A. Additional paid leave

    B. Health benefits for adult children

    C. Domestic partner benefits

    D. All of the above

42. The global company you work for has many business units in the Middle East and has a high number of Muslim employees. The leaders of these units have requested that the company add a 401(k) investment option that is compliant with Islamic religious law. As the plan fiduciary, what should be your response?

    A. Let the leaders know that there is a process for evaluating funds based solely on the economic interests of the employer.

    B. Refuse to add the option because you cannot consider religion in the selection of investment funds.

    C. Agree to add the option as part of a mix of socially responsible funds.

    D. Agree to add the option, provided it makes sound economic sense and does not increase the cost of the plan to employees.

43. Using the information in question 42, how should you communicate your decision to employees?

    A. Hold an all-employee meeting, tying in global workers via technology.

    B. Train the supervisors on sensitivity, as well as the nature of fiduciary responsibility, and then have them notify their workforce.

    C. Meet one-on-one through site visits.

    D. Post it on the company intranet.

44. Under what conditions would you recommend to your employer a "black-out period" for employee stock option plans?

    A. Just prior to a major announcement that may affect the company stock price

    B. When a merger with a competitor has been announced

    C. When a plan's fund manager is being replaced

    D. All of the above

45. Giant retailers such as Walmart and Amazon have been making strides toward purchasing healthcare facilities and insurers. This is an example of which type of strategy related to total rewards?

A. To provide prescription coverage to their already large market share of elderly customers

B. To capitalize on the predicted increase in Medicare use

C. To diversify their brand

D. To create a low-cost point of care for employees

46. Which of the following statements is true regarding discretionary bonuses?

A. Discretionary bonuses must be included in weighted overtime calculations.

B. Discretionary bonuses do not have to be included in the calculation of overtime.

C. Discretionary bonuses may be deferred and thus taxed at a lower rate than regular pay.

D. Discretionary bonuses are allowed only for highly compensated employees.

47. The global engineering and construction company for which you are VP of HR has tasked you with decreasing facility costs in four key areas of the world. Which HR action should be the first strategy you explore?

A. Laying off workers

B. Designing telecommuting programs

C. Consolidating branches

D. Hiring contract workers

48. Which compensation strategy should you recommend to establish total rewards for senior leaders?

A. Building a compensation committee

B. Hiring an external consultant

C. Seeking advice from the board of directors

D. A combination of all three

49. During the annual budgeting process, you need to estimate the baseline increase to employee health insurance costs. What amount should you apply?

A. 4 to 6 percent

B. 10 to 12 percent

C. 14 to 16 percent

D. 20 percent and above

50. What is the primary purpose of a compensation committee?

A. To determine the wage ranges for all corporate positions

B. As a court order to remedy compensation discrimination

C. To make recommendations for executive pay

D. To determine bonuses for a board of directors

Chapter

11

SPHR Practice Area 5: Employee Relations and Engagement

THE SPHR EXAM CONTENT FROM THE EMPLOYEE RELATIONS AND ENGAGEMENT FUNCTIONAL AREA COVERED IN THIS CHAPTER FOCUSES ON THE ABILITY TO "DEVELOP AND/ OR MONITOR STRATEGIES IMPACTING EMPLOYEE SATISFACTION AND PERFORMANCE INCLUDING DIVERSITY AND INCLUSION, SAFETY, SECURITY, AND LABOR STRATEGIES." EXAM CONTENT CONSISTS OF THE FOLLOWING RESPONSIBILITIES:

✓ 01   Design and evaluate strategies for employee satisfaction (for example: recognition, career path) and performance management (for example: performance evaluation, corrective action, coaching)

✓ 02   Analyze and evaluate strategies to promote diversity and inclusion

✓ 03   Evaluate employee safety and security strategies (for example: emergency response plan, building access, data security/privacy)

✓ 04   Develop and evaluate labor strategies (for example: collective bargaining, grievance program, concerted activity, staying union free, strategically aligning with labor)

IN ADDITION TO THE RESPONSIBILITIES LISTED ABOVE, AN INDIVIDUAL TAKING THE SPHR EXAM SHOULD HAVE WORKING KNOWLEDGE OF THE FOLLOWING, USUALLY DERIVED THROUGH PRACTICAL EXPERIENCE:

✓ 51 Strategies to facilitate positive employee relations

✓ 52 Methods for assessing employee attitudes, opinions, and satisfaction

✓ 53 Performance management strategies

✓ 54 Human relations concepts and applications

✓ 55 Ethical and professional standards

✓ 56 Diversity and inclusion concepts and applications

✓ 57 Occupational injury and illness prevention techniques

✓ 58 Workplace safety and security risks, and strategies

✓ 59 Emergency response, business continuity, and disaster recovery strategies

✓ 60 Internal investigation, monitoring, and surveillance techniques

✓ 61 Data security and privacy

✓ 62 The collective bargaining process, strategies, and concepts (for example: contract negotiation, costing, administration)

25. During the collective bargaining process, the union demands that all members receive an additional paid holiday. Which strategy is most effective for HR to use during negotiations?

    A. Resolve this issue before moving on to the next.

    B. Survey employees to see whether that is what they really value.

    C. Table the discussion until you have seen all union demands.

    D. Immediately agree, since this issue has a relatively minor impact on company financials.

26. A manager has been asked to use a forced distribution appraisal tool and must allocate her employees according to a predetermined scale. She complains that all of her employees' performance is satisfactory—none are above average, and none are below average. Which of the following is most likely occurring?

    A. Bias

    B. The error of averages

    C. The manager is not paying close enough attention to employee performance.

    D. The error of central tendency

27. Using the same scenario as in the previous question, how should HR respond?

    A. Work with the manager to complete the performance reviews, asking relevant questions for accuracy.

    B. Train the manager on how to effectively collect and deliver constructive feedback.

    C. Train the manager on the types of rater bias and how to avoid them.

    D. All of the above

28. One performance management struggle of a major electronics parts manufacturer is the ability to make abstract concepts, such as culture and initiative, measurable. Which HR solution should you recommend to their leaders?

    A. To be legally defensible, they should measure only what is quantifiable.

    B. They should work with line supervisors to clarify the abstract concepts and then design specific tools for measurement.

    C. They should use 360-degree feedback to collect information on all performance measures.

    D. All of the above

29. What is the final step in a performance measurement system?

    A. Feedback

    B. Pay increases

    C. Quarterly reviews

    D. Promotion

30. The company you work for is struggling to develop cohesive teams that are focused on organizational results as opposed to individual results. Which of the following performance measurement components is most likely contributing to the problem?

    A. The company leaders may not have a clear vision of successful performance outputs.

    B. The company culture is too competitive.

    C. The company has too many disparate business units.

    D. The company's performance appraisals are highly individualized.

31. Which of the following should be the starting point for a talent management cycle?

    A. Establishing performance benchmarks

    B. Creating skills training for current performance

    C. Tying employee pay levels to performance

    D. Writing meaningful performance appraisal templates

32. Which of the following types of feedback is more likely to be expected of members on an executive team?

    A. Regular peer to peer

    B. Weekly meetings with the CEO

    C. Annual 360 degree

    D. Quarterly from the executive team facilitator

33. What is the primary purpose of a union security agreement?

    A. To protect employees' right to organize

    B. To create a perpetuation contract

    C. To ensure the union remains funded

    D. To protect union members from security risks

34. The collective bargaining process at the casino for which you are HR is coming up. You have been asked to prepare data related to increasing the allowance for employee footwear. Which of the following should you bring to aid in the negotiation?

    A. Total number of employees and how many employees bought new shoes in the last year

    B. Total number of union members, current price of approved footwear, and number of employees who used the allowance during the last contract period

    C. Total number of union members, research related to lower-cost footwear, and current uniform allowance thresholds

    D. None of the above, because the union rep will come with that supporting data.

35. An employee at your company posted a disparaging message on her personal Facebook page related to unlawful immigrants. Many of her co-workers—who were Facebook friends—saw the message and were offended because they had family members whose immigration status was in question. For the rest of the week, the co-workers stopped talking to the employee, were avoiding her at lunch, and tensions were running high. Eventually, an employee complained to HR. How should HR respond?

   A. Meet with the involved staff to help mediate the situation and to remind them all of appropriate workplace behaviors.

   B. Discipline the employee for discriminatory online behavior.

   C. Hold an all-employee meeting about diversity and sensitivity.

   D. Do nothing, because it was an off-duty situation.

36. As the HR director for a large media outlet, you have been asked to participate in the collective bargaining process. The union members have just rejected a tentative settlement that cut member wages by 10 percent. You were instructed to respond with a new proposal that cut wages even further, by 23 percent, and to notify the union that unless accepted, the company would have to start the process of selling or shutting down the business. This is an example of what type of management bargaining strategy?

   A. Conventional

   B. Strong-arm

   C. Ultra-concession

   D. Unlawful

37. Giving union leaders a decision-making voice and access to company financials are characteristics of what type of union-management relationship?

   A. Concession

   B. Conventional

   C. Conciliatory

   D. Cooperative

38. What is the primary advantage for employers when it comes to negotiating lump-sum pay increases during the collective bargaining process?

   A. It limits the compounding effect of labor agreements over time.

   B. It helps manage the cost of labor during the contract period.

   C. It can include traditional cost of living increases.

   D. All of the above

39. Which of the following wage cost-cutting strategies during collective bargaining would be most effective for a large retailer that depends on entry-level and low-skilled workers?

   A. Lump-sum payments

   B. Two-tier pay systems

   C. Cost-of-living increases

   D. Wage freezes

40. Which of the following types of benefit negotiation strategies during the collective bargaining process is *most* likely to help a company appear more financially secure to investors?

   A. Successfully negotiating a voluntary employee benefit agreement

   B. Deferring employee wage increases until the next contract negotiation

   C. Entering into health insurance captive accounts

   D. All of the above

41. What is the primary advantage to union members of making the union—rather than the employer—responsible for their health benefits once they retire?

   A. Their benefits are guaranteed upon retirement.

   B. They receive equivalent or better benefits upon retirement.

   C. Their benefits are better protected.

   D. Their retiree benefits will be less costly.

42. What is an employer seeking to negotiate if they ask a union to expand job classifications so employees can work outside of their normal job scope?

   A. Benefits

   B. Work rules

   C. Cost shifting

   D. Security clauses

43. With the recent NLRB rule changes allowing for an expedited election process, which of the following union avoidance strategies should HR consider?

   A. Begin to screen applicants to determine whether they are pro-union.

   B. Embed policies in the handbook that prohibit social media posts about work.

   C. Hire a professional union avoidance firm immediately when notified of an election.

   D. Build and maintain perpetual avoidance strategies.

44. The retail restaurant chain for which you have just been hired has a social media policy that prohibits employees from making "disparaging, false, misleading, harassing, or discriminatory statements about or relating to the employer and other parties." This is the *best* example of which of the following?

   A. An unlawful policy

   B. Creating an affirmative defense against a claim of harassment

   C. A code of conduct statement

   D. A discriminatory policy

45. Which of the following intrinsic motivational constructs is made up of meaning, competence, self-determination, and impact?

   A. Psychological empowerment

   B. Self-actualization

   C. Personal competencies

   D. Emotional intelligence

46. High degrees of employee job satisfaction are most positively correlated with which of the following job attitudes?

   A. Conscientousness

   B. Organizational commitment

   C. Positivity

   D. All of the above

47. "A relatively enduring state of mind referring to the simultaneous investment of personal energies in the experience or performance of work" is the definition of which of the following employee conditions?

   A. Job satisfaction

   B. Organizational commitment

   C. Employee engagement

   D. Job involvement

48. While observing employees doing their work as part of the job analysis process, you noticed that productivity increased. When you stopped observing the employees, productivity went back down to normal levels. This is the best example of which of the following?

   A. The Hawthorne effect

   B. Job inflation

   C. Employee fear of getting in trouble

   D. McClelland's need theory

49. A manager wants to reward Lisa, one of his graphic designers, who is highly conscientious, easy to work with, and able to work independently on complex design projects. Which of the following is the *best* example of an extrinsic reward that would support Lisa's intrinsic sense of motivation?

   A. Giving her a pay increase

   B. Setting limits on how often Lisa should be responding to after-hours emails

   C. Granting her more time to work on creative projects

   D. Changing her schedule so she can better work with co-workers in different time zones

50. Which of the following conditions is likely to occur as the result of the high-profile sexual harassment cases in the news?

   A. An increase in the number of harassment claims filed

   B. Changes to how non-disclosure agreements are used by employers

   C. A review of internal practices to reduce favoritism

   D. All of the above

51. The CFO at the large media services agency for which you work has been accused of sexual harassment. After the investigation, the accuser signed a confidentiality agreement and was paid a six-figure settlement. Which of the following statements is true?

   A. The confidentiality agreement was unlawful.

   B. The company may not deduct the settlement fees on their corporate taxes.

   C. The CFO should be fired.

   D. The company will be obligated to keep the accuser employed.

52. Which of the following are representative of the types of diversity that must be managed within an organization?

   A. Employee attitudes

   B. Age

   C. Personality characteristics

   D. All of the above

53. Which of the following elements are addressed by developments in the study of organizational neuroscience?

   A. Change management

   B. Unconscious bias

   C. Diversity and inclusion

   D. All of the above

54. Which of the following employees would be the best choice to serve as the head of a company's diversity council?

   A. The CEO

   B. The HR director

   C. The VP of operations

   D. The operations manager

55. Which of the following are elements of an effective performance management system?

   A. Performance appraisals

   B. Goal-setting

   C. Coaching

   D. All of the above

56. You recently received a complaint about the quality manager from one of his direct reports that he was behaving unprofessionally. This was out of character for the quality manager, as he normally is easy to work with, so you hesitated to open a formal investigation. A week later, you receive another, related complaint that made you realize you had to intervene. In looking at his file, it had been more than a year since his last performance appraisal, so you decided to start there. Which of the following methods should you use that would *best* address the manager's recent behavioral issues?

    A. Multisource feedback

    B. BAR scale

    C. Critical incident

    D. Observation

57. Which of the following is a form of performance feedback bias that is most often present when reviewing telecommuting employee performance?

    A. Cognitive

    B. Face time

    C. Horn effect

    D. Negative emphasis

58. "Takes shortcuts around established procedures" and "Never deviates from established procedures" are two examples from what type of performance rating scale?

    A. Comparison

    B. Checklist

    C. Narrative

    D. Behaviorally anchored

59. Using the example from question 58, the behavioral examples on the scale are called what?

    A. Key performance indicators

    B. Critical incidents

    C. Standard work audits

    D. Behavioral statements

60. A new supervisory position has opened up at the grocery chain where you work. Senior leaders asked you to review the most recent performance appraisals to help identify which employee should be promoted. Upon doing so, you noted that the majority of the eligible employees all had been lumped together in the top of the scale distribution. This is an example of what type of rating scale error?

    A. Halo effect

    B. Forced distribution

    C. Horn effect

    D. Range restriction

61. For an employer who wants to be able to use performance feedback to make promotion decisions—such as the one in question 60—which of the following rating tools would be most effective?

   A. BARS

   B. Forced distribution

   C. Checklists

   D. Likert scales

62. With regard to job burnout, employers should seek to help employees use their stress to enhance performance, up to a maximum point. This is an example of employers helping employees do what?

   A. Synthesize stress

   B. Eliminate stress

   C. Optimize stress

   D. Reduce stress

63. Stress at work is related to which of the following job outcomes?

   A. Absenteeism

   B. Higher use of health insurance

   C. Negative job attitudes

   D. All of the above

64. What is the most important benefit of a return-to-work (RTW) program?

   A. They reduce the overall cost of a workplace injury.

   B. RTW programs can be built to serve employees with work-related and non–work-related injuries or illness.

   C. RTW programs reduce the risk of a lawsuit.

   D. RTW programs eliminate the need for modified duty.

65. Conducting workplace threat assessments is what type of strategic HR activity?

   A. Planning

   B. Response

   C. Business continuity

   D. Education

66. Unexpected loss of key employees, pandemics, and disaster recovery are threats that share the need for which of the following types of plans?

   A. Strategic plans

   B. Risk management plans

   C. Business continuity plans

   D. Health and safety plans

67. The communication tower industry has a high incidence of workplace fatalities. The employers joined together and established two goals: to reduce workplace fatalities by 25 percent and to reduce workplace accidents by 4 percent. These employers are most likely engaged in which risk management strategy?

A. Engaging in an OSHA partnership

B. Negotiating a collective bargaining agreement

C. Complying with a works council agreement

D. Completing a risk assessment

68. Irregular or unnatural body movements at work is the focus of what type of risk management activity?

A. Addressing workplace diseases

B. Complying with OSHA's general duty clause

C. Ergonomics training

D. All of the above

69. The Department of Labor reports that victims of intimate partner violence (IPV) lose nearly 8 million days of paid work per year in the United States, resulting in more than $1 billion in lost productivity for employers. As a result, many employers are implementing policies that include information related to domestic violence. Which of the following elements should be included in an IPV policy?

A. Protection and restraining order process

B. Security concerns

C. Leave availability related to dealing with IPV

D. All of the above

70. Which of the following should be a *first* step in preventing abusive conduct and harassing behaviors at work?

A. Take all claims of bullying or harassment seriously.

B. Train employees on how to report bullying behaviors.

C. Embed workplace civility initiatives into the culture.

D. Establish an anti-harassment policy.

71. The telecommunications company you work for recently spun off its wireless division. Your CEO asked you to commission a study that compares the remaining top talent with major competitors in the same market. This is an example of which talent management technique?

A. Behavioral benchmarking

B. Equity research

C. Comparative appraisals

D. Gap analysis

72. Talent management approaches have evolved beyond the single performance appraisal into a more holistic experience that draws from multiple disciplines. Best practices, 360-degree feedback, and leadership self-awareness are all examples of which of the following such disciplines?

   A. HR, business, strategy

   B. Industry, academics, associations

   C. Business, HR, psychology

   D. Psychology, organizational behavior, coaching

73. Complete the following sentence: Talent management systems are unsustainable when there is a lack of _____ planning.

   A. Top level

   B. Strategic

   C. Action

   D. Workforce

74. Before executive compensation can be both defined and measured, there are several factors that must be considered. Which of the following measures would most likely be included in a company's *equity* philosophy when designing an executive performance evaluation system?

   A. Measures of diversity

   B. Measures of compensation

   C. Measures of business strategy

   D. Measures of culture

75. Which of the following statements are true regarding the requirements for executive performance appraisals?

   A. The NYSE requires that CEO performance be evaluated.

   B. NASDAQ does not require CEO performance evaluations.

   C. The SEC only requires that the criteria for executive compensation be clearly outlined.

   D. All of the above

Chapter

12

SPHR Practice Exam

1. One of your production managers uses incentives to reward employees for meeting operational objectives. This is the *best* example of which of the following leadership styles?

   A. Charismatic leadership

   B. Transactional leadership

   C. Laissez-faire leadership

   D. Authoritarian leadership

2. Consensual romantic relationships at work represent what type of risk?

   A. Intimate partner violence

   B. Unlawful treatment

   C. Sexual harassment

   D. None, because it's consensual

3. The international gas utility company for which you direct HR does not have an organized health and safety program for its workers. What should be your first step?

   A. Focus on becoming compliant with international, federal, state, and local safety standards.

   B. Identify the employees who are most at risk and begin safety efforts with them.

   C. Obtain approval for a company-wide incentive program based on zero accidents or injuries.

   D. Meet with the workers' compensation brokers to assess the costs of lack of a safety program.

4. The food distribution center for which you work has seen an increase in the number of loading-dock workers reporting ankle injuries. What strategy would be most effective to reduce or eliminate the risk?

   A. Require employees to wear high-top steel-toed work boots.

   B. Review the injury records for patterns of unsafe behaviors.

   C. Conduct a root-cause analysis with a committee made up of dock workers.

   D. Ask the occupational clinic to come in and provide safety training.

5. The major Internet provider for which you are the VP of human resources has just experienced the largest customer and employee data breach in the history of the United States. In an effort to comply with the Securities and Exchange Commission (SEC), you should first do what?

   A. Evaluate the areas where the company's data is still at risk for hackers

   B. Research credit monitoring services to offer affected individuals.

   C. Wait to notify investors until the executive team can sell their shares of company stock.

   D. Assess the depth of the data breach and notify investors as soon as is practicable.

6. Which of the following are examples of the physical assets that must be secured to prevent a cybersecurity attack?

   A. The employees

   B. The buildings

   C. The workstations

   D. The power lines

7. Establishing a hierarchy of assets helps companies do what when it comes to data protection?

   A. Identify priorities when it comes to building a robust data security program

   B. Determine what skills in data security personnel to hire for

   C. Write policies that protect critical assets

   D. Purchase external layers of protections, making the data harder to breach

8. The hospital for which you work has hired an outside agency to staff the parking lot security posts. The guard works only at night and is unsupervised. Recently there has been a rash of attacks in the area against security guards in general. What steps should you take to protect this contingent worker from becoming a victim of workplace violence?

   A. Allow him to carry his personal gun while on duty.

   B. Install security cameras that are monitored from the inside.

   C. Make a business case to the board of directors that this post should have two workers at all times.

   D. Ask the employment agency to cover the costs of additional security recommendations.

9. A major sandwich restaurant hires 15-year-old workers to operate a meat slicer. This may violate which of the following?

   A. The Food and Drug Administration

   B. Food Safety Management

   C. The Fair Labor Standards Act

   D. The Occupational Safety and Health Act

10. An employee has shared with her manager that she has been prescribed medicine for her bipolar disorder. Which labor laws may need to be considered on her behalf?

   A. The Americans with Disabilities Act

   B. The Occupational Safety and Health Act

   C. The Drug-Free Workplace Act

   D. Both A and B

11. A winery employs hundreds of seasonal, temporary workers that are processed through a staffing agency. Many of them will be working with hazardous chemicals. Which of the following should you do *first* to comply with OSHA's hazard communication standard?

    A. Ask the temporary agency to provide general hazardous material–handling training.

    B. Ensure that the same protections offered to regular workers are offered to temporary workers.

    C. Ask the agency to come inspect the facility to ensure it is a safe work environment.

    D. Communicate with the agency regarding what types of protection will be needed.

12. A software developer in the Midwest has decided to offer voluntary microchipping of their employees. The chips will be medically inserted into the individual's right hand and will allow employees to open doors, clock in, and even make purchases in the company cafeteria. What type of data is being collected?

    A. Biometric

    B. Personal

    C. Identity

    D. Medical

13. Using the information from the previous question, what type of risk is the microchipping employer exposed to?

    A. Identity theft

    B. Privacy concerns

    C. Health risks

    D. All of the above

14. Which of the following mitigation efforts will improve data security?

    A. Purchasing EPL insurance

    B. A computer monitoring system of employee keystrokes

    C. Writing a policy that prohibits the sharing of passwords

    D. Not collecting the data at all

15. In the wake of recent workplace violence episodes in the news, your executive team has requested that you put together a written plan that addresses what steps to take should an incident occur at one of your locations. You will most likely need what type of plan?

    A. Disaster recovery plan

    B. Incident response plan

    C. Business continuity plan

    D. All of the above

16. Your company has a written plan that details the manual workarounds for the company's accounting and payment systems should there be an emergency. This is an example that would be included in what type of plan?

    A. Business continuity

    B. Critical incident

    C. Disaster recovery

    D. Injury and illness

17. To comply with SEC rules at your place of business, you should do which of the following?

    A. Link executive pay to monthly performance measures.

    B. Disclose executive pay rates to all employees.

    C. Publish the ratio of executive to employee pay to shareholders.

    D. All of the above.

18. Which of the following statements is true about OSHA's Strategic Partnership Program (SPP)?

    A. It is a coalition of employee groups and unions.

    B. It is mandatory.

    C. It requires top management support.

    D. All of the above

19. Of the following, which is *most* important when it comes to building an effective safety management program?

    A. Creating a safety culture

    B. Relevant policies, procedures, and rules

    C. Top management support

    D. Approval for personal protective equipment

20. A large employer with multiple facilities all across the United States has decided to raffle off a car at the end of the year. Employees will automatically get one entry for each week that they work without injury. Which of the following is the employer at risk for?

    A. Tax code violation

    B. Discrimination

    C. Retaliation

    D. None of the above

21. To be removed from OSHA's routine inspection list, which program should you recommend your employer join?

    A. Voluntary Protection Program

    B. Strategic Partnership Program

    C. Alliance Program

    D. Consultation Program

22. Employers have which of the following obligations with regard to international assignee protection?

  A. They must carry kidnap and ransom insurance for high hazard areas.

  B. They have a duty of care to take all reasonable steps to protect their expatriates.

  C. They must have a written crisis management plan in place.

  D. Employers have the same obligation for international assignees as they do for home country nationals.

23. Why might it be a good idea to work with an insurance broker if a company decides to place employees on international assignments?

  A. The broker can help build crisis response plans.

  B. The broker may have connections to negotiate in a crisis situation.

  C. The broker may have access to international resources should a medical emergency arise.

  D. All of the above

24. Which of the following strategies would best be served by implementing an RTW program at your place of work?

  A. The ability to coordinate different types of leave

  B. Compliance with OSHA standards

  C. The need to reduce injuries and accidents in the workplace

  D. The desire to reduce the overall costs of workplace injuries

25. Under what conditions may an injured worker's pay be reduced when accepting a modified duty assignment?

  A. Only if the injured worker is temporarily stationed at a job that normally pays a lower rate

  B. It depends on the laws of the state in which the injury occurred

  C. Only if they are doing so for a nonretaliatory reason

  D. All of the above

26. An injured worker has been told by his workers' compensation doctor that he is able to go back to work at full duty. The employee disagrees. What should you recommend?

  A. Sending him back to a doctor of his choice for a final recommendation

  B. Discussing an IME with the workers' compensation insurance

  C. A referral to the company's labor attorney

  D. Termination of employment if he does not return

27. Collective bargaining is best understood as which of the following?

  A. Implied contract

  B. Union responsibility

  C. Employer responsibility

  D. Statutory right

28. Freedom of speech, due process, and workplace safety are all examples of which of the following?

    A. Employee responsibilities

    B. Employee rights

    C. Employment contract clauses

    D. Constitutional rights

29. Which of the following agreements may employers have the *most* legal trouble enforcing?

    A. Nonsolicitation of current employees

    B. Arbitration agreements

    C. Employment contracts

    D. Noncompete agreements

30. Under what conditions would you recommend to your employer that they adopt a nonpiracy agreement?

    A. For a high-tech organization to prevent employee poaching

    B. For a work environment with legally protected trade secrets

    C. For companies doing business in international waters

    D. Never—nonpiracy agreements are unlawful.

31. When an employer terminates the rights of an employee for a discriminatory reason, which of the following is said to have occurred?

    A. Constructive discharge

    B. Wrongful discharge

    C. Reduction in force

    D. Discharge without cause

32. In the absence of an employment contract or collective bargaining agreement, when may an employee expect to only be terminated for cause?

    A. If they are a protected class individual

    B. If there is a progressive discipline policy in the handbook

    C. If their behavior was first investigated by management

    D. None of the above

33. An employee has been terminated for "just cause." Which of the following reasons is most likely?

    A. The employee refused to forge his boss's signature on a document.

    B. The employee violated the employer's anti-harassment rules.

    C. The employee was late because he went to vote in the presidential election.

    D. The employee was a whistleblower who filed a report of corruption that turned out to be inaccurate.

34. Augustine filed a grievance with HR because he believed that a supervisor gave Amy—Augustine's co-worker—a higher raise than Augustine received because the supervisor is trying to date Amy. This is an example of which of the following?

    A. Sexual harassment

    B. Distributive justice

    C. Discriminatory treatment

    D. Both A and B

35. In compulsory arbitration, which of the following conditions is nearly always included?

    A. The employee exchanges the right to sue the employer.

    B. An arbitrator is selected from the American Arbitration Association (AAA).

    C. There is a written arbitration agreement reviewed by legal counsel.

    D. All of the above

36. Which of the following should *not* be included in an employee's regular personnel file because of privacy concerns?

    A. Application for employment

    B. Historical records older than three years

    C. Medical benefits claims data

    D. Performance reviews

37. Of the following recognition programs, which is *not* entitlement-oriented?

    A. Service awards

    B. Employee of the month

    C. Sales awards

    D. Longevity bonus

38. Multicultural work teams, training, and mentoring systems may all be part of what type of human resource program?

    A. Diversity program

    B. Climate program

    C. Anti-harassment program

    D. Equal Employment Opportunity program

39. Discourteous behavior can quickly escalate to which of the following problems?

    A. Unlawful harassment

    B. Violation of a company's code of conduct

    C. Workplace violence

    D. All of the above

40. The company you work for gives all employees an annual bonus right around Christmas time. The amount is dependent upon company profitability. This effort is best represented by which of the following?

   A. A generous employer

   B. An entitlement-oriented incentive

   C. A company recognition program

   D. A way to keep overtime costs down

41. Under which of the following conditions may an employer avoid a claim of defamation when providing an employment reference for a former employee?

   A. When the information shared is truthful

   B. When the employer provides only dates of employment and a job title

   C. When the employer has received written authorization from the employee to disclose personnel information

   D. All of the above

42. In a union environment, an employee who believes that he has been unfairly passed over for promotion should file which of the following?

   A. A complaint

   B. A grievance

   C. A charge of discrimination

   D. A charge of harassment

43. An employee is called to his supervisor's office, believing that he will be disciplined. Accordingly, he requests that his union steward be present for the meeting. His supervisor denies the request, violating which of the following employee rights?

   A. Statutory

   B. Due process

   C. Weingarten

   D. Privacy

44. What recourse is available for an employee who was denied his Weingarten rights and, in the process, was terminated?

   A. Reinstatement

   B. The right to sue for criminal damage

   C. The right to sue for civil damages

   D. Back pay and reinstatement

45. Which of the following is occurring when a third party settles disputes that occur as the result of differences in the interpretation of a collective bargaining agreement?

   A. Collective bargaining

   B. Labor negotiations

   C. Labor strike

   D. Grievance arbitration

46. Engineers, nurses, and physicians would most likely belong to what type of union?

    A. Nongovernmental

    B. Professional

    C. Industrial

    D. Services

47. Janitors, building cleaners, and meatpacking workers are examples of which groups targeted by unions over the last several years?

    A. Low skilled

    B. Professional

    C. Contingent

    D. Part-time

48. A shift of a union's focus to issues of pay equity and flexible work arrangements is most likely an effort to organize which type of worker?

    A. Millennials

    B. Blue collar

    C. Women

    D. Liberal

49. Which disciplinary approach establishes the expectation in employees that they will progress through a series of steps when being disciplined?

    A. Positive

    B. Progressive

    C. Coaching

    D. Self

50. Which of the following are formal systems designed to obtain employee feedback?

    A. Suggestion systems

    B. Focus groups

    C. Surveys

    D. All of the above

51. Technological methods with which to obtain employee feedback include which of the following?

    A. Focus groups

    B. Teleconferencing

    C. Videos

    D. Instant messaging

52. Internal methods of communicating with employees include which of the following?

    A. Intranet postings

    B. Newsletters

    C. Instant messaging

    D. All of the above

53. Taylor has been frequently absent from work over the last three months, so much so that she has violated the company's attendance policy. The supervisor has come to you for advice on how to proceed. Which of the following options puts the company at the most risk?

    A. Discuss with the supervisor the reasons for the absences

    B. Review with the supervisor any relevant documentation

    C. Review the days missed to look for trends

    D. Proceed directly with the discipline

54. Which of the following is the role of a supervisor—not human resources—when disciplining an employee?

    A. Make the decision to discipline

    B. Train managers on disciplinary actions

    C. Design disciplinary procedures

    D. Understand labor laws related to employee rights

55. The best discipline could be described as which of the following?

    A. Training

    B. Self-discipline

    C. Progressive

    D. All of the above

56. Chuck has been struggling with having a positive attitude at work. You and his supervisor met with Chuck to make him aware of the behavioral expectations. As a result, Chuck's attitude improves. This approach is a characteristic of which type of discipline?

    A. Counseling

    B. Progressive

    C. Positive

    D. Mentoring

57. Of the following, which is the most challenging issue when implementing a positive discipline approach?

    A. Gaining employee buy-in

    B. Monitoring for consistent practices

    C. Writing a legally compliant policy

    D. The time it takes to train managers

58. You are the senior labor relations specialist at your place of work, and the company has an existing progressive discipline policy and practice. Under this policy, which of the following employee offenses would most likely lead to immediate termination?

A. Falsifying an employment application

B. Insubordination

C. Safety rule violation

D. Excessive tardiness

59. Why might a manager be reluctant to discipline an employee?

A. Fear of conflict

B. Guilt

C. Fear of lawsuits

D. All of the above

60. Which of the following are mandatory notices for an employee who has been discharged?

A. COBRA notification

B. Severance agreement

C. Employee Change in Status form

D. Both A and C

61. To be effective, HR policies should be which of the following?

A. Effective

B. Relevant

C. Legal

D. All of the above

62. You received an urgent call from management saying that the surveillance system caught an employee downloading a customer list to a thumb drive. What should you advise?

A. Confront the employee and immediately search them and their belongings.

B. Call the police.

C. Confront the employee and show the proof of the theft.

D. Nothing; employee surveillance is unlawful.

63. How are procedures different from policies?

A. Procedures are general guidelines for employee behaviors.

B. Policies are more specific than procedures.

C. Procedures are more specific than policies.

D. There is no difference.

64. Your company handbook includes the statement "Employees are prohibited from alcohol use at work." This is an example of which of the following?

A. Policy

B. Procedure

    C. Rule

    D. All of the above

65. Which of the following phrases should be eliminated from a company handbook?

    A. Permanent employee

    B. Probation period

    C. No social media use

    D. All of the above

66. "This employee handbook is not intended to be part of a contract..." is being used in an employee handbook to preserve which of the following?

    A. Employee rights

    B. Employer rights

    C. Employment at will

    D. The public policy exception

67. Your company CEO recorded a "state of the company" video and asked you to post it on the company intranet. This is an example of what type of communication?

    A. Upward communication

    B. Downward communication

    C. Electronic communication

    D. Digital communication

68. A safety suggestion system is an example of which of the following?

    A. Employee survey

    B. Downward communication

    C. Upward communication

    D. Incentive

69. The large hotel you work for asks guests to complete cards commenting on the level of service they received from the workers. These results are most likely used by human resources to do what?

    A. Recognize employees

    B. Discipline employees

    C. Refine procedures

    D. All of the above

70. Which of the following requires employers to provide jobs and a workplace environment that are free from recognized safety and health hazards?

    A. An emergency action plan

    B. The Control of Hazardous Energy standard

    C. The General Duty standard

    D. The Hazard Communication standard

71. Workplace violence, theft, and computer hackers are all classified as which of the following types of risk?
    A. Security
    B. Health
    C. Safety
    D. Financial

72. Which of the following types of risk is associated with embezzling?
    A. Legal
    B. Safety and health
    C. Security
    D. Workplace privacy

73. The controller of your organization was caught paying herself for additional vacation time that was never authorized or approved. Additionally, she coded the transactions so that they did not show up under G&A payroll but rather as a production expense. This is an example of which of the following?
    A. Fraudulent activity
    B. Deception
    C. Forgery
    D. Misrepresentation of financial statements

74. Natural disasters and terrorism are both threats to which of the following?
    A. Employee safety and health
    B. Resource availability
    C. Business continuity
    D. All of the above

75. A review of the human capital management plan (HCMP) is most likely to occur in what type of audit?
    A. Risk assessment
    B. HR
    C. GAAP
    D. Internal revenue (tax)

76. As the HR manager for a small construction firm, you have begun to notice an increase in falls at various work sites. So far, no one has been seriously injured; in fact, the employees joke about their "close calls." Which of the following should you do?
    A. Discipline employees for not taking safety risks seriously
    B. Conduct worksite inspections to identify potential fall hazards
    C. Retrain employees in your company's fall protection procedures
    D. Nothing yet, as no injuries have occurred

77. The manager of the marketing department established a goal for his staff that directed them to double unique web traffic to the website within 90 days. If they accomplish this goal, the department will evenly split a bonus among them. The manager is *most* likely using which performance management technique?

   A. SMART

   B. MBO

   C. 360

   D. Forced distribution

78. Why is it important to have a nonunion philosophy statement?

   A. It supports an open door policy for employees to discuss wages and working conditions directly with the employer.

   B. It gives employers the opportunity to respond to dissatisfiers prior to the relationship becoming adversarial.

   C. Once a union has petitioned for an election, an employer's right to communicate is restricted.

   D. All of the above

79. One of the company's best performers is extremely self-managed and able to follow all rules and procedures with very little direction or feedback. This employee is most likely high in which personality characteristic?

   A. Neuroticism

   B. Conscientiousness

   C. Awareness

   D. Emotional intelligence

80. Organizational citizenship behaviors are marked by which of the following individual characteristics?

   A. Sportsmanship, altruism, and conscientiousness

   B. Courtesy, civic virtue, and pride

   C. Conscientiousness, courtesy, and altruism

   D. Conscientiousness, civic virtue, and emotional intelligence

81. The investment of physical, emotional, and cognitive resources *best* describes which of the following?

   A. Employee engagement

   B. Job satisfaction

   C. Organizational commitment

   D. Employee relations

82. Which of the following terms describes an organization that is rigidly devoted to polices, rules, and procedures?

    A. Centralized

    B. Formal

    C. Decentralized

    D. Bureaucratic

83. Which of the following conditions is most likely to improve employee productivity according to humanistic theories of motivation?

    A. More qualified supervisors

    B. Improved tools and equipment

    C. Management attention and feedback

    D. Equal rewards

84. The consideration of employee inputs, work processes, and outputs are at the heart of which category of organizational theories?

    A. Systems

    B. Humanistic

    C. Bureaucratic

    D. Relational

85. Which of the following intervention strategies should you recommend to an employer wanting to improve creativity and innovation in the workplace?

    A. Create a bonus program.

    B. Increase diversity.

    C. Improve the quality of tools and equipment to encourage these outcomes.

    D. Allow employees to adjust their schedules based on project needs.

86. The desire to do something that matters is an example of what type of reward?

    A. Psychological

    B. Direct

    C. Extrinsic

    D. Intrinsic

87. Which of the following management techniques should you recommend to an employer that requires immediate compliance from their employees, such as for air traffic controllers or emergency dispatchers?

    A. Decentralized

    B. Self-direction

    C. Open systems

    D. Traditional

88. The customer service representatives at your business are experiencing high degrees of burnout because 90 percent of their calls are from disgruntled customers. Which of the following is the most likely source of their burnout?

    A. Low emotional intelligence

    B. High degree of emotional labor

    C. Negative collective affect

    D. Low pay

89. An employee complains to their supervisor that another employee is always late, stating that "it must be because he is lazy and just doesn't want to come to work." The next day, the complaining employee was late, and when asked why, he stated that "construction on his normal commute was heavier than usual that day." The complaining employee is most likely making what type of error?

    A. Values-based

    B. Discrimination

    C. Bias

    D. Fundamental attribution

90. The president of the company you work for wants to embark on a cost savings initiative throughout all departments. All employees will receive a percentage of the savings at the end of the year. This is an example of what type of compensation program?

    A. Deferred compensation

    B. Gain-sharing

    C. Discretionary bonus

    D. Commission

91. Which of the following theories of motivation looks at how people compare their efforts with their rewards?

    A. Equity

    B. Intrinsic

    C. Extrinsic

    D. Systems

92. Many employees are struggling to perform under the new management structure that has recently been put into place. Their primary concern is that they don't know how long the new structure will hold, simply because the company has tried it before and it didn't work. As a result, they are hesitant to invest too much effort into the new requirements. This is an example of which of the following conditions of change?

    A. Freezing

    B. Norming

    C. Change uncertainty

    D. Change avoidance

93. Organizational development is made up of which of the following scientific domains?

    A. Social psychology

    B. Industrial-organizational psychology

    C. Applied psychology

    D. All of the above

94. Fill in the blanks: _____ are a creative tool used for brainstorming that is more restrictive than _____.

    A. Focus groups; employee surveys

    B. Nominal groups; the Delphi technique

    C. Employee surveys; focus groups

    D. Mind-maps; the Medici approach

95. A local gym recently sold the rights to another company to use their name, supply chain resources, and workflow processes in another city. This is an example of what type of business structure?

    A. Subsidiary

    B. Merger

    C. Joint venture

    D. Franchising

96. Which of the following types of budgets starts from scratch each year?

    A. Incremental

    B. Bottom up

    C. Zero-based

    D. Top-down

97. Cost savings, availability of talent, and specialized expertise are all reasons for HR to recommend which of the following staffing strategies?

    A. Co-sourcing

    B. Temporary workers

    C. Professional employer organizations

    D. Part-time workers

98. Which of the following is an example of a business operating expense?

    A. Salaries

    B. Rent

    C. Software licenses

    D. All of the above

121. A business case can help management make better-quality decisions because it does which of the following?

    A. Communicates how a plan will influence operational efficiencies

    B. Provides multiple options for solving a business problem

    C. Describes possible risks that could result from taking action

    D. Quantitatively analyzes relevant HR trends

122. Under what conditions should you recommend that an employer require an employee to take a polygraph test?

    A. If you believe an employee is under the influence of a drug at work

    B. If you believe the controller embezzled funds

    C. If an employee accuses another employee of violent behavior

    D. Never, because polygraph tests are unlawful.

123. The company you work for prefers a flat-line decision-making structure. They strive to grant as much decision-making power to the employees as possible and tie pay directly to performance outcomes when possible. This is most likely what type of organization?

    A. A high-involvement organization

    B. A learning organization

    C. An Internet start-up

    D. A nonprofit

124. Which of the following job characteristics contribute most to a sense of employee ownership over outcomes?

    A. Task significance and autonomy

    B. Autonomy and feedback

    C. Skill variety and task identity

    D. Task significance and feedback

125. During training, you notice that an employee rapidly learns the new material that is exciting. After she has mastered the task, there is really not much else to learn. She most likely is experiencing which type of learning curve?

    A. Positively accelerating

    B. S-shaped

    C. Plateau

    D. Negatively accelerating

126. A large network software firm creates a program for women in leadership. Participants meet every month for a year to provide peer support toward taking on more leadership tasks or roles. At the end of the third year, more than 100 women have graduated from the program. This company is engaged in which of the following?

    A. Diversity-based networking

    B. Learning circles

    C. Executive groups

    D. Incubators

127. Many states have recently adopted laws that forbid employers from asking applicants about their prior salary history. This is known as what type of law?

    A. Anti-harassment laws

    B. Wage and hour laws

    C. Pay equity laws

    D. Anti-discrimination laws

128. Employee behavior will be affected by wages based upon which of the following?

    A. If they can live comfortably on their base wages

    B. If they are making more in their current jobs than they could working for competitors

    C. The perception of what was earned versus what was discretionary

    D. The perception that they are paid what they are worth

129. The HR manager for whom you are responsible got upset after a disgruntled employee yelled at her. By the end of the day, however, she understood that the employee's anger had nothing to do with her and that he was just reacting to the situation. The HR manager is demonstrating which of the following elements of emotional intelligence?

    A. Emotional regulation

    B. Emotional labor

    C. Self-awareness

    D. Emotional support

130. Which of the following statements regarding emotional intelligence (EI) is *false*?

    A. EI is related to other types of intelligence, including IQ.

    B. Employees have different levels of EI.

    C. EI can be learned.

    D. EI is highly predictive of employee performance.

131. Which generation is more likely to value money and flexibility as career goals?

    A. Generation X

    B. Boomers

    C. Millennials

    D. Traditionalists

132. The diversity manager at the Fortune 500 company for which you work has asked for the EEO 1 reports showing the demographics of the new hires over the last six months. The diversity manager is considering what type of diversity?

    A. Deep-level

    B. Surface-level

    C. Trait-based

    D. Biological

133. The values and attitudes held by employees has been shown by research to be positively correlated with overall performance. This is an example of what type of diversity at work?

  A. Deep-level

  B. Surface-level

  C. Trait-based

  D. Biological

134. Under which condition may an employer adopt a fluctuating work week to calculate employee pay?

  A. For exempt employees to keep track of time

  B. If the employee schedules actually fluctuate

  C. For nonexempt workers who are paid a flat, biweekly sum

  D. Never, because fluctuating workweeks are prohibited under the Fair Labor Standards Act.

135. Of the following pairs of words, which are most likely to positively affect the collective attitude of a team?

  A. Job involvement and employee engagement

  B. Job enlargement and job enrichment

  C. Fair pay and feedback

  D. Social pressure and emotional contagion

136. You recently were informed that your company is being acquired by a major competitor. You have been authorized to put together an executive agreement that will pay the CEO to stay on board for a period of three years after the deal is finalized. This is an example of which executive compensation benefit?

  A. Golden handcuff

  B. Golden parachute

  C. Golden life jacket

  D. Golden handshake

137. Which of the following is the proper definition of phantom stock?

  A. Employees are offered stock options as incentives but are not allowed to exercise them until they are fully vested.

  B. Employees are incentivized based on the stock price but never actually earn shares.

  C. Employees are offered stock shares at the strike price.

  D. Employees are offered equity shares but must earn the ability to trade.

138. The large construction company for which you work is struggling to find foremen in the ever-growing economy. They realize they are at risk to lose the ability to complete the several jobs they have on the books and so decide to increase field employee pay to the 90th percentile of the midrange market wage. This is an example of which of the following risk management strategies?

    A. Mitigation

    B. Avoidance

    C. Acceptance

    D. Transference

139. Which of the following HR docs run the risk of creating an implied employment contract?

    A. Job offers

    B. Job descriptions

    C. Performance reviews

    D. All of the above

140. Predicting the consequences of an electricity outage at your place of work is the primary focus of which of the following business continuity planning tools?

    A. Hazard assessment

    B. Rapid response plan

    C. Business impact analysis

    D. Prevention plan

141. The large manufacturer for which you work recently automated the high-hazard job that was the primary source of injury for employees. This is an example of what type of hazard control?

    A. Administrative

    B. Engineering

    C. Training

    D. PPE

142. Glare and shadow controls are possible abatement strategies for which type of workplace hazard?

    A. Lighting

    B. Machinery

    C. Electricity

    D. Housekeeping

143. The major hospital for which you work has asked you to create an educational resource for local employers to help prepare for an influenza pandemic. Which of the following would you recommend employers do to help prevent the spread of disease?

    A. Mandate flu vaccines for all employees.

    B. Encourage employees to stay home when sick.

    C. Provide hand sanitizer to kill the germs.

    D. All of the above

144. The rise of sexual harassment claims in the news in 2018 is *most* likely going to lead to which of the following conditions?

    A. More enforcement of existing anti-harassment laws

    B. Increased training obligations of employers

    C. An increase in claims of workplace harassment

    D. Higher employee fines for wrongdoing

145. Tension headaches, absenteeism, and erratic behaviors are all signs of which of the following workplace safety hazards?

    A. Substance abuse

    B. Autoimmune disorders

    C. Soft tissue injury

    D. Stress

146. Your American employer has asked you to identify the risk of global illness for expatriates working across the globe. Which HR tool should you use?

    A. An international broker

    B. Government resources

    C. A self-inspection

    D. A job hazard analysis

147. Which of the following groups contribute to the design and enforcement of workplace health and safety standards for multinational employers across Europe?

    A. OSHA

    B. Works councils

    C. Labor unions

    D. All of the above

148. Of the following HR tools, which is the *first* that you should use when trying to identify predictors of success in a job?

    A. Job analysis

    B. Job specifications

    C. Job descriptions

    D. Job evaluation

149. Which of the following is quickly becoming the primary way employers vet job candidates in the 21st century?

    A. Online videos

    B. Apps

    C. Social media

    D. Job boards

150. What is a major advantage of having a return-to-work program for individuals with a non–work-related injury?

    A. Increased compliance with workers' compensation laws

    B. Preparing for stronger labor laws related to safety

    C. Better individual management of work responsibilities

    D. All of the above

Appendix

Answers to Practice Test Questions

PHR Practice Area 1: Business Management

1. D. There are four basic elements to the acronym VUCA: volatile, uncertain, complex, and ambiguous. VUCA describes the environment in which competent HR professionals must perform.

2. A. The sales and marketing organizational functions, while closely related, have distinct roles in the transfer of company products or services to the customer. The sales function serves the near-term needs of the customer. The marketing function serves the longer-term goals of placement, product, price, and promotion.

3. B. The operational role of a human resource professional refers to work related to running the core business. This would include tasks such as processing payroll, hiring, disciplining employees, and other tasks related to day-to-day operations. These tasks are typical for a PHR-level professional.

4. D. A code or statement of conduct can serve many purposes. It may serve to define proper behavior when there is a conflict of interest in an ethics policy. It may also describe expected standards of behavior in both the employee handbook and the IIPP.

5. D. Workforce analytics is growing in popularity as a tool that employers use to gather data on a macro level about the workforce. Analytics are future-focused in that employers use the data gathered to both predict behaviors and make decisions about effective HR programs.

6. A. Change management is a critical process used to effectively manage the change required to implement strategic initiatives. Authoritarian and transformational are management/leadership styles, not strategies. Risk management is the practice of forecasting and responding to risks facing an organization.

7. D. Workforce expansion as a structural change is often the result of business growth or decline. In this case, HR will need to address communication methods between corporate and the new facility, help build a cohesive team identity, and formalize a cohesive management approach to the challenges inherent in multi-establishment businesses.

8. A. A cost per hire metric is useful when needing to calculate the true costs associated with recruiting and selection. Factors to include are advertising, labor rates to screen résumé and interview candidates, costs for pre-employment testing, and administrative costs associated with hiring.

9. C. An important role of human resource practitioners is to reinforce a company's standards to supervisors. In this case, reminding the supervisor that he is responsible for modeling appropriate behavior may be a good first step toward changing behaviors.

10. B. Employee handbooks help to protect the organization from predictable risks based on litigation statistics and recommended best practices in compliance with various labor laws. They are not specifically required by law and are only one step toward defending against claims of discrimination. While handbooks certainly help to mitigate and offset

risks, similar to an insurance policy, they typically do not go into as much detail as standard operating procedures, compliance checklists, or full HR audits.

11. D. Trending and forecasting are critical activities in enterprise risk management. They help to predict the areas of greatest vulnerability based on the legal climate. Updates based on trends cannot necessarily be gleaned from litigation statistics alone, and unemployment statistics are a different set of compiled numbers than litigation information.

12. A. Retaliation continues to account for the largest number of discrimination charges filed with the EEOC, followed by Race and Disability (FY 2016). This information is critical when developing risk management strategies such as policies prohibiting retaliation from supervisors and prompt investigation of discrimination claims under any of the statutes enforced by the EEOC.

13. C. Once a member of Congress (MOC) agrees to sponsor a bill, it is assigned to a committee to determine whether it is viable. If a bill is deemed viable, it is then sent to a subcommittee, which makes any changes to the bill and either sends it back to the full committee or allows it to die without taking further action. Unifying or influencing members of Congress for or against a bill is known as *lobbying*.

14. A. Lobbying can be an activity as simple as writing to an MOC or as elaborate as the hiring of a professional firm or industry group. It is designed to influence the development of law that serves the core interest of the affected group. Administrative laws are regulations that are developed outside of the traditional bill process through Congress, such as agency and executive orders. Corporate governance efforts reflect various influences, such as finance laws and social responsibility, in the development and implementation of compliance efforts.

15. D. A code of conduct seeks to communicate the company expectations of employees. These may include standards for professionalism, specific policies, and general work rules. An ethics or values statement strives to communicate the standards a company seeks to uphold in its business practices.

16. B. The ways in which goods or services are produced are included under the production layout function of an organization. Consider that all work is production—even services such as sales and marketing. Scheduling involves the availability of goods or services during peak demands. Capacity is determining how much of a good or service can be provided based on inputs, and the facility location is where these goods and services will be produced.

17. A. Capacity is the process of determining how much of a good or service can be provided based on inputs, such as the availability of material, labor, and equipment, when considering the needs of the customer. The ways in which goods or services are produced are included under the production layout function of an organization. Scheduling involves the availability of goods or services during peak demands, and the facility location is where these goods and services will be produced.

18. D. Long-term successful companies are able to identify changes in technology that influence their industry-specific demands. Other external scanning factors include the labor pool, legal and regulatory activity, and the economic environment.

19. B. While both B and D are correct, it is important to consider interdepartmental support from a strategic perspective. Processing payroll is an operational task that can be done internally or externally. Formulating models that help to predict labor needs is a better example of the application of information from other departments in the achievement of organizational outcomes.

20. B. The task of forecasting involves analyzing data from the past while anticipating future needs to generate projections, in this case, in the form of a budget. Forecasting by nature is subject to error, but experienced forecasters become adept at interpreting data to make reasonable decisions.

21. C. A general partnership (GP) is one in which the partners are active in the daily operations of the business. In a limited liability structure, the partners act more as investors than managers. A joint venture is similar to a GP but is usually formed to manage a specific project, such as an overseas endeavor or investment in a new product. A corporation is not a partnership agreement.

22. A. The old adage "What's in it for me?" applies to employees in any situation involving change. Communicating the "why" of any organizational change, either directly or through a front-line manager, often goes a long way to helping employees shift from the status quo to the new normal with less resistance than they might exhibit if asked to comply without question.

23. B. HR's role in change management is to address the human challenges any changes will face before they take root. Helping employees understand the need for the change, communicating how the change will affect an employee's role, dealing with resistance, and/or dealing with outright refusals to embrace the change are all areas where HR can lead in a change management intervention.

24. C. Supply chain management is the operational business function concerned with acquiring raw materials all the way through to customer delivery and support. It includes the functions of purchasing, inventory, and shipping and receiving.

25. A. In this scenario, the company may need to address staffing shortages or surpluses as the managers execute the business goals. For this reason, HR should meet regularly with managers to first identify the workforce needs and then to update the managers on progress being made toward addressing those needs.

26. D. Human capital metrics are those that provide data to help forecast human resource needs and measure current state. Human capital is seen as a resource that may be used to achieve organizational goals, so factors such as organizational climate, skillset of the workforce, and outputs may all be measured and used to design effective business strategies.

27. C. A values statement does not need to include a plan of action but, rather, a declaration of the expected standards of company and employee behaviors. It should be oriented toward what is important to the company and what should be important to the employees.

28. D. A business unit is a way to logically sort and order separate segments of a company. By doing so, organizations may develop specific strategies and focus resources on the subunits to help the company compete in their relative markets and achieve organizational goals.

29. A. Assets include any financial or other resources that an organization owns or that may be used toward the achievement of business goals. Assets are also used to measure the tangible and intangible value of a company.

30. C. In a series of numbers, the mode is the value that occurs most frequently, so the correct answer is 5.

31. B. Under conditions of transparency and trust, a company would seek to build a culture that allows for the free exchange of ideas, without fear of retaliation or punishment for disagreement. This would include coaching supervisors to allow employees to challenge the way things are done, especially if the employees have ideas on how to make a process or business condition better.

32. C. Any leadership development program must be aligned with company strategy and serve to communicate and reinforce the mission, vision, and values. In this way, HR would need to undertake an evaluation of the current leadership in relation to strategic outcomes before making a decision about hiring and terminations or populating the leadership pipeline. Additionally, HR would be responsible for coaching an under-performing manager to help bridge the gap between the current and desired states.

33. D. Ethical dilemmas most typically occur when there are conflicting values. This is why reliance upon individual ethics is less successful in organizational decision-making than establishing a corporate code of ethics from which all leaders are expected to operate. HR is expected to "lead the leaders" by communicating and modeling the expected standards of ethical behaviors and company values.

34. A. A small-business startup may not be able to afford an above-market pay strategy, and offering a creative culture will not alter the qualifications of the available labor pool. Influencing the skillset of the workforce population by offering internships, providing relevant equipment to local schools, and investing in the baseline skills necessary for workers will all aid in creating a qualified workforce for future hires.

35. A. Key external partnerships for companies facing large reductions in force or layoffs are state unemployment offices. Services that may be offered include wage replacement, retraining, résumé development, and job placement assistance.

36. C. An external scan includes a review of the variables that can or will influence the achievement of business objectives. It includes a scan of the general business environment, which may shed light on other elements to review, such as the economic environment and legal and regulatory practices that affect your industry.

37. B. Strategic workforce planning takes into account both the skillset of current employees and the availability of skills in the labor force population. From this, training needs can be assessed, the value of the job/skills can be reviewed (compensation), and diversity can be analyzed to meet strategic objectives.

38. D. Evidenced-based management is built from organizational science. Originally employed in the medical field to build best practices, it has evolved to help form guidelines for many organizational behaviors, including decision-making using evidence from science, organizational history, experience, and company values.

39. B. One type of experiential evidence that is available to make decisions is cognitive heuristics. Heuristics are simple, efficient guidelines that are built—in this case—from past experience and are used to guide decision-making from experts on the job. A supervisor who has led a production department for several years, for example, may already know approximately how many employees she will need to hire for during peak season.

40. C. The Delphi technique is a systematic decision-making process that draws upon the collective wisdom of subject-matter experts. Key to this technique is the facilitator, who gathers all feedback and rationale and keeps track of proposed changes. This iterative process allows for a collective "best solution" to be identified while taking in many perspectives.

41. A. Research has shown that high-quality leader-employee relationships help to reduce resistance to change. HR may be tasked with helping to improve trust in order to help employees commit to and cope with organizational changes.

42. B. Employers generally have four choices when approaching proactive risk management strategies. In the case of legal risks, purchasing employment practices liability insurance transfers part of the risk to another party, should a claim of unlawful conduct arise.

43. D. The practice of gathering employee data through workforce analytics continues to grow. HR practitioners must understand the internal and external risks and advise management on how to best address them. Issues such as privacy, data protection, and permissions are all areas in which HR may provide advisory support.

44. C. The term *churn* relates to the amount of turnover at a place of employment. A churn model can be built to help employers predict employee turnover (such as how often a position turns over and the reasons for the change), thus giving HR information to build retention practices. Data to inform churn models include length of service, type of training, years to promotion, and pay.

45. D. Those with a "stake" in the success (or failure) of a business are known as the stakeholders. These include suppliers, employees, customers, and the communities in which a business operates.

46. C. Corporate governance is a system of rules and behavioral guidelines that a company agrees to comply with. This system can include legal and nonlegal components.

47. A. A human resource information system is designed to manage HR-related tasks such as service awards, attendance, résumé tracking, and performance and training documents.

48. C. Human capital is a resource that an employer may use to compete, similar to financial and other types of resources. Human capital refers to employee knowledge and talents that add value to an organization.

49. A. Leading economic indicators are signs that predict changes to the economy that businesses must prepare to respond to.

50. D. Group consensus is a decision-making process in which a group of people come to an agreement or come to the same conclusion about an idea or a process.

PHR Practice Area 2: Talent Planning & Acquisition

1. D. The contrast error occurs when a rater compares other candidates to each other and rates them based on their differences, rather than the qualifications necessary to perform the work.

2. B. The gut feeling error occurs when a rater relies on intuition to make a decision about a candidate's qualifications, rather than focusing on the applicant's qualifications as they relate to the work.

3. A. The knowledge of predictor error occurs when the rater knows that a candidate scored particularly high or low on an assessment test that appears to be a valid predictor of future success on the job.

4. D. The negative emphasis form of interviewer bias occurs when the interviewer allows a small amount of negative information to outweigh other job-related criteria. It is important for HR to suspend judgment and encourage the supervisor to look at the fit between the candidate and the job and between the candidate and the organization.

5. C. A bona fide occupational qualification is classified when an individual's protected-class characteristic such as age, sex, or religion is "reasonably necessary to the normal operations of the business." In this case, the employer must comply with the federal regulations governing their industry.

6. B. The purpose of BFOQs is to allow employers to make employment decisions based on protected-class characteristics when those characteristics are "reasonably necessary to the normal operations of the business." Perception of outcomes does not validate a BFOQ.

7. D. Title VII of the Civil Rights Act identified not only protected-class groups but also unlawful employment actions such as discriminatory recruiting, compensation, and training. The Civil Rights Act of 1991 amended Title VII providing, among other things, remedies for intentional discrimination and a definition of the concept of business necessity.

8. D. Title VII of the Civil Rights Act of 1964 originally identified five protected classes: race, color, religion, national origin, and sex. It has been amended, and other laws have evolved to include age, pregnancy, disability, and military status.

9. B. The ADEA prohibits discrimination against people 40 years of age or older in employment activities, including hiring, job assignments, training, promotion, compensation, benefits, and other terms and conditions of employment. The OWBPA amended the ADEA in 1990 to include a prohibition on discrimination against older workers related to benefit plans.

10. B. The ADEA specifically prohibits discrimination against individuals 40 years of age and older.

11. C. The ADA applies to employers with 15 or more employees, and it served in part to define the term *disability*. The disabilities defined included both physical and mental impairments.

12. A. Covered entities under the ADA are identified as employment agencies, labor unions, joint labor-management committees, and employers with 15 or more employees.

13. D. The amendments to the ADA described the intent of the law related to the definitions of disability and major life activities. It also gave direction related to mitigating measures and clarified the concept of "regarded as." In this question, those who are "regarded as" having a disability and therefore were subject to unlawful employment practices are protected under the ADA as though they were actually disabled. For example, an employee with a facial disfigurement that does not impact a major life activity or require accommodation, and who is removed from a receptionist position out of concern for a negative reaction by customers, may be entitled to protection under the ADA.

14. D. *Disability* is broadly defined under the 2008 amendments. The definition includes those with a physical or mental impairment, a record of past impairment such as cancer in remission, and those who are not disabled but perceived to be disabled, such as crossed eyes that do not substantially limit their ability to perform the work.

15. D. The definition of a disability includes physical or mental impairments that substantially limit one or more major life activities. Major life activities fall into two categories: general activities, such as performing manual tasks, and major bodily functions, such as bodily systems performance.

16. B. The 2008 amendments to the ADA mandate that the EEOC develop and implement regulations and guidance for employers to follow in compliance with the ADA.

17. D. Many of the original labor laws have been amended over the years to take into account necessary clarifications of content and to codify court decisions. The Civil Rights Act of 1991 amended several major labor laws, including Title VII of the Civil Rights Act of 1964. The OWBPA amended the ADEA, and the ADA Amendments Act of 2008 amended the ADA.

18. B. The Civil Rights Act of 1991 established a sliding scale for compensatory and punitive damages based on company size. The limit for total compensatory and punitive damages for employers with 101–200 employees is $100,000.

19. B. GINA responded to the ability of medicine to identify genetic predisposition to particular diseases. Title I of GINA generally prohibits group health plans and health insurance issuers from discriminating based on genetic information, and it affects compliance with both the Health Insurance Portability and Accountability Act of 1996 (HIPAA) and the Employee Retirement Income Security Act (ERISA).

20. B. Executive orders are presidential proclamations that, when published in the Federal Register, become law after 30 days.

21. A. Several executive orders affect equal employment compliance by employers, and most of these relate to the expansion of those identified for protection against unlawful discrimination. EO 11246 and its amendments specifically prohibit employment discrimination on the basis of race, color, religion, sex, sexual orientation, gender identity, or national origin.

22. B. Several executive orders affect equal employment compliance by employers, and most of these relate to the expansion of those identified for protection against unlawful discrimination. EO 11375 was an amendment to EO 11246 that expanded coverage to include gender.

23. D. Several executive orders affect equal employment compliance by employers, and most of these relate to the expansion of those identified for protection against unlawful discrimination. EO 13152 amended EO 11478 to define "status as a parent" referring to an individual's relationship with a person younger than 18, or older than 18 if incapable of self-care.

24. C. The race/ethnicity categories were expanded in 2007 to include seven categories required for reporting on the employer EEO 1 report.

25. B. The Office of Federal Contract Compliance Programs (OFCCP) is responsible for the identification of affirmative action plan components. In the 2003 revision, OFCCP included factors such as the organizational profile, job group analysis, and determination of protected-class availability as well as setting placement goals, identifying problem areas, and preparing a schedule for internal audits in defining the necessary components of a compliant affirmative action plan (AAP).

26. C. Although both reengineering and restructuring may involve workforce expansion or reduction, reengineering focuses workforce planning efforts on what the customer is willing to pay as part of the process of building products or providing a service. For example, a customer would not be willing to pay for unnecessary wait time, so a process may need to be reengineered to eliminate elements that result in wasted time.

27. D. Job analysis identifies the knowledge, skills, abilities, tasks, duties, and responsibilities necessary to complete the work of an organization or departmental unit. This information is used to write job descriptions, create meaningful performance feedback systems, and properly compensate employees for the work being performed.

28. B. Internal talent, external talent, and alternative staffing methods are the three options for hiring qualified talent to fill open positions within an organization. They include options such as internal promotions, previous applicants, traditional recruiting outlets such as the Internet and newspapers, and alternative methods such as job sharing, telecommuting, and temporary workers.

29. D. A professional employer organization acts as a company's HR department. It becomes the employer of record and then leases the employees back to the organization to complete the work. An employer does not transfer all risk, as co-employment issues can arise.

30. B. The IRS has established guidelines to help determine whether an individual is an employee or an independent contractor. This classification is important, as it determines, among other things, who is responsible for the taxes owed to the IRS. Degree of control measures include behavioral controls (when and where work is done), financial controls

(who pays taxes and what expenses are reimbursed), and contractual controls (under what conditions the individual may be let go and a determination made on employment benefit obligations, such as pension or health insurance).

31. D. A robust staffing plan begins with the end in mind. It is usually in response to a strategic plan that has the potential to require skill development and resource allocation of the human talent to achieve organizational goals.

32. B. When sourcing and recruiting for qualified talent to fill open positions within an organization, HR must consider both actively looking individuals and passively available individuals. Particularly with hard-to-fill positions or in times of low unemployment, tapping into the currently working applicant pool may be a necessary staffing strategy.

33. B. The primary purpose of recruiting is to fill the open position with the best-qualified candidate for the job. This cannot be accomplished without a clear idea of the job specifications. Because line managers are often better acquainted with which KSAs are necessary, HR should work closely with them to determine the skills being sought during the recruiting process.

34. C. Job bidding is the process used by employers to allow employees to express an interest in a position prior to it becoming available. Job posting is an internal job announcement that provides basic information about an open position.

35. A. Social media and other online recruiting strategies involve the use of various Internet sources and virtual behaviors to fill open positions within a company. It helps to build the employer brand while accessing personal and professional networks to publicize job openings.

36. D. The UGESPs were jointly developed by several agencies with the intent to provide compliance guidelines related to employee selection procedures. They state, among other things, that any selection tool that has an adverse impact on a protected-class group is discriminatory unless the employer can show that the tool is both job-related and a valid predictor of future success on the job.

37. C. While this may be an example of discriminatory hiring practices because of the 4/5ths rule defined by the UGESPs, this adverse impact must be validated by the tests of job-relatedness and validity.

38. D. A weighted application form allows for easy identification of candidates with skills that are most important for the open position. They are designed to help reduce bias in the selection process, directing the focus to the job-related requirements of the jobs versus personal characteristics.

39. B. While all options are possible answers, B provides the best reason as to why interviews are important in the selection process. Rating candidates on their overall job and organization fit is the primary purpose of an interview. Although communicating position specifics certainly may be a by-product of the interview process, it most likely occurs during the prequalifying stage of the interview process.

40. D. Applicant tests are designed to predict future success on a job based on different characteristics. These characteristics should be job-related and valid. In this scenario, an integrity test would assess an applicant's honesty, work ethic, and attitude toward employee behaviors.

41. C. Applicant tests are designed to predict future success on a job based on different characteristics. These characteristics should be job-related and valid. In this scenario, the applicant is given a physical assessment test designed to determine whether the candidate is physically able to perform specific job duties.

42. C. In *Griggs v. Duke Power*, the employer used a high school diploma requirement as a pre-employment test. Although the test was not intentionally discriminatory, it still excluded members of a protected-class group and did not accurately predict future success on the job. Therefore, the court ruled that the high school diploma requirement was found to be discriminatory in effect.

43. A. The UGESPs require that employment tests be both reliable and valid. A test is considered to be reliable when it measures results consistently over time. A test is considered valid if it predicts what it intends to predict.

44. B. This pre-employment test is legally valid because it accurately correlated employee test results with future performance.

45. B. While many former employers are reluctant to provide detailed performance information about past employees, they are safe in providing factual information that is given in good faith. Examples of the types of information that may be collected in an employment reference check include dates of employment, position title, and whether the employee is re-hireable.

46. C. Negligent hiring occurs when an employer knows or should have known about an applicant's prior history, which endangers others with whom the employee comes into contact. Once an employer finds out about such history, they must take steps to safeguard others.

47. B. Employment at will means that an employee or employer can terminate employment at any time and for any reason. An employment contract specifically negates employment at will, as the employer and employee are entering into an agreement that defines services, compensation, and other terms and conditions of employment.

48. B. Form I-9, Employment Eligibility Verification, is the form required by the Immigration Reform and Control Act that employers must use to verify an employee's identity and right to work in the United States. It is a post-hire document that must be completed within three days of the employee's first day of work.

49. B. Employee digital conduct—including posting reviews, complaining about wages, and even having negative things to say about the company—may in fact be protected activity. The case filed by the Equal Employment Opportunity Commission against IXL Learning Inc. is just one example of how a protected-class worker may be the victim of unlawful retaliation based on their digital behavior.

50. D. The rights of employees while online may be protected by many agencies, including the National Labor Relations Board (NLRB) and the Equal Employment Opportunity Commission (EEOC). Under the NLR Act, employees must be allowed to engage in protected concerted activity, even when online. However, the NLRB did rule that online posts that are not intended to be read by co-workers are not protected (*XL Learning, Inc. and Adrian Scott Duane*, Case 20-CA-153625, JD(SF)-21-16.) The EEOC took a different stance and filed suit on behalf of the complainant in the same case, stating that the platform did not matter; the basis for retaliation claims remains constant.

51. C. The primary purpose of the interactive process under the Americans with Disabilities Act is to help a disabled worker and their employer communicate. It may include identifying employee restrictions, identifying job needs, scheduling changes, scheduling time-off requests, and many other elements necessary to help meet the needs of both the employer and the employee.

52. C. It may be reasonable to reassign an employee who is out on protected leave under the ADA. It is important that the employer has first tried to accommodate the worker in his current position and met any leave of absence requirements under other laws.

53. C. The Equal Employment Opportunity Commission has directed employers to individually assess candidates who have been convicted of a crime. Data to evaluate includes the nature of the conviction, the length of time that has passed since the conviction, and the job requirements.

54. A. Background screening is typically a post-offer, pre-hire HR activity. This means that an offer of employment has been extended but is conditioned on the ability of the individual to successfully pass a background check when required for the job.

55. D. The primary purpose of properly validating employment tests is to ensure the tests accurately measure the job requirements. This will help employers accomplish the other options, including aiding in the recruitment of qualified staff and helping employers manage compliance risk with various labor laws.

56. D. A workforce plan is designed to address the human resource/staffing needs of a company. It is future oriented, aimed at aligning the current skillset of the workforce with business strategy while creating a plan to address a skills gap where necessary.

57. B. The process and outputs from a job analysis directly influence the ability of HR to perform in all other competency areas. The data from a job analysis will be used to properly compare wages in the relevant labor market, identify the job relatedness of pre-employment tests, and help employers build job descriptions, policies, procedures, and rules to comply with labor law.

58. C. Under the Americans with Disabilities Act, job-essential functions are typically determined by the percentage of time spent doing the tasks, the frequency with which the tasks are performed, and how important each task is to overall job outputs.

59. B. Both job posting and job bidding are used to recruit internally. Job posting is an internal job announcement made when a job is open, whereas job bidding allows for employees to express an interest in a position before it is available.

60. D. Onboarding is a more robust employee socialization tool than its relation, orientation. Onboarding is a process that can occur over many months, designed to welcome, orient, and help a new hire adjust to the organization, its culture, and its norms.

61. B. Universities and colleges in the United States have highly diverse student populations. Applicants from this recruiting source may come from all over the world, speak different languages, and vary in age, majors, and intelligence levels.

62. C. Prequalifying questions can be an effective way to screen for minimum job requirements before allowing an applicant to continue through the selection process, thus resulting in a pool of more qualified candidates for processing.

63. A. A cognitive ability test is one that attempts to identify general mental ability, also known as *intelligence*. These types of tests are used to predict performance on a job.

64. C. *Aptitude* is a term that applies to an employee's natural ability to learn new things or to apply new knowledge to a job. In other cases, the term may apply to a function that the employee is naturally inclined to do well.

65. D. Personality profiles are used to identify both traits and behaviors of individuals. The most common of them often identify the conscientiousness of a person, their typical motivators, and their orientation toward extroversion or introversion. In all cases, the tests should be based on validated, job-related work criteria before being used in selection.

66. B. For HR to adequately prepare a workforce plan, they must access federal and state reports related to labor market characteristics. These governments collect demographic data, wage data, and knowledge/skills data that may be used by employers to help align a staffing strategy with business targets.

67. A. Jobs in STEM domains are projected to continue to grow, and federal, state, and local agencies recognize the skills gap. In response, these agencies are creating partnerships with businesses to influence the development and availability of these critical skill sets. Strategies include investing in elementary schools to help students learn these skills early and advocating for immigration reform that allows for more STEM visas.

68. D. A skills inventory is a tool used primarily to assess the skillset of the existing workforce. By creating and maintaining the inventory, HR can provide data to management to help create a workforce plan that is aligned with business strategy.

69. A. The employer brand in its most basic form helps to build the company identity. The brand includes the company's mission, vision, and values, and it communicates why current employees should stay while developing a desire of both passive and active candidates to work there.

70. D. The employer brand is a valuable commodity to accomplish several HR functions. This includes marketing the company to qualified applicants, helping to develop employees into brand ambassadors, and providing content for employee training programs designed to embed company culture at all levels.

71. A. The reputation a company acquires is communicated to existing and potential applicants. This phenomenon is also known as company branding and serves to help attract candidates who want to work in that type of environment. The brand also allows employers to build selection systems that help measure individual characteristics beyond technical skills.

72. C. HR must take care to avoid inadvertently creating an employment contract when using offer letters to bring on new candidates. This can be done by including at-will employment language in the letter and to avoid making promises of continued employment or future pay.

73. B. An employment contract is a binding agreement between two parties—the employer and employee—that will typically include the reasons an employee may be terminated. An offer letter will have a statement of at-will employment, meaning that either the employer or the employee may terminate employment at any time and for any lawful reason.

74. A. Anchoring bias occurs when a party to a negotiation affixes (anchors) a high starting price in the other party. In this case, HR used the first piece of information to inform their judgment and subsequent decision-making.

75. A. Social media is an excellent vehicle through which HR can recruit passive candidates (candidates not actively seeking employment). When used properly, it communicates why people should come to work at that organization in addition to simply posting current openings.

76. D. Calculating an accurate cost per hire must include any external and internal expenses associated with the hiring process.

77. B. Of the four steps to organizational socialization, metamorphosis is the final stage. During this stage, the employee becomes an established contributor, marked by a clear understanding of the organizational culture and their job tasks.

78. C. In many cases, job sharing is an effective option for certain jobs and employees. By documenting the agreement between two employees—including performance expectations and length of time for the arrangement—the employer and sharing employees have a good sense of the scope of the flexible work arrangement, thus increasing the chances for success.

79. D. Phased retirement is an alternative staffing arrangement in which employees have flexible options. To retain a highly knowledgeable and skilled workforce that continues to age, phased retirement may be an effective solution for employers.

80. B. Forecasting is an activity that seeks to align the conditions of supply and demand of talent with business strategy. This allows employers to make decisions about staffing levels to achieve business objectives.

81. D. Successful onboarding activities go beyond the operational activities of orientation, such as watching safety videos and giving new hires a copy of the employee handbook. Sometimes referred to as *organizational socialization*, the onboarding process can take anywhere from 30–120 days and helps the new employee engage with their job, co-workers, and the company culture.

82. D. There are many advantages to a successful onboarding program, and HR is often tasked with taking the lead in these efforts. Studies have shown that onboarding helps improve employee loyalty by helping new hires understand what is expected of them and creating a support structure for questions or concerns.

83. B. Study after study shows that the key factor for employee turnover is the relationship they have with their supervisor or manager. For this reason, it is important for HR to help leadership engage in positive employee relations activities and give them the tools to properly manage employee performance.

84. D. Diversity recruiting is a method used to ensure an organization is staffed with the most qualified talent for a position. This increases organizational competitiveness as well as customer satisfaction. Bias occurs when a decision-maker gives preference to one group over another, often based on unfair stereotypes or heuristics. All three are based on preconceived, incorrect notions of how related groups behave or perform.

85. C. Bias can be both conscious and unconscious, and all humans are capable of it. While not illegal unless a recruiter makes a hiring decision based solely on gender, it is still important that recruiters take steps to neutralize unconscious bias when searching for top talent. This may include searching for female names or creating search strings such as "women in the medical field" to help avoid unconscious bias in the recruiting process.

86. A. It is never best practice to ask candidates to reveal private information related to their social media accounts, and doing so may violate both state and federal laws.

87. B. A bona fide occupational qualification (BFOQ) allows employers to consider otherwise protected characteristics if the employer can show that the characteristic is related to successful job performance. In the case of the FAA, courts have ruled that the factor of age is "reasonably necessary to the operation of business," particularly for safety sensitive functions.

88. C. The Immigration Reform and Control Act (IRCA) requires that employees complete Form I-9 within 72 hours of the first day of work for wages. For HR, it may be necessary to remind employees of these requirements, tell them of the repercussions if they fail to comply, and provide support where possible to help keep them working.

89. C. The Office of Federal Contract Compliance is tasked with managing affirmative action plans (AAPs) and programs. While the components of AAPs may differ depending on the type, in general, federal contractors or subcontractors with more than 50 employees and a government contract (or subcontract) in excess of $50,000 must have a written AAP.

90. D. While establishing goals of an affirmative action program is necessary, employers are prohibited from establishing quotas for hires. Additionally, any type of discrimination based on age or military status is unlawful, as is requiring individuals to self-identify their protected class (asking them to voluntarily self-identify is lawful).

91. D. There are many priorities for HR as they are tasked with managing employee records. Both security and accessibility are elements of a compliant program; however, properly protecting employee confidential information must be HR's first concern.

92. A. The process for destroying records is not one that may be taken lightly; however, employers should not keep records beyond when they are allowed to destroy them. In this example, it is important that you consider any pending litigation that may affect the retention requirements of the documents.

93. C. In this scenario, it appears that you may not be adequately recruiting for the proper skillsets of the job. Conducting a thorough job analysis with the R&D team will help identify the essential knowledge, skills, and abilities; find appropriate recruiting sources for the job posting; competitively price the job; and ultimately find a more qualified candidate for the role.

94. A. Job descriptions with the corresponding essential functions are critical tools in helping a physician determine what modifications may be necessary for an injured worker to return to work. Inaccurate or outdated job descriptions may result in an employee being taken off work, which corresponds to higher workers' compensation costs and lower injured worker morale.

95. A. When there are multiple jobs to analyze and limited HR resources to do so, a questionnaire is a useful job analysis method. The surveys may be open ended or highly structured, allowing you to collect the necessary data depending on the quality of existing information.

96. C. Exempt employees have certain duties tests that qualify them to be exempt from overtime pay, meals, and rest breaks. By including the duties that support an exempt status, employers may be less likely to improperly classify these workers and will also be more likely to successfully defend a wage and hour claim under the Fair Labor Standards Act.

97. B. Employee self-service not only can help the initial process but can be available for employees to periodically update their records as new skills are acquired. While this approach may require some face-to-face interaction and training, it is a better long-term option than the others.

98. A. Former employees may be an excellent recruiting source under the right conditions. It is important for HR to consider the reason the employee left, however, before inviting them back to work. For those who left for personal reasons or left in good standing, it may be a great option, especially as they already know the culture, many of the people, and, in most cases, the job fundamentals.

99. D. For employees needing to relocate to accept a job offer, HR is tasked with offering relocation assistance. This can take on many forms, including those listed. It may also include helping a spouse find employment, offsetting childcare costs, and negotiating the coverage of moving expenses.

100. D. Combining key words related to an open position along with search terms AND, OR, and NOT form the basis for Boolean searches for talent. Recruiters should be proficient in basic Boolean search techniques—and the legal ramifications—to cast a wide net for qualified talent.

101. A. Some studies have shown that a new hire makes a decision to stay at their job within the first three weeks of employment, making this time period of significant importance to an employer's retention efforts. Onboarding programs that follow new hires into their jobs will contribute to organizational socialization activities, helping employees better understand the company, products/services, and individual roles. Managers must participate in this activity, so gaining their buy-in at the program design stage is imperative.

102. B. Whether voluntary or involuntary, affirmative action programs and plans are aimed at increasing the opportunity and presence of protected-class individuals in the workplace. This diversity is considered both a social and moral obligation and serves business outcomes by including and reflecting the communities in which businesses operate and their customer base.

103. D. In this case, you must first know how many employees work for the company, as that drives which labor law record-keeping and retention requirements you must comply with. For example, employers with 15 or more employees are subject to the record-keeping requirements of the Americans with Disabilities Act, whereas employers with 20 or more employees are subject to the requirements of the Age Discrimination in Employment Act.

104. B. There are many rules and guidelines that govern the employment of minors at any time during the year. The Fair Labor Standards Act is the primary federal law governing this HR practice, but special documentation—such as work permits—may also be required at a state level.

105. D. Employee onboarding programs serve specific employer and employee needs, affecting outcomes such as engagement, socialization, compliance, and turnover. For this reason, HR must build in measurement tools to identify both what is and is not working and to refine the program in response to the measures.

106. B. Due diligence at its core is a type of investigation HR does when a corporation is restructuring via merger or acquisition. It includes gathering and analyzing data related to the transaction including assets, liabilities, and/or pending lawsuits.

107. D. When two companies join together to become a single business entity, there are many advantages. These advantages include reducing the market share of the competition by eliminating competitors and market redundancies and increasing profitability by eliminating duplicate jobs.

108. A. The Department of Labor's Bureau of Labor Statistics is responsible for monitoring the trends within all labor markets. The DOL regularly gathers and analyzes data, publishing reports and recommendations that employers may access to help make decisions related to wages, layoffs, labor supply and demand forecasts, and many other factors.

109. A. The Americans with Disabilities Act (ADA) applies to employers with more than 15 employees. Employees undergoing treatment/rehabilitation for substance abuse and alcoholism are covered under the ADA, and the request is short term. With regard to the essential functions, the employee is clearly qualified to do the tasks as he is able to do every other day of the week, so the employer should comply with the accommodation.

110. A. Job descriptions will typically include the knowledge, skills, and abilities statements. According to the Department of Labor, knowledge statements reflect the application of an organized set of principles, theories, models, or procedures.

111. D. The Department of Labor defines skills as *developed capacities* that are used by the employee to facilitate performance. In the case of the HR generalist, hiring criteria based on competencies would include a measure of an individual's active listening skills.

112. C. The purpose of analyzing the labor market is to gain an understanding of the external conditions and trends that may affect a company's strategic plan. Identifying what is relevant to your employer involves comparing current and future staffing needs against labor market data.

113. C. A workforce plan takes into account the skills of current employees when compared with a company's strategic direction. This includes assessing the internal workforce to identify skills gaps that may be incorporated into a workforce plan to develop skills necessary to achieve company objectives.

114. D. The use of digital badges in onboarding can be an effective way to accomplish many things. This includes helping new hires establish in-house credentials to increase loyalty and engagement. Digital badges are also a way for HR to track who has completed training and reach out to those who perhaps are falling behind. Finally, HR can design courses with benchmark knowledge about the new hire's job, role, or company products and services so that new hires all start out with the same/similar knowledge baseline.

115. A. In this case, HR must understand what the market—and their competitors—are paying for similar jobs within the relevant geographic and industrial landscape. This knowledge will help a company avoid under-paying or over-paying for talent.

116. B. Turnover has many associated costs, both direct and indirect. Direct costs are easier to measure and often tangible, such as the cost of HR staff's time to recruit or monies owed the exiting employee. Indirect costs are less tangible, and thus more difficult to measure, but can have significant impact if not properly accounted for in an employer's retention plan.

117. D. In most cases, if a state has different record-keeping requirements than the federal government, the state laws must meet or exceed the federal guidelines.

PHR Practice Area 3: Learning and Development

1. D. The function of learning and development pivots upon the effective management of the human talent of the organization. It includes training and development activities as well as individual and organizational interventions that are aligned to business and strategic management.

2. B. Copyrights protect the owner of the original work for the life of the author plus 70 years. Employers that pay employees for the development of original work as part of their normal job duties own the copyright because the company paid for the work to be done.

3. A. Under the Copyright Act of 1976, authors retain the copyright to original work for their life plus 70 years. After that the work goes into the public domain and may be used without violating the copyright.

4. D. A design patent is designed to protect exactly what the name states—new, original, or ornamental designs of manufactured items.

5. A. A utility patent protects those processes or machines that are useful from a functional perspective. They are usually limited to 20 years.

6. B. The purpose of organizational development (OD) is to examine the processes and people who impact the ability of a company holistically to produce desired results. This examination is followed by systematic activities—called *interventions*—designed to make necessary changes at both the individual and organizational levels.

7. D. Change management is a strategic intervention that helps employees deal with and implement changes that are the result of strategic decisions. These changes may include the introduction of new technology, creating a more efficient process, or altering the organizational hierarchy/reporting structure.

8. A. Managing changes within an organization requires the systematic application of a change management theory that will help move both individuals and processes in the direction necessary for results. The change process theory developed by Kurt Lewin described three stages for change, including the following:

Unfreezing, or identifying and communicating the need for change

Moving, or examining and managing resistance

Refreezing, or the stage where the change becomes the new norm

9. D. The evaluation stage of the ADDIE training model consists of many factors. It includes gathering the participants' thoughts on how well or how poorly the training was delivered, as well as evaluating whether the training achieved the desired outcomes.

10. A. In the first level of Kirkpatrick's training evaluation model, participants are asked for their "reactions" to the training content and logistics. This reaction-level 1 training would seek both information about the training facility and feedback on the trainer.

11. C. Peter Senge described five disciplines that enable a company to cultivate a learning organization, including the concept of personal mastery, which is the development of subject-matter experts (SMEs) in their chosen field. SMEs are resources for the organization to draw upon in the application of their core competency toward desired business results.

12. B. Peter Senge described five disciplines that enable a company to cultivate a learning organization, including the concept of mental models, which refers to an individual's or organization's perceptions of how things should be done. These perceptions provide a model for employee behavior, and they may produce both positive and negative effects.

13. D. TQM is a type of organizational intervention that focuses on the structure and behaviors of the organization, most often through the filter of the customer. TQM is dependent upon continuous improvement and adaptations to the needs and desires of the customer.

14. D. Dr. Ishikawa significantly contributed to the TQM movement and is well known for the analytical tools used in an intervention. Examples include the following:

Checksheets—Relevant data is recorded and then counted based on number of occurrences.

Histograms—These charts are used to identify patterns in information.

Pareto charts—These graphically represent the 80/20 rule, which states that 80 percent of the problems are caused by 20 percent of the causes. This means that allocating resources toward that 20 percent will result in a high return on investment.

15. C. A Pareto chart is a graphical representation of the 80/20 rule, which states that 80 percent of the problems are caused by 20 percent of the causes. This means that allocating resources to correct the deficiencies should result in a higher return on investment.

16. A. A cause-and-effect diagram visually represents possible causes of a specific problem in a process. For example, identifying the root cause of a workplace injury would involve diagramming the possible causes that led to the injury for analysis.

17. B. Six Sigma began as a philosophy used by engineers to study process defects, and it can be used to measure products or services. It is a systematic way to identify exceptions to processes by defining the issues, measuring the company's performance, analyzing gaps between desired and actual performance, implementing improvement solutions, and controlling the new process until the changes are firmly rooted in place.

18. B. High-involvement organizations are those that create a culture of accountability and continuous feedback. This results in a flatter structure with fewer reporting structures, often made up of self-directed work teams accountable for outcomes.

19. B. Interventions are designed to shake up the status quo. In a human process intervention, employee socialization factors and the individual contributions to desired outcomes are analyzed and systematically addressed using tools such as development activities, TQM, and Six Sigma. Common processes that are addressed include enhancing an individual's ability to work well as part of a team, conflict resolution training, and management by objectives. They differ from human resource interventions, which may include activities related to other HR functions, such as compensation, workforce planning, and employee relations.

20. B. In this example, the root cause of employee turnover is lack of leadership accountability. A leadership evaluation and development program will help define performance expectations, identify under-performing leaders, and help them develop more effective leadership skills.

21. A. Skills training provides employees with specific information that is needed to do their jobs. It is often used as a talent management technique. Talent management involves several strategies and activities designed to direct the efforts of the workforce toward desired outcomes. It includes analyzing the fit between the person (skills) and requested tasks (job), offering feedback, and designing solutions for deficiencies such as training or job redesign.

22. C. Supervisory training takes into account the skills and responsibilities necessary to manage workers. It is often used as a talent management technique designed to enhance supervisory effectiveness that, in turn, improves retention and increases other positive outcomes.

23. D. Mentoring programs take into account all of these. A good mentor acts as a trainer and a coach, providing feedback from a position of experience without authority. While not a supervisor in the true sense of the word, a mentor provides feedback to the employee about how well or how poorly they are doing in the context of the issues that the employee brings to the discussion and the employee's desired career development. A mentor serves broad, long-term career needs, whereas a coach focuses on the development needs of an employee in a specific area.

24. C. A mentor is typically focused on the growth of the employee in the context of his or her career needs. A coach is usually focused on developing an employee or manager in a particular area.

25. B. Peer-to-peer coaching can be a successful strategy when performance and decisions are tied to a workgroup or management tier. A peer group understands the unique needs of both the job and the organization, providing a level of support that is both relevant and meaningful.

26. C. Virtual coaching can be a successful approach for executives or managers with time or distance barriers, requiring the individual to be self-managed. It is most successful when augmented by face-to-face sessions and tied to clearly communicated outcomes and expectations. It is a form of personal coaching that may combine elements of e-learning, such as videoconferencing and email.

27. D. A leadership program identifies high-potential (HiPo) employees for development as leaders. It involves training and development activities, such as coaching and mentoring, focused on both skill and career development.

28. B. Task-level training provides information specific to a job process or task as opposed to the behaviors of an individual or an organization.

29. C. Organizational-level training may encompass the entire organization or a business unit. It can be the result of new strategic initiatives or in response to a needs assessment recommending risk avoidance. Task-level training provides information specific to a job process or task. Individual-level training focuses on individual performance.

30. B. Individual-level training focuses on individual performance and may take into account developmental needs. Organizational-level training may encompass the entire organization or a business unit. It can be the result of new strategic initiatives or in response to a needs assessment recommending risk avoidance. Task-level training provides information specific to a job process or task.

31. D. A training needs assessment is a process that begins with identifying the goals of training. From there, data can be gathered and analyzed, the performance gap identified, and training solutions proposed in accordance with instructional outcomes.

32. B. A training needs assessment is a step-by-step process that begins by identifying goals, outcomes, and deficiencies. Once relevant data is gathered and analyzed and the performance gaps between actual and desired performance have been identified, multiple options for closing the gap can be considered and proposed.

33. B. Learning curves are a graphical representation of the rate of learning over time. A positively accelerating learning curve occurs when the learning accelerates over time rather than diminishing, as with a negatively accelerating learning curve. An S-shaped learning curve combines elements of both positive and negative curves, and a plateau occurs when learning levels off after an initial increase. Consider the following:

Positive—Increases

Negative—Decreases

S-shaped—Increases and decreases

Plateau—Flattens out

34. C. Of the three main learning styles, visual learners (and trainers) tend to prefer information that is communicated via visual aids such as formal presentations, charts, and graphs.

35. A. Tactile learners are often at their best when they are able to use their hands to understand training content. This can be accomplished by on the job training but also by "touching" a keyboard when learning new content.

36. A. Tactile learners often use their body's senses to absorb new information. This can be aided by movement, or frequent changes of position during class sessions.

37. D. The Fair Labor Standards Act defined the four conditions that must be met for an employer to avoid paying wages for training time. These conditions include that attendance is outside regular working hours; attendance is voluntary; the course, lecture, or meeting is not job-related; and the employee does not perform any productive work during attendance.

38. B. Studies have shown that increasing the diversity of work teams has significant impact on the generation of creative and innovative ideas.

39. D. Supervisory training usually involves topics related to interactions with employees. It is a talent management strategy that seeks to impart to the supervisor the skills necessary for effective management of people and processes.

40. D. Job enrichment is the process of assigning new responsibilities or tasks that challenge the employee to use their skills or to develop an aptitude for others. It includes using job factors, such as skill variety, task identity, task significance, autonomy, and feedback.

41. C. Onboarding is about much more than simply having a new hire fill out the paperwork or technical training. It involves activities that help the employee make a connection to the work but also to management and co-workers. Doing so gives the employee resources to access in times of uncertainty or stress.

42. D. The psychology of creativity points to the presence of individual expertise and organizational business structures that allow for mind-wandering. These two elements contribute to enhanced creative work activities such as problem-solving and brainstorming. Employees who lack project management skills may be unable to bring their creative ideas to fruition. The absence of any of these may inhibit the development of an innovative workforce that considers multiple options and perspectives.

43. B. Workforce collaboration is an ongoing activity that relies upon the ability of individuals to connect. Especially with a remote, virtual, or other-than-headquartered workforce, technological solutions are a major step toward keeping teams in touch with each other.

44. C. One advantage of e-learning training options is that employees do not have to waste time traveling to and from training locations.

45. D. Job shadowing is a training method in which a person learns a new job by watching (or shadowing) a person performing the tasks.

46. D. There is a growing trend acknowledging that organizational levels are not the key factor in the development of mentoring relationships. Reverse mentoring occurs when a more senior-level employee is learning or being mentored by a junior-level employee.

47. B. According to a 2018 Leanin.org survey of more than 8,000 working adults, many men are hesitant to begin to mentor female employees. The survey found that since the scandals that prompted the #metoo movement, the number of men unwilling to mentor females has more than tripled.

48. D. A well-crafted electronic communications policy will provide guidelines for employee behaviors as well as protect the company from liability. A statement that reminds employees that they must respect copyrighted materials, may not use company electronic communications to disrupt the work of others, and should have no reasonable expectation of privacy are all important elements of this type of policy.

49. B. The purpose of a training needs assessment is to identify and help establish the objectives of human resource development activities. The process of conducting the needs assessment will identify the current competencies of the employees while also identifying the required skillsets for current or future company needs. This information will help employers make informed decisions about what type of training will be most effective in bridging the gap.

50. C. Micro-learning provides employees with short bursts of training rather than requiring them to gather in a traditional classroom environment. This allows employees to access information on demand where necessary, often from their more readily available mobile devices.

51. C. A dual career ladder allows employees with superior skills to advance within the company without having to enter a management role. Often tied to advanced licensing or certifications, it is an effective way to help employees create depth in their careers as well as achieve pay increases for skill development activities.

52. B. All individuals learn at different paces. Trainers who understand the variables associated with how quickly or how slowly a person learns are better positioned to design training that will meet overall performance needs.

53. D. Stretch goals are those that require an employee to improve their knowledge or competencies beyond that required of their current position. A research project will help her gain knowledge about a specific subject, and tying the goal to business strategy will help her better understand the internal needs of the business.

54. A. Setting performance goals are often part of an effective performance appraisal process. Goals that are specific, measurable, achievable, relevant, and time bound are known as SMART goals. A relevant goal is one that is connected to something important, usually a company or department need or the larger mission/objectives of the organization.

55. B. Coaching is a highly individualized activity that is dependent upon the specific needs of the individual being coached. The process involves direct (often face to face, although that's not necessary), one-on-one communication about specific employee skills, relationships in the workplace, career development, or other needs of the employee to improve overall performance.

56. A. When implementing an executive coaching program, it is helpful to gather information about how the executive is perceived. This information can be used alongside other tools—such as personality profiles—to maximize the coaching session outcomes. Decisions about evaluation, program delivery, or strategic objectives are often decided before a program is implemented.

57. D. At the heart of any good mentorship program is a partnership between the mentor and employee or executive. The mentor agrees to provide meaningful, constructive feedback and be available to the employee as agreed. The employee agrees to actively participate and engage, using the feedback to improve performance and other outcomes.

58. Understanding a person's leadership style is another tool that may be used in the development of a management development program. In this case, the sales manager is demonstrating a laissez-faire leadership style, one that is characterized by a hands-off, laid back approach to managing employees.

59. A. Individuals with a transactional leadership style practice a "this for that" form of leadership and are generally more likely to be motivated by tangible rewards or threats of discipline.

60. C. Instructional designers must be careful to avoid violating the Copyright Act when creating training material. Generally, using short quotations, content from legislative reports or guidelines, and original work for training would all be considered legitimate. Reproducing artwork or similar items—such as a cartoon—without permission from the owner would be a copyright infringement.

61. B. In this example, how well or how poorly a portfolio is being managed can effectively identify employee training needs, especially as this is the primary activity of this job function.

62. C. Language barriers in training will continue to emerge as the labor force population becomes increasingly diverse. For this reason, it is important that HR anticipate the need and create training content that ensures all participants may fully benefit from a training program. This may include offering content that is in multiple languages.

63. D. Building a leadership pipeline is a critical function for many employers, especially those facing an overall shortage of workers. Asking employees to self-identify, as well as asking supervisors for their recommendations, are good starting points for succession planning.

64. B. A job task or process analysis is an important early step in the design of effective training programs. This type of analysis can help employers define the learning objectives, as well as design training delivery and evaluative outcomes.

65. A. The Americans with Disabilities Act requires employers with 15 or more employees to engage in the interactive process to accommodate individuals with disabilities. In this case, asking the employee what she needs will start the conversation toward a reasonable solution, one that gives her the knowledge she needs to do her job effectively.

66. B. Gathering unfiltered employee feedback is a critical outcome of an employee focus group. For this reason, it is best that a focus group is facilitated by someone other than their direct manager so that employees are comfortable sharing their opinions without fear—real or perceived—of reprisal.

67. C. Collaboration is often required when facilitating employee focus groups. For this reason, U-shaped seating in which employees can all see and talk to each other will best facilitate the discussion.

68. A. Embarking on a mentorship program requires careful planning to ensure success. When creating pairs, it is important that the mentee believes that their mentor truly has their best interests at heart so they are comfortable exposing their weaknesses for development purposes.

69. A. Coaching and mentoring differ in that coaching is an on-the-job training activity meant to provide real-time, transactional feedback on employee behaviors. Mentoring is a long-term program that is often more transformative in nature, helping the employee maximize skills, address weaknesses, identify motivators, and create career paths.

70. B. External coaches are usually reserved for exempt-level or high-performance employees. This option usually involves private coaching sessions with a professional who seeks to modify behavior or improve specific outcomes.

71. B. The function of career management programs is to help support the workforce planning needs of the organization. It includes identifying current and future staffing needs, assessing employee skills, and designing the necessary training and development programs for employees to serve the current and future needs of the business.

72. D. Executive coaching is focused on individual needs, strengths, and weaknesses as opposed to business needs, goals, objectives, or strategies.

73. C. An increasing challenge of using fast-track programs for high-potential workers is the message it sends to employees who are not selected for training. It is important that HR design a selection program that does not discriminate against protected-class workers and that all employees have the opportunity to be considered for any fast-track program. For those not selected, HR is instrumental in controlling the message to minimize low morale and prepare others for future programs based on skill development.

74. D. Replacement planning is generally used for attrition plans that are less than one year in scope. It is a tool used to assess the best candidate available to fulfill immediate needs or as backup for critical positions.

75. C. A succession plan is a long-term view that seeks to identify employees with the development potential to groom into future roles. It involves creating specific plans and setting goals to prepare the employee for future leadership vacancies.

76. C. Process flow mapping is one tool used in organizational development to redesign how a work process is completed. It is characterized by a series of steps that visualize a process from start to finish.

77. A. A successful organization development intervention first and foremost requires a proper plan. This includes starting with the end in mind by identifying targets and then establishing implementation milestones that can be measured.

78. C. Almost any type of OD intervention will require HR to step in to both lead and implement change. HR is often called upon to serve as or find a change agent, someone who deliberately causes change within a department or organization.

79. D. With the limited time and financial resources of companies today, it stands to reason that focusing succession planning efforts on jobs that are most difficult to fill, such as leadership roles, is a best practice.

80. B. Critical roles that are either important for business operations or represented by hard-to-find skills should be placed in a priority position when HR is tasked with building replacement or succession plans.

PHR Practice Area 4: Total Rewards

1. C. Elements of total rewards packages fall within two categories: monetary and nonmonetary. Examples of monetary compensation include base pay and retirement contributions. Examples of nonmonetary compensation include nontangible rewards, such as job satisfaction.

2. B. Direct compensation includes payments made to employees that are associated with wages and salaries. They include variable pay and pay for performance. Indirect compensation includes fringe benefits, such as vacation and sick pay.

3. D. Procedural justice is a pay equity concept in which employees perceive the procedures used to determine pay rates as either fair or unfair. It may also include how bonuses are distributed and the method used to determine pay increases.

4. B. Pay openness refers to the degree of secrecy around the ability of employees to discuss their wages. It directly affects the perceived fairness of employer compensation plans. Under some conditions, such as state laws and in union environments, it may be unlawful to forbid employees to disclose their pay rates.

5. B. There are two basic orientations of compensation philosophies: performance-based and entitlement. Companies that are oriented toward performance-based pay systems believe that compensation should be tied to effort, inputs, and results. Entitlement-oriented companies are more likely to provide cost-of-living or seniority increases, preferring to reward based on factors less related to performance.

6. B. A compensation strategy involves the organizational choices that must be made in the application of resources to attract, retain, and motivate employees.

7. C. The Securities and Exchange Commission requires clear and concise information related to executive compensation. This includes the disclosure of the amount and type of compensation paid to the top five executives and the criteria used in reaching executive compensation decisions.

8. A. Fiduciary responsibility is a term that applies to those in a position of responsibility. In an HR context, it applies to professionals who are tasked with advising, managing, and/or administering total rewards programs.

9. C. External factors, such as the economy and the availability of talent in the labor market, affect compensation decisions such as base pay, perks, and benefits.

10. D. The Fair Labor Standards Act (FLSA) affected three distinct areas related to compensation: establishing a federal minimum wage, restricting child labor, and limiting working hours through overtime pay and exemption status.

11. C. The FLSA has two categories of coverage: enterprise and individual. Enterprise coverage applies to organizations with at least two employees and at least $500,000 in annual sales. Individual coverage applies to employers engaged in interstate commerce.

12. D. The FLSA regulations apply to workers who are not already covered by another law. These include railroad and airline employers, who are subject to wage regulations identified under the Railway Labor Act.

13. D. The FLSA requires that employers define the pay status of all positions within the organization. Based on the job responsibilities, a position may be exempt from the payment of overtime for working more than 40 hours in a week.

14. C. Positions may be exempt from one or all of the FLSA requirements. For this reason, it is important for employers to conduct a duties test used to determine job responsibilities for the purpose of defining exemption status.

15. B. Some states have established their own minimum wage that is higher than the federal minimum of $7.25. Where federal and state laws have different minimum wage rates, the higher standard applies.

16. A. Compensatory time, or comp time, may be used by public employers to compensate employees instead of overtime pay. Instead of being paid time-and-a-half their regular rate of pay for hours worked in excess of 40 in the workweek, they are rewarded with the equivalent of paid time off, calculated at the overtime rate of time-and-a-half.

17. B. There are several types of compensable time for hourly workers defined under the FLSA. They include waiting time, which is time spent by employees who have been asked to wait for an assignment. On-call pay is compensable if an employer places significant constraints on an employee who may be called in for duty. Travel time pay may be compensable for any time beyond an hourly employee's regular commute.

18. C. While the FLSA does not specifically require meal/rest periods, if they are provided, they are subject to a determination of compensability. Rest periods of less than 20 minutes must be paid to (nonexempt) hourly workers.

19. A. An employee runs the risk of losing their exemption status if an employer makes an improper deduction from their paycheck. This means the employer would be obligated to pay for all hours worked in the period that the unlawful deductions were made. The FLSA has a safe harbor provision for unintended payroll errors that could affect exemption status.

20. B. There are several types of exemption statuses identified under the FLSA. The executive exemption applies to employees who have managing the organization or business unit as their primary responsibility, including directing the work of others, and who have the authority to hire and fire.

21. D. There are several types of exemption statuses identified under the FLSA. The professional exemption applies to employees who have advanced knowledge in a field of science or learning acquired through education. This exemption also applies to creative professionals whose primary responsibilities include invention, imagination, originality, or talent.

22. C. Base pay is the most basic form of direct compensation, often communicated in terms of an hourly rate, an annual salary, or a salary amount stated in the organization's payroll period.

23. D. Performance-based compensation includes programs designed to reward the efforts of employees.

24. C. Pay differentials are used as incentives for employees to work in less desirable jobs. Examples include shift pay, on-call pay, and hazard pay.

25. B. A reporting premium may be required by state law or an employment agreement. It applies to employees who are called or scheduled to work, report in as required, and find that there is no work available.

26. C. Base pay and variable pay are the two main types of compensation. Incentives, bonuses, and pay for performance are all examples of variable-pay programs.

27. B. Performance-based pay must have a direct line of sight between the employee's performance and reward. Doubling the unused days would be counterproductive to the desired outcome, and cashing out an employee's unused pay limits their flexibility in the future. Using a performance management system to track and influence pay increases directly links employee performance to outcomes. It is still important, however, that employers do not unintentionally violate the Americans with Disabilities Act by discriminating against covered employees for absences related to a qualified disability.

28. C. Gainsharing programs are designed to improve labor or production costs. Working with employees and committees, opportunities are identified and implemented with the gains shared among the employees. Gainsharing includes programs such as Improshare, the Scanlon plan, and profit-sharing.

29. C. Variable pay is also known as earnings at risk. It implies that a portion of the pay must be earned by meeting specific criteria. Commissions provide incentives to sales employees by paying them a percentage of the sales price for products and services sold to the customer.

30. B. Bonuses are often discretionary in nature, being provided to employees based on differing variables. These variables may include profit-sharing, spot awards for individual performance, or bonuses based on specific criteria such as employee referrals.

31. D. Job evaluation is an attempt to remove subjectivity from the process of determining the value of jobs. It identifies objective criteria and measures them against the level of importance to both the job and the organization.

32. B. The ranking method requires evaluators, such as supervisors, to compare the value of jobs to one another. It is a rather subjective method used to evaluate jobs, as evaluators may be influenced by factors unrelated to the work being done.

33. D. Using multiple sources to glean information about compensation and benefits ensures that representative data is collected from the relevant market. Government surveys, employee needs surveys, and commissioned surveys are all examples of source information.

34. C. When a new hire makes more than the incumbent, wage compression has occurred. It may be the result of high demand for a certain skillset, or it may occur when an organization's pay practices, such as merit or cost-of-living increases, fail to keep pace with labor market conditions.

35. A. Voluntary benefits, such as healthcare and retirement, are often offered by employers to attract and retain qualified individuals. Employers offer mandated benefits such as workers' compensation insurance and Medicare deductions in order to comply with federal or state laws.

36. D. The Family Medical Leave Act (FMLA) was passed to provide job protection for eligible employees who are faced with a serious illness in themselves or a family member. It allows covered employees to take 12 weeks of unpaid leave within a 12-month period, in most cases obligating the employer to reinstate the employee to the same or similar position upon return.

37. D. FMLA applies to all public agencies and schools, as well as employers with 50 or more employees working within a 75-mile radius.

38. D. COBRA amended ERISA in 1996 by requiring businesses with 20 or more employees to provide health plan continuation coverage under certain circumstances. ERISA is the federal law that sets minimum standards for most voluntarily established pension and health plans in private industry to provide protection for individuals in these plans.

39. C. Payroll, compensation, and benefits often make up the largest operating expense for employers. They are also critical factors in determining employee attraction and retention. Therefore, employers should view compensation and benefits as both an expense and a strategy.

40. B. A compensation philosophy is a specific statement related to compensation and benefits within an organization. It serves to guide the direction of strategic decision-making about one of the highest operating costs within the organization.

41. A. Internal conditions, such as willingness and ability to pay, affect how HR should structure the compensation philosophy. For example, if an organization does not want to lead the market in pay for entry-level workers, either because they can't or because the market is flooded with talent, a compensation philosophy should not reflect competitive rates.

42. B. The Fair Labor Standards Act (FLSA) requires that all hourly, nonexempt workers be paid overtime for any hours worked over 40 in a week.

43. A. The Portal-to-Portal Act amended the FLSA in 1947. It clarified what was considered to be compensable time, and it established that employers were not required to pay for the regular commute time of employees.

44. C. Discretionary bonuses are often given without the formality or benchmarks of traditional gainsharing programs, such as Improshare or Scanlon. While the amount of the bonus is based on individual attributes (years of service), it applies company-wide and is therefore a group incentive built on shared financial rewards.

45. D. Compensable factors are those characteristics of jobs that have value. The job evaluation process attempts to identify these factors and then assign a value aligned with the compensation strategy and task importance.

46. A. The Hay system is a complicated point factor classification method of job evaluation. It uses three factors: knowledge, problem-solving, and accountability to value jobs within an organization.

47. D. Survey data is often necessary to determine cost-of-living adjustments (COLA) to pay. It relies on factors such as inflation to determine how much pay must grow in order for employees to maintain their current lifestyle.

48. D. Benefits fall within two classifications: those that are required by law and those that employers choose to offer. Total rewards include both direct and indirect compensation options along with the identification of intrinsic and extrinsic rewards.

49. D. Mandated employee benefits, or those required by law, often have some level of wage replacement calculation for qualifying employee events such as disability, injury, retirement, or unemployment.

50. D. Employees needing time off for routine or short-term conditions do not generally have protection under the ADA. The FMLA applies to employers with 50 or more employees, and workers' compensation covers employees who have a work-related injury. Any slight tweak could alter their eligibility, however. For example, the FMLA could apply in this situation if the employer had 50 or more employees for each working day during each of 20 or more calendar workweeks in the current or preceding year, and the ADA may come into effect if the injury becomes debilitating.

51. B. While notifying employees of their eligibility, rights, and responsibilities is mandatory, employers are not required to use DOL forms such as WH-380, WH-381, or WH-382. However, if a substitute form is used, it must include all of the information required by the regulations.

52. B. A defined benefit plan promises a specified monthly benefit upon retirement. A defined contribution plan specifies a contribution amount, but not necessarily a specified amount upon retirement, as these accounts are subject to contributions minus investment gains or losses.

53. A. While retirement benefits are considered voluntary, once employers opt to provide them there are regulations with which they must comply. ERISA requires that employers file three reports: a summary plan description, an annual report, and reports to individual participants of their benefit rights.

54. B. Delayed vesting refers to requiring employees to complete a minimum number of years of service before they can claim ownership of the portion of employer contributions in their retirement plans. In cliff vesting, a specified period of time must be completed; in graded vesting, partial ownership of employer contributions occurs in accordance with a vesting schedule.

55. C. In addition to setting standards for those responsible for safeguarding pension funds, ERISA defines funding requirements for pension plans. Once accrued obligations have been determined, employers must make quarterly deposits to a trust fund established expressly for this purpose.

56. C. The OWBPA amended the Age Discrimination in Employment Act in response to several discriminatory factors of the time. It includes a prohibition of discrimination against older workers, and it defines the conditions under which an employee may waive their right to sue for discrimination.

57. D. While it is mandatory for employers to offer COBRA continuation of health care to eligible ex-employees who have experienced a qualifying event, they are not obligated to continue to pay the insurance premium on the employee's behalf. Therefore, employers may charge up to 102 percent of the group's premium to the employee.

58. C. While group health plans can require an employee to take a physical at the time of enrollment, it is specifically prohibited from using information gathered in that exam to restrict enrollment or charge more to otherwise eligible employees.

59. C. The IRS issued guidance that defined waiting periods for group health plans. It includes the requirement that plans and insurance issuers offering group coverage may not use a waiting period that exceeds 90 days.

60. C. The Pension Protection Act of 2006 (PPA) requires that pension plans offered by employers be fully funded. This is to avoid shortfalls of funding should the company go out of business or as the workers retire and begin to collect their payments.

61. A. There are many reasons a company may choose to outsource payroll processing. There is also much debate about whether payroll is an HR function or an accounting function. Regardless, with an HR department of one person, outsourcing payroll will allow for up-to-date expertise and efficient processing of this critical employee need.

62. C. HR professionals responsible for payroll must be certain to understand the difference between voluntary and involuntary deductions. In this example, an employee may elect to have a portion of their pay withheld to fund a 401(k) retirement account.

63. B. For smaller employers, it can be difficult to keep up with the complex, changing payroll and tax-related regulations. For this reason, it is a significant advantage to outsource the payroll function for a small company.

64. A. Of the options listed that may be outsourced, COBRA represents the least valuable HR activity for companies, mainly because it addresses the needs of employees who are no longer employed.

65. D. There are many elements HR must consider when generating a request for proposal for COBRA outsourcing services. Eligibility tracking, COBRA notices, and monitoring coverage periods are just a few compliance pieces that HR must ensure are being managed, either in-house or with a service.

66. D. Most employers are having to explore cost containment strategies as the price of employee benefits continues to skyrocket. In this needs assessment, the employees are worried about the cost. To address their concerns while balancing the value of these programs to the employer, you should explore all cost containment options before making a recommendation.

67. C. The Affordable Care Act, also known as Obamacare, allows employers to require a 90–calendar-day waiting period for new hires before they may enroll in company healthcare plans.

68. D. Under the Affordable Care Act, employers cannot require employees to wait more than 90 days to be eligible for company health benefits. The 90-day period includes weekends and holidays (calendar days).

69. A. Employee self-service programs have significant advantages when it comes to benefits open enrollment. By consolidating information into one database, redundancies may be eliminated and thus productivity increased.

70. B. The long-term management of an employee self-service system is a key consideration. Many HR professionals are not technical experts, and many small employers do not have IT staff on site should issues arise. For that reason, HR should pay particular attention to the troubleshooting process once a system "goes live." Failure to do so could result in lost productivity, frustration, and under-utilization of the features.

71. C. While all of these are sources for wage data, the best option would be industry surveys. Available for purchase, these surveys provide a more detailed view of the nature of the competitive pay structures. These surveys may include the employer size, types of benefits, and the nature of commission and bonus structures.

72. D. Employer pay systems and practices must be internally and externally competitive and equitable. In this way, their practices are more likely to be based on needs (employee and market) and compliant with federal, state, and local regulations.

73. D. Under the IRS's guidance, eligibility conditions will not be considered to be designed to avoid the 90-day waiting period obligation provided that coverage is made effective no later than 13 months from the employee's start date.

74. A. The needs of the employees when preparing for open enrollment season will drive many outcomes. For example, if employees no longer value a particular offering, the employer may be able to reduce costs by no longer offering the benefit. Employees also have differing needs when it comes to the use of technology, many preferring a face-to-face approach over a technological solution. By first understanding what the employee needs and wants, HR may design solutions that can positively impact both the employer and the employee.

75. D. Engaging employees throughout the open enrollment process can be done in several ways. By putting relevant information out early in the process, HR can help avoid the "information saturation" that so often occurs with administrative-heavy practices. Offering incentives and following up with those who have not yet participated can also help HR meet timelines.

76. C. Employees are much less likely to ask questions about their personal needs in a group meeting format. Face-to-face sessions, either with HR or with a broker who understands the plans, is a much more effective way to help employees select a benefits plan that will meet their needs while also giving the employer an opportunity to explain the rationale behind any unpopular changes.

77. C. Time and financial support seem to be the two primary needs of employees who are dealing with the loss of a loved one; some grief experts recommend at least 20 days of bereavement for the loss of close family members. For this reason, many employers are updating their traditional bereavement practices. Especially for employers operating in states with short-term disability programs that offer wage replacement, reminding the grieving employee of other types of leave benefits can help.

78. D. Cyberattacks against company health and retirement plans are on the increase—both for employers that collect and store the data as well as any third-party vendors that may have access. Risks in this example include a breach of privacy laws related to medical information, negligence should the data be compromised, and identity theft should sensitive information such as Social Security numbers fall into the wrong hands.

79. C. The amount a retiree will receive upon retirement is dependent upon the individual's average earnings on jobs that are covered by Social Security.

80. A. The practice of coordination of benefits eliminates coverage redundancies while ensuring the covered individuals get the most out of all plans.

81. D. A Health Insurance Purchasing Cooperative is a type of employer alliance. Businesses band together in a single bargaining unit that may then leverage its size to get more affordable rates than the individual businesses would by negotiating independently.

82. C. A pregnant worker with paid sick time benefits through her employer would receive partial wage replacement first through her employer's benefit.

83. D. Any individual or individuals with discretionary decision-making authority about an employer's group health plan are expected to make decisions that are in the plan's participants' and beneficiaries' interest only. These responsibilities are defined not only by title but for any individual or group of individuals with the ability to exercise discretionary authority.

84. B. The Fair Labor Standards Act requires that employers keep payroll records for at least three years.

85. C. President Obama signed the Lilly Ledbetter Fair Pay Act in 2009 to extend the filing time for those who believe they have been the victim of compensation discrimination under the Equal Pay Act. The EEOC states the following: "The deadline for filing a charge or lawsuit under the EPA is two years from the day you received the last discriminatory paycheck (this is extended to three years in the case of willful discrimination)."

PHR Practice Area 5: Employee and Labor Relations

1. C. Common law doctrines are case laws and precedents that help employers make decisions. In the case of employment at will, courts have established that either party may terminate the employment relationship at any time and for any reason, provided that it is not based on an unlawful practice.

2. B. Respondeat superior is the common-law doctrine that holds employers responsible for the actions of their employees, regardless of whether the employer's actions were negligent or reckless. Consider respondeat superior in cases of sexual harassment where the employer was unaware of the employee's actions or a charge of negligent hiring when an employee acts outside of the expected standards of behavior. In both of these examples, the employer potentially "should have known" of the employee's behavior.

3. A. Constructive discharge takes place when a supervisor attempts to make working conditions so intolerable that an employee feels they have no choice but to quit. It may be in the form of shift changes, unreasonable requests, denial of time off, or other circumstances related to the employee's working conditions. It is an unlawful employment practice.

4. B. There are two basic forms of sexual harassment: hostile environment and quid pro quo. Quid pro quo means "this for that," often occurring when an employer or their representatives require something of an employee in exchange for a work benefit.

5. A. In *Harris v. Forklift Systems* the Supreme Court found that the standard for determining sexual harassment falls somewhere between that which is merely offensive and that which results in tangible psychological injury. While each case would be considered on its merits, *Harris v. Forklift Systems* gives the courts and employers the opportunity to consider all factors of the work environment in determining whether unlawful harassment has occurred.

6. D. USERRA provides several protections for reservists and other active military personnel, including the right to an escalator position upon return and the continued accrual of pension benefits.

7. C. An employment contract is most often a written agreement binding the employer and employee to a relationship for a specified period of time. A signed agreement, it spells out the job duties, rate of pay, benefits, perks, and separation terms along with many other terms and conditions of employment.

8. A. Employee relations are about the employees or, more specifically, about balancing their needs with the needs of the employer. Proper communication and meaningful feedback will aid in change management efforts and build a relationship on which organizational outcomes can be achieved.

9. C. Organizational climate and culture factors represent to an employer how and why certain things work within their organization. The ability to "feel out" the climate is built on observations and feedback. A company's mission, vision, and values help define the culture. Threaded throughout both factors are management behavior and the quality of the relationships formed by employees at all levels.

10. D. For many employees, work-life balance remains a priority, providing an opportunity for employers to respond. Compressed workweeks, telecommuting, flextime, job sharing, and part-time work are all flex scheduling options from which employers can choose to help increase employee retention.

11. A. Policies are used to communicate broad guidelines that are designed to direct organizational behavior. Procedures provide details about how to go forward in implementing the policy, and rules state what employees may or may not do to comply with the policy. In this example, the policy would prohibit unlawful harassment, the procedure would state how employees should report unlawful harassment, and the work rule would give an example of prohibited conduct, such as posting an offensive joke.

12. B. Effective employee relations programs work to prevent the need for disciplinary action. They accomplish this through clear communication and strong performance management efforts with their employees. Companies that lack an employee relations focus often rely on discipline as their only tool in effective performance management.

13. D. All of these answers can help employers avoid the cost of defending a claim of wrongful discipline or discharge. Compulsory arbitration, however, requires that, as a condition of employment, the employee agree to submit any future conflict to an arbitrator for resolution, rather than having the conflict work its way through the court system.

14. D. Mediation is often used as the first step in ADR efforts. Because it is not binding, the parties may choose to move to the next step, which is usually arbitration.

15. C. The Sherman Act was originally used to control business monopolies. It allowed companies, in relatively broad language, to sue each other to stop a specific business action, and employers used it to break strikes. In 1914, the Clayton Act was passed to limit the impact of the Sherman Act by exempting labor unions from its application.

16. C. The violence of the labor movement is often lamented as being driven by union organizers and organized crime, but it is forgotten that employers often used force to break up organizing activity, which had no real protection under the law. The passage of the National Labor Relations Act in 1935 changed that, granting workers the right to organize. It established unfair labor practices and created the National Labor Relations Board to oversee the organizing process.

17. D. A Republican majority used the Taft-Hartley Act to respond to the broad reach of President Roosevelt's New Deal initiatives. It gave a legitimate voice to employers who felt the unions had too much power.

18. A. Unfair labor practices are defined by the NLRA as unlawful practices used by employers throughout the organizing process. Threatening to shut down or move operations, intimidating employees, coercing them to vote against a union, or spying on organizing activity are all classified as unfair labor practices.

19. A. The National Labor Relations Board was created as part of the National Labor Relations Act to enforce its provisions. It responds to charges of unfair labor practices or petitions for representation through the organizing activity.

20. C. A union may petition the NLRB for an election if 30 percent or more of the employees in the anticipated bargaining unit sign authorization cards.

21. C. In August 2000, the NLRB decided a case that extended the rights guaranteed by the NLRA to temporary and contingent workers. These rights include the right to organize and the right to be free from retaliation for participating in union-organizing activities.

22. C. In positional bargaining, each side takes up a "position." This means that one side must lose something for the other side to gain. It is considered an adversarial process.

23. B. Integrative bargaining looks at all of the issues on the bargaining table, allowing for trade-offs to avoid a bargaining impasse. Principled bargaining is focused on finding mutually beneficial solutions, bargaining based on the interests of both parties as opposed to relative positions.

24. C. A collective bargaining agreement functions as a binding employment contract or agreement made on behalf of the employees by their representatives—that is, the union. A CBA may include doctrine related to membership, management, and general terms and conditions of employment.

25. D. A nonunion philosophy is an action plan, not just a statement. It outlines strategies to involve employees in the decision-making process so that they have a say in decisions that affect their pay and working conditions. If employees have a positive perception of the process, they are less inclined to vote in a group to represent them. Furthermore, pay is one of the top items at the negotiating table.

26. B. As with any type of organizational intervention, HR will be most successful when they have identified the needs of the workforce as they relate to the desired outcome. For that reason, building employee feedback systems in which to gather information about the needs is the best first step.

27. C. Absenteeism reports reflect several characteristics of job dissatisfiers, including stressed-out workers, supervisory conflicts, and the feeling of being undervalued by the company. It is one of many job satisfaction measures that include turnover, employee surveys, and customer satisfaction reports.

28. B. Tactical accountability makes use of both internal and external data to guide employer actions. HR helps to integrate these efforts into the regular day-to-day activities of the organization.

29. C. Common law doctrines are established through precedents founded through case law. Employment at-will allows either the employer or the employee to terminate the relationship at any time and for any reason other than those that are unlawful.

30. B. Employment at will allows either party to terminate the employment at any time and for any reason. However, there are specific exceptions to this doctrine. The duty of good faith and fair dealing requires that both parties have an obligation to act in a fair and honest manner in the execution of the agreement.

31. A. Promissory estoppel occurs when an employer promises an employee or potential employee a reward for an employee action and then fails to follow through on the delivery. This may result in the employer being obligated to make good on the agreement or pay equivalent damages. Contract exceptions occur when there is an employment or other type of contract that specifies the conditions under which a person may be terminated.

32. B. Respondeat superior means that an employer may be held responsible for the actions of their employees, particularly when the employee acts within the scope of their employment.

33. A. Constructive discharge occurs when an employer makes working conditions so intolerable that an employee feels that they have no other choice but to quit. It is an unlawful employment practice.

34. B. Sexual harassment is often in the eye of the beholder, and it is dependent on factors such as the severity and frequency of the conduct. The EEOC prohibits "unwelcome sexual advances, requests for sexual favors, and other verbal or physical conduct of a sexual nature," especially if it interferes with an employee's ability to do their job.

35. C. In *Faragher v. City of Boca Raton*, the Supreme Court found that employers are responsible for the actions of their employees and have a responsibility to control them. This exists even when the harassment does not result in an adverse employment action against the employee. An affirmative defense may be raised by an employer when it can show that it has a policy in place prohibiting harassment, it promptly investigates and takes appropriate action, and that employees have a grievance procedure to report claims of harassment. Without these elements, an employer may be liable for its employees' actions even when the employees are acting outside the normal scope of their employment.

36. A. The Glass Ceiling Act established a commission to determine whether a glass ceiling, that is, a barrier to senior-level positions for women and minorities, existed. They also were tasked with identifying these barriers. The commission found that there were societal, internal structural, and governmental barriers for women and minorities in employment.

37. C. The Uniformed Services Employment and Reemployment Rights Act (USERRA) grants employees on military leave the right to have their jobs back when they return. It also protects them for a period of time after they return from discharge without cause, depending on the length of their leave.

38. C. Employee involvement strategies allow employers to manage the knowledge of their human talent at all levels effectively. While employees should be allowed to develop to their fullest potential within their jobs, employers need to maximize the talent for the most efficient production of their goods or services. Delegating authority in a relevant process will allow employees to apply their talents toward the good of the company.

39. A. Part of communicating information with employees is ensuring that they receive the correct information. Without effective communication strategies like open door policies, informational staff meetings, brown bag lunches, and newsletters, the employees most often rely on the grapevine to exchange information.

40. B. A key characteristic of a skip-level interview as an employee feedback initiative is to remove the direct supervisor from the chain of communication. The goal is not to spy or play "gotcha" but rather to create an open forum that removes any perceived obstacles to the free exchange of information, increasing the content's validity as a result.

41. A. Positive employee relations strategies are more than just good business. These strategies help to foster a learning organization, where information is freely shared and discussed. If employees do not feel respected or do not trust "management," they will not provide meaningful feedback or participate in employee relations strategies.

42. C. Employee recognition programs are designed specifically to recognize the efforts of employees. Incentive programs should be self-funded and focused on desired behaviors, and diversity management programs address diversity in the workplace.

43. B. Work-life balance presents opportunities for positive employee strategies such as compressed workweeks, flex time, job sharing, and part-time work. With flex time, employees are allowed to work hours that are more suited to their personal schedules.

44. D. A reference guide is one of the many tools used to implement work procedures. It is often a compilation of data around a specific process that organizes large amounts of information into a single reference document.

45. D. An employee handbook is many things, not the least of which is a tool that communicates information in compliance with labor laws and risk management. It protects the employer on many levels. Communicating the expectations to employees through a handbook establishes those expectations, serves notice to employees where required, and establishes the guidelines for both employee rights and responsibilities.

46. B. Performance improvement from an HR perspective aligns organizational needs with employee behavior. Discipline should not be the only tool used to manage employee behavior. Employees are entitled to fair and equitable treatment and access to the resources necessary to do their jobs (employee needs). The employer requires employees to perform to the minimum standards of behavior.

47. A. Alternative dispute resolution (ADR) is a group of methods used to solve litigation without legal intervention. They may be part of employment contracts, CBAs, and employee handbooks, with parties agreeing to utilize one or more of these methods should a dispute arise.

48. B. A peer review panel is a technique used to solve disputes that arise in an employment relationship. A panel is assembled using employees and managers who have been trained in the company's policies, procedures, and rules, and who make decisions that can be binding to both parties.

49. D. An effective absenteeism policy communicates the standards to the employees and shares with the employees what they can expect when they miss work.

50. C. Terminating an employee requires careful analysis of the specifics of each case. Specifically with regard to absenteeism, employees may be protected under the FMLA or ADA. There are a few circumstances, however, in which the danger presented to the employer or other employees is greater than the risk of wrongful termination, such as theft, violence, or illegal acts.

51. D. HR is often tasked with creating a toolbox of resources for employees and managers to use in the day-to-day operations of the company. Discipline is most often used to help manage the performance—or lack of performance—of individual workers.

52. C. Weingarten rights were granted by the NLRB in response to a case where an employee was investigated and interrogated without the representation of her union. This established that employers who fail to allow union representation at a meeting where discipline is likely to occur have committed an unfair labor practice.

53. B. Not all employers will offer benefits or be required to comply with the Family Medical Leave Act. The at-will policy statement, however, protects the right of the employer and the employee to terminate the relationship at any time and for any lawful reason.

54. C. Inclusiveness is a necessary part of an employee involvement strategy, particularly in a diverse workgroup. A brainstorming session gives equal opportunity to the talent, seeking to merge the project needs with the abilities of the department.

55. C. Positive employee relations strategies, such as special events, recognition, and diversity, all help to promote a positive organizational culture. They do so by recognizing shared accomplishments, celebrating successes, and including all degrees of diverse thinking that must exist for an organization to compete effectively.

56. D. An employee management committee can be an effective way to engage in participative management techniques. It can be used to solve problems (such as a load configuration committee), coordinate interdepartmental efforts (such as in a merger), and allow for employee input on decisions that affect their work. However, the prudent employer understands how best to structure the committee to avoid a claim of an unfair labor practice.

57. A. Due process is a legal concept that in the context of employment protects an employee's right to fair treatment, particularly when there are established procedures in place regarding discipline. It is considered a best-interest practice to help protect employers from claims of wrongful discipline or discharge.

58. D. Economic strikes are those that are called in an effort to obtain better pay, hours, or working conditions from the employer. They are lawful strikes.

59. D. Employers must take care to not violate the National Labor Relations Act by interfering with employees' right to organize. This includes discriminating against an employee for participating in union activities.

60. B. Featherbedding is an unfair labor practice in which unions require more employees than are necessary to do the work.

61. C. Union avoidance strategies begin with noticing the first signs. Unusual or secretive congregating employees, aggressive complaints about working conditions or wages, strangers in the company parking lot, and union slogans are all signs of potential union-organizing activity.

62. D. If an employer intentionally or unintentionally accepts evidence that a majority of the employees have signed union authorization cards, it may result in the employer voluntarily recognizing the union, losing their ability to present their case to employees prior to a formal election. A demand for recognition usually occurs once a union has a sufficient number of signed authorization cards. It is important that the person who is presented with the demand letter does not respond in a way that could be construed as recognizing the union as the bargaining agent. A neutrality agreement is an agreement from the employer not to say or do anything to oppose the union, and a card check election means that the employer agrees to recognize the union based on the number of signed authorization cards.

63. C. There are many tactics unions use to begin the organizing process. Of them, few are as effective as having an existing employee working from within, using their influence and company knowledge to encourage participation in the organizing efforts.

64. D. Within seven days after a union election has been directed by the National Labor Relations Board, employers are required to provide the union with a list of employee names and addresses.

65. A. Union security clauses require members of the union to provide financial support to the union, usually through the payment of dues. In a union shop, employees are required to join a union within a grace period after hire. In an agency shop, all employees must either join the union or pay dues if they choose not to join. In a closed shop, new hires must join the union prior to being hired.

66. B. Employee relations activities are specifically geared toward increasing employee job satisfaction. This can be measured by using techniques such as ROI, turnover, and absenteeism analysis.

67. D. Employee surveys are designed to gather information about both the culture and the climate. Both of those factors are based on subjective interpretations of the receiver, but are no less important than objective analysis.

68. A. Tactical accountability measures are those that measure the effectiveness of employee relations activities on the overall application of ER strategies. Measuring these outcomes can be difficult, as it is often necessary to attempt to quantify the risk avoidance efforts.

69. A. The concept of exclusive jurisdiction is simply the assignment of one union over a group of workers, such as craft workers or commercial drivers. Exclusive jurisdiction is a principle in which unions do not attempt to organize a group that is already represented by another union.

70. D. The Worker Adjustment and Retraining Notification Act was passed primarily to protect workers by requiring some employers to provide 60 days' notice of covered plant closings and covered mass layoffs.

71. A. The Sherman Anti-Trust Act was designed to prohibit business monopolies, which included any sort of business relationship that restricted trade. The courts ruled that strikes and boycotts were covered by this mandate.

72. B. In *NLRB vs. Sturgis*, the courts established that a union can organize a bargaining unit of an employer's regular employees and temporary employees, but only if both the employer and the staffing agency consent.

73. D. Many companies and unions are finding that a cooperative approach to the shared responsibilities for employees is more effective than the adversarial efforts of the past. In a joint management initiative, unions offer skills and compliance training and health and safety inspections as part of their services.

74. B. Of the list presented, the best reason an employer may use workplace surveillance is to protect employees and other stakeholders from unauthorized access to sensitive data.

75. C. Both employee rights and responsibilities are governed by case law and statutes. Employee rights include the right to a work environment free from harassment and the right to vote. Employee responsibilities include the duty of diligence, the duty of obedience, and the duty of loyalty.

76. A. Handbooks are often written from the perspective of managing risk for an employer. As a result, many handbooks are not written at an appropriate reading level for employees.

77. C. The needs of employers and employees vary from company to company and even from worksite to worksite. For this reason, HR should make an honest attempt to communicate the handbook and accompanying polices in a way that best serves the needs of the employer/employee relationship.

78. C. An HR audit can be used for several purposes, all of which are named here. In risk management, however, the primary purpose is to analyze an organization's business practices to identify and mitigate/eliminate risks.

79. D. The term *risk management* is often used interchangeably with the term *safety*. However, risk management in an organization seeks to identify risks in all facets of human resource management, not just compliance with the Occupational Safety and Health Act.

80. A. The Occupational Safety and Health Act established responsibilities of employers in three main areas. Employers must provide a workplace free from recognized hazards that may cause death or serious injury, employers must comply with safety and health standards, and employers must comply with standards/regulations that affect their individual actions and behavior.

81. D. The OSH Act of 1970 established three permanent agencies: NIOSH, OSHA, and OSHRC. All three are charged with furthering the safety and health rights of American workers. NIOSH conducts safety and health research, OSHA creates and enforces safety and health standards, and OSHRC is an independent agency that adjudicates enforcement actions brought by employers.

82. A. The primary purpose of requiring employers to document certain types of injuries and illnesses is to identify and respond to emerging trends. Records include exposures to hazardous substances, documentation of safety training, and OSHA logs that record injuries and illnesses.

83. B. The Mine Safety and Health Act established mandatory safety and health standards for mine operators and the monitoring of mine operations throughout the United States. Similar to OSHA, it seeks to conduct research and provide resources that enhance the safety and health of mine workers.

84. C. There are three types of environmental health hazards: chemical, physical, and biological. Chemical hazards are those that put an employee into contact with potentially hazardous substances. Physical hazards are those that could cause physical or bodily harm, such as slips, trips, or fall conditions, to an employee. Biological hazards are those that affect the bodily systems, such as bacteria or contaminated water.

85. A. In a risk assessment of security, human resources professionals address four types of risks: financial, physical, informational, and human. Information assets can be compromised at all four levels. For example, employees can leak confidential information (human), hackers can break into a company database (physical), or a fire could erupt, damaging records (financial).

86. C. Business continuity planning is the act of developing, monitoring, and implementing systems to respond to unplanned events. It focuses largely on containment of hazards and steps to continue critical business operations as needed.

87. C. Workplace violence policies and procedures are put into place to help managers recognize the signs of stress and offer solutions where appropriate.

88. A. Administering effective RTW solutions can help the employee transition back into their job and reduce the overall cost of a workers' compensation claim. Modified duty assignments that align the employee's work with their specific medical restrictions will allow employees to return to work sooner rather than later.

89. B. Employer security issues are many and include the need for data protection, protecting both employees and customers from identity theft, and compliance with the Electronic Communications Privacy Act of 1986.

90. A. Employees have a reasonable expectation of privacy in the workplace. This is established based on factors such as privacy policies and precedent. Any monitoring of electronic media must be in accordance with the law and be communicated to the affected employees via a policy statement.

91. C. Assessing business continuity risks includes the creation of plans that respond to a crisis throughout specific phases. It begins with a plan to direct employees at the time of a crisis and includes OSHA's emergency action plan. This is followed by a disaster recovery plan and then a continuity of operations plan. All plans must be regularly maintained and communicated.

92. B. An independent medical exam is useful for employers who want to determine whether an injured worker is fit to return to work. Impartiality is important to help prevent fraud and to deal with the challenges that are presented through improper diagnosis or treatment.

93. D. Substance abuse policies are merely written words if they lack support from top management. They are part of a broader program that may include the types of drug screening that the employee may expect on the job and the return-to-work process.

94. A. Legal risks have a broad reach, which are threaded throughout all HR activities. Compliance with labor laws, including those regulating safety and health, workplace privacy, staffing, and training, are all part of the scope of risk assessment in HR.

95. B. There are several different types of tools available to HR to use in assessing risk. In this scenario, a prompt and thorough investigation can help assess the risk and direct the employer response.

96. D. There are several forms of work-life discrimination that can occur in the workplace. Giving favor to a male candidate over a female candidate based on perceived future performance is a form of disparate treatment that falls within the category of caregiver or childcare discrimination.

97. B. Employers that have federal contracts in excess of $100,000 must follow specific guidelines regarding substance abuse in the workplace. These guidelines include developing a written policy, establishing an awareness program, and notifying contracting agencies of violations of illegal drug offenses.

98. A. The National Institute of Occupational Safety and Health is part of the Department of Health and Human Services. It is charged with researching and evaluating workplace hazards and recommending ways to reduce the effect of those hazards on workers.

99. B. Employers are required to record all work-related illnesses and injuries that fall within certain guidelines. According to OSHA standard 1904.5, an employer is not required to record an injury or illness when it occurs to an employee who was present in the workplace as a member of the general public.

100. A. OSHA establishes inspection priorities based on the nature and severity of the hazard for employees. Imminent danger classifications are considered high priority and exist when there is reasonable certainty that immediate death or serious injury may occur as a result of the hazard.

101. B. An OSHA inspection takes place in three parts: the opening conference, the facility tour, and the closing conference. During the facility tour, the employer can be expected to provide copies of any written safety and health programs and records, such as OSHA logs and employee exposures to hazards.

102. C. Biological hazards are those that affect the employee through exposure to bacteria, fungi, viruses, molds, and other detrimental environmental health hazards.

103. C. Training is not always the best solution to abate workplace hazards. When an employee has an injury or potential injury, the first step must always be to address the welfare of the individual by offering immediate medical care. A workstation evaluation and subsequent ergonomics training may be recommended afterward to prevent similar injuries from occurring in the future.

104. C. An employer's ergonomic injury rate can be calculated to assess the success of prevention efforts. Measuring an EIR both before and after safety training or assessment efforts will help determine business impact. The EIR is calculated by dividing the total number of hours worked by all employees during the period (700,000) by the total number of injuries multiplied by 200,000 (7,000,000).

105. A. Although workers' compensation laws have been expanded from their original intent, the primary purpose was to ensure that workers received medical care and other types of compensation should they be injured on the job.

106. C. State laws can vary from federal law in many ways, particularly in the area of leave management. However, under federal law, employers may run the 12 weeks of unpaid leave an eligible employee is entitled to under the Family Medical Leave Act along with any time off for a work-related injury/illness.

107. A. Modified duty is typically a short-term solution for injured workers to allow them to return to work with restrictions. Employers are not obligated to offer modified assignments. Reasonable accommodation is typically a longer-term solution that may be required in accordance with the Americans with Disabilities Act.

108. D. An employer who utilizes modified duty must be aware that the practices used to accommodate an injured worker may also have to be used to accommodate a disabled worker.

109. A. The Fair Labor Standards Act was the first regulation that established guidelines for the use of child labor. The act included descriptions of hazardous conditions for minors.

110. D. A risk assessment is a highly useful tool that can be tailored to identify specific types of threats that can occur against an employer. These threats may include threats against the safety and health of employees, the presence of any union-organizing activity, and risks associated with being out of compliance with various labor laws.

111. C. An audit of the employer's selection practices focuses on risks associated with legal compliance in employer selection procedures. These risks include the proper use of reliable and valid pre-employment tests that do not result in disparate impact against protected-class groups.

112. B. As with many risks associated with business, having written plans and procedures prior to their need is a best practice. Such resources may be consulted for input, and any training needs can be identified (and implemented) as needed.

113. D. Biometric data are built around employee characteristics that are difficult to falsify. They include facial recognition, retina scans, and fingerprints.

114. C. There are currently no specific OSHA standards for occupational heat exposure at the federal level. However, under the General Duty clause, Section 5(a)(1) of the Occupational Safety and Health Act (OSHA) of 1970, employers are required to provide their employees with a place of employment that "is free from recognizable hazards that are causing or likely to cause death or serious harm to employees."

115. A. There are many variables that affect the safety standards that must be applied at a place of work. These variables include industry- and state-specific requirements as well as the nature and frequency of hazards. For this reason, a formal risk assessment will help you identify hazards and research the laws that outline safety responsibilities.

116. B. The primary goal of any health and safety self-inspection is to identify and correct hazards to prevent an incident.

117. B. Personal protective equipment is generally a last step toward eliminating/reducing a safety hazard.

118. C. Ergonomic injuries are most likely to occur in jobs that require repetitive motion. This includes long-term exposure to vibration.

119. B. OSHA recommends that employers conduct job hazard analyses to identify both hazards and controls. Administrative controls include written policies, procedures, rules, signage, and training.

120. C. OSHA defines the direct cause of injuries as the "unplanned release of energy...." In this case, the force of the contact between the forklift and the driver's ankle was more than his ankle could absorb.

121. A. Part of accident and injury investigations includes determining the direct and indirect causes. OSHA defines indirect causes as unsafe acts or unsafe conditions. In this case, that would be the employee's lack of attention while operating the forklift.

122. D. The first priority when responding to a workplace incident is to secure the area so no other injuries may occur.

123. B. Group bias is a real concern for accident investigators. To avoid contamination of what really happened, it is a best practice to separate the witnesses and interview them one on one.

124. D. The purpose of a written injury and illness prevention plan is to communicate the top-level commitment of the executive team to an overall safety management system. The plan will describe the elements of this program, including a commitment to regular hazard analyses and preventative efforts to reduce worker exposure, along with a description of safety meetings or trainings to prevent injury.

125. B. The narrative method of performance appraisals requires a more descriptive approach to documenting employee performance. Variations on this method include essays or critical incident reviews.

126. D. There are many different ways employers may choose to time the delivery of performance feedback. The most common include after the introductory period is complete, quarterly, and annually.

127. C. This is not a recordable injury because the employee received first-aid treatment only and was able to return to work on his next scheduled work day. OSHA does not require employers to count the day of the injury.

128. D. Discrimination becomes unlawful when it is based on non–job-related criteria such as gender, age, or religious affiliation. Simply being in a position of authority over a romantic interest does not automatically mean that the supervisor is discriminating.

129. A. A valid, nondiscriminatory, and effective performance appraisal process takes into account job-related behaviors and improvement feedback.

130. C. The halo/horn bias occurs during performance appraisals when competence in one area serves as the primary behavior in a performance review, often to the exclusion of negative behaviors.

Chapter 6: PHR Practice Exam

1. A. Lagging economic indicators confirm that a change has already happened in an economy, such as the unemployment rate. Leading indicators are signs that predict a change in the economy, such as the forecasting of a rise or fall in interest rates.

2. A. Anchoring bias occurs when greater weight is given to the first piece of information received. In salary negotiations, this would occur when the applicant asks for a high salary amount, thus fixing (anchoring) that amount as the starting point for negotiations.

3. C. Demographic data is used to make many types of organizational decisions, from recruiting sources to the types of benefits a company should offer. This type of data is often communicated in statistics, such as age, gender, income, or ethnic background.

4. D. Forecasting is a planning tool used to predict future outcomes based on data. It can be used to drive data-based decisions that—while imperfect—can narrow the target for planning purposes.

5. B. Cascading goals are those that flow from the top down. These goals are further cascaded when each department then creates individual goals based on the desired organizational outcomes.

6. C. A company's mission statement describes the primary purpose of an organization. In this case, Zappos defines itself less as an online retailer and more by its commitment to customer service.

7. A. Modular organizational structures are less traditional than their counterparts. What makes modular structures different is that many of the components are outsourced, and stakeholders (suppliers, customers) often become part of the "whole" organization.

8. D. The operations function of a business is responsible for producing the goods or delivering the services of an organization. Many companies use the term *production* to refer to its business operations unit.

9. A. Return on investment is a financial formula HR may use to evaluate the financial success (or failure) of an intervention, strategy, or program. It uses inputs such as total expenses and compares them to outcomes. HR may use this to look back on the value of a program or to forecast the benefit of taking on a new project.

10. D. Recruiting sources may come from within the organization or outside. When jobs are filled internally, employees are moved from one job to another.

11. B. Growing in popularity, paid volunteer time-off policies are used by employers to encourage employees to serve in the communities where they work.

12. B. In *Griggs v. Duke Power*, the courts found that an employer's use of an otherwise neutral employment "test"—in this case a high school diploma requirement—was a discriminatory practice because it resulted in under-representation of a protected-class group.

13. B. The job description is the readable form of all the data collected during the job analysis process. It includes a summary of the job, the job competencies, and the specifications necessary in order to perform the essential functions in a satisfactory manner.

14. D. The Americans with Disabilities Act (ADA) defines essential functions as those that are the primary reason for the existence of the job. In identifying what is essential, employers may consider the percentage of time spent on each task, the frequency of the task (daily, weekly, etc.) and how important the task is to the overall purpose.

15. B. Insourcing occurs when an employer brings in services that it used to outsource. It is an event that HR will need to help manage via many activities of workforce planning, including job design, recruitment, and selection.

16. C. Job design has impacts on both the organization through efficiencies and the employee by increasing job satisfaction. In job enlargement, an employee's current job responsibilities are expanded, generally without a change in status or increase in pay.

17. A. The process of formalization involves sorting and grouping a job's tasks, duties, and responsibilities by conducting job analyses.

18. D. Judgmental forecasts involve the use of historical and present data to anticipate future conditions. Managers may be called upon to estimate based on their expertise, or general "rules of thumb" may be applied to this planning activity.

19. B. Moving employees from one location or one job to another can be an effective way to avoid layoffs. In workforce planning, it is important that HR look at the whole staffing picture to avoid hiring in one department while laying off in others. While not a perfect strategy every time, it can be effective for managing workforce imbalances.

20. C. Many HR professionals are solo practitioners and must find ways to outsource tasks to make time for other responsibilities. Recruiting and selection can be time-consuming, so outsourcing it to a professional staffing agency may be a good strategy under these circumstances.

21. A. A workforce plan is part of an overall human resource strategy that serves to identify the gap between the skillsets of the current employees and the skillsets needed to achieve organizational goals.

22. B. Talent management refers to the selection and cultivation of talent throughout the employee life cycle. It begins with actively integrating new hires into their roles within the organization and continues through the development of new skills as necessary.

23. C. Training interventions are often a useful way to help employers achieve their strategic goals. For this reason, it is often useful to begin with the training objectives in mind, allowing for training design that will effectively target those goals.

24. B. Employee development plans must take into consideration not only what the employee needs but how those needs align with the company strategy. Needs assessments allow the company to identify the skillsets of current workers and plan for the development (or recruiting) for the future.

25. A. A task analysis is used when building training content to compare the needs of the job with the skillsets of the workers. In this way, instructional designers may be more likely to design training that is effectively transferred to the job.

26. B. A gap analysis focuses on the areas in between current and desired states. In training, it is used to build training objectives with content that addresses the gap (or gaps). In organizational development, a gap analysis may be used to generate intervention strategies to take a company from current to desired future state.

27. B. A performance improvement plan (PIP) is used to support employees struggling with performance while also holding them accountable to past behavior and future outcomes. Future discipline, re-training, and possible termination are all elements that may be written into the action items of a PIP.

28. D. There is not a one-size-fits-all solution to increasing diversity in hiring practices. Modifying education or experience requirements can encourage more diverse candidates to apply. Using keyword searches such as *women in tech* can increase visibility of underrepresented groups, and ensuring you use diverse sources for advertising can help improve the results of an employer's hiring practices.

29. A. Studies have shown that women tend to only apply for jobs for which they are an exact fit. Onerous experience requirements that are not absolutely necessary may discourage women from applying for a job.

30. D. Individuals generally will act in response to intrinsic or extrinsic motivators. Intrinsic motivators are those that come from within and include personal or job satisfaction or taking pride in their work.

31. C. Autonomy is similar to empowerment in that employees are permitted the freedom to act independently when making decisions about their jobs. Hackman and Oldham identified autonomy as one of the factors that lead to job satisfaction.

32. D. According to Hackman and Oldham's job characteristic model, offering employees feedback on how well or how poorly they are performing gives them a sense of ownership and responsibility for their job outcomes.

33. B. Herzberg's studies found that job satisfiers and dissatisfiers are not opposites, nor do they even exist on the same continuum. He found that what satisfies employees and what dissatisfies employees act independently of one another.

34. A. B.F. Skinner believed that all individual behavior occurs in response to conditioning. When we are conditioned through reward (recognition, food, money) or punishment (removal of something desired or strong consequences), we act in ways that will deliver (or avoid) the expected result.

35. C. Instructional design is about much more than writing training content. The process must address the needs identified through the training needs assessment, the desired outcomes of training, and the logistics (method, location, etc.) of the training sessions themselves.

36. A. Effective instructional design relies on a systematic approach that first identifies the training needs. In the ADDIE model, this *analysis* phase establishes the benchmarks from which the *design* and *development* stages may begin. After content has been developed and logistics defined, training may be *implemented* and eventually *evaluated* for effectiveness.

37. C. The focus of any training design must be on the transfer of learning, and there are many ways an instructional designer may achieve this. In customized training, content is most often built from scratch to accommodate specific training outcomes or work environments. Tailored training is a bit simpler in that it takes existing off-the-shelf content and modifies it to suit the participants and outcomes.

38. B. Proprietary rights refer to ownership of all property, including that of an intellectual nature. Licensing occurs when the property owner grants the licensee permission to use the content in the manner agreed upon. This means paying the per-seat (or per-license) fees in accordance with the provider's policy.

39. C. Synchronous learning is a type of e-learning in which training is conducted online and participants interact at the same time.

40. C. Micro-learning is characterized by short bursts of content delivery, often through the use of videos. Content must be narrowly tailored with clear learning outcomes, which makes this training easy to sort and order into a training database for easy access and modification. It also helps make updating content easier.

41. C. On-the-job training (OJT) occurs when a trainee receives instruction while working, usually from a trainer or more experienced employee.

42. D. Simulation training is an interactive training method that is designed to provide realistic opportunities for trainees to practice the necessary skills without endangering co-workers or the public.

43. B. Classroom-based training can be an effective way to communicate to small groups of trainees. The face-to-face instruction allows for questions and answers, while the classroom setting is conducive to formal presentations.

44. D. Performance management is a process that includes setting goals, measuring progress, and providing regular informal and formal feedback to employees. Performance management may include a formal appraisal and development plan, all three of which are part of a robust talent management system.

45. D. Having a performance system in place that is fair to all employees requires multiple elements. Supervisors must understand the nature and types of natural bias and be trained to avoid discriminatory practices. The performance instruments and rating systems must be valid and job-related. Job descriptions must be relevant, accurate, and up to date to ensure that employers are measuring what should be measured.

46. C. To calculate turnover, divide the number of terminated employees by the total number hired within that same period and then multiply the result by 100 to achieve a percentage. In this example, it would be $15/50 = 0.3 \times 100 = 30\%$.

47. C. A progress review is a type of performance evaluation that is informal. It involves regularly reviewing an employee's progress toward goals and providing recommendations for improvements as needed.

48. D. Rensis Likert developed an easy system for creating scales on performance reviews. It may be numerical or response-based. A disadvantage is that not all supervisors have the same interpretation of the scales, creating inconsistency in ratings between both supervisors and employees. An advantage is that it provides for more consistent responses than narrative forms of review.

49. A. Forced distribution is an employee evaluation system in which supervisors are "forced" to group employees in a certain way, and most often compared against others in the same work group.

50. D. The Department of Labor made significant changes to the Family Medical Leave Act in 2008. Among those changes, employers may require the use of all accrued time and they may deny any perfect attendance awards to those whose FMLA time disqualifies them, so long as they also do so for non-FMLA leaves. The 2008 final rule also clarified that light-duty work assignments may not be counted as time off under the FMLA.

51. D. By passing the Family Medical Leave Act, Congress effectively addressed the job security needs of employees who need to care for a sick family member. It required employers with 50 or more employees to provide up to 12 weeks of unpaid leave to eligible employees.

52. B. The IRS established the standard by which employers may be considered an "applicable large employer" for purposes of complying with the various elements of the PPACA. It applies to employers with at least 50 full-time employees in the preceding calendar year.

53. A. The original intent of the Equal Pay Act was to address gender inequality in pay between women and men doing the same work.

54. C. Willful violators of the requirements under the Fair Labor Standards Act may face criminal charges as well as fines of up to $10,000.

55. C. The Portal to Portal Act was an amendment to the Fair Labor Standards Act. It clarified what was—and was not—compensable time for purposes of calculating wages and overtime for nonexempt employees. This included the requirement to pay employees for time spent putting on company equipment or uniforms.

56. B. There are many competing demands on how long payroll records should be retained by employers. The Equal Employment Opportunity Commission, the Fair Labor Standards Act, and the Age Discrimination in Employment Act all require that payroll records be kept for three years.

57. C. Many employees who leave a company for better pay do so at the expense of the total value of their employment with their current company. By utilizing a hidden paycheck—a statement that outlines the total value of an employee's pay when non-salary options are included—employees may better understand what they are actually gaining (or losing) by leaving.

58. D. The employee burden should be understood for HR to create accurate budgets. This refers to the additional costs to employee base wages that is made up from benefits and taxes.

59. C. The decision to outsource the important task of payroll requires much assessment. Because employees depend upon their paychecks being delivered accurately, how the vendor will handle any mistakes should be of significant importance when choosing a service.

60. A. A defined benefit plan is one in which the participants know exactly how much the employer will contribute to their retirement funds. It could be paid in a lump-sum payment or as regular recurring payments.

61. B. In a contributory plan, both the employer and the employee may make retirement contributions.

62. B. An employer work-life balance program is an excellent way to offer expanded benefits to workers. Programs such as unlimited time off and alternative work schedules are increasing in popularity as the workforce needs are changing.

63. D. Many types of insurance premiums are based upon the likelihood that an employer will experience more claims than similar employers in their industry. Employers with higher incidents of employee injuries, higher use of state unemployment insurance, and more claims made under Employment Practices Liability Insurance will result in an employer paying more for their policies.

64. C. Employee benefits may be either mandated and voluntary. Mandatory benefits include the employer paying into an employee's Social Security account via a tax on payroll and carrying insurance for an individual who gets injured on the job.

65. B. As with all HR activities, offering benefits carries with it a certain degree of risk. Benefits specialists should understand both existing and emerging labor laws related to the administration of benefits.

66. C. It seems that health insurance costs have continued to rise over the last several years, prompting employers to look for ways to save. HR, as a true business partner, should be armed with information before recommending any cost savings strategy. For benefits, this includes conducting needs assessments to ensure company health insurance is doing what it is designed to do—attract and retain qualified workers.

67. C. While higher wages are attractive to employees, they are considered taxable income. Many benefits, however, have better tax treatment, and thus $1 in benefits is often taxed at a lower rate (if at all) than $1 in wages.

68. D. The term *strategy* defines how an employer is able to compete in their relevant market. It may include how they compete with their competition via differentiation or cost leadership but also how they compete for skilled workers.

69. D. Employer benefits can take on many forms. The most popular seem to be health insurance and retirement offerings, although company housing, gym memberships, and other lifestyle benefits are also used by employers to attract and retain employees.

70. B. Incentive pay is a form of indirect compensation that can be monetary or nonmonetary. Incentive pay is often used to reward or motivate individual employees.

71. D. While not many, there are conditions under which employers may pay employees less than minimum wage. Employers may obtain a certificate from the Department of Labor that authorizes them to pay full-time students enrolled in vocational education programs less than the federal minimum wage.

72. A. Direct compensation is payments made directly to exempt and nonexempt workers in the form of base pay. In most cases, base pay must be tied to minimum wage laws.

73. D. With the increasing responsibilities of human resources, it becomes necessary to rely on multiple resources. This is particularly true for smaller HR departments that still must meet the very real and important task of managing employee compensation. Strategies such as training supervisors on timekeeping, adopting employee self-service programs, and outsourcing payroll may all be helpful.

74. B. As with most HR program delivery, technology has had a significant impact on the ability of companies to control the cost of compensation and benefits programs. Both direct deposit and self-service systems can help reduce processing time, leaving HR free to conduct the highly valuable face-to-face activities required of a functioning department.

75. B. HR professionals are held to a higher standard, having fiduciary responsibility to a company's stakeholders. Making business decisions based on personal preferences would be an example of a breach of that responsibility.

76. D. Minimum wage is only one of the various conditions that affect employee pay rates. Often, state, city, or regional locations have prevailing wage requirements that the employer must comply with. Collective bargaining agreements often include minimum rates of pay for certain bargaining units or job classifications.

77. D. Head count is the term used to communicate the number of employees an employer has on their payroll at any given time.

78. A. Constructive discharge occurs when an employer or its representatives makes conditions intolerable enough that a reasonable person feels they have no choice other than to quit.

79. B. Qualified privilege protects employers that provide former workers with references, provided that the information is job-related, truthful, and clear.

80. A. Employees who do not trust the employer procedures used to make decisions about pay indicates that there is a real (or perceived) lack of internal equity in the pay system.

81. C. Competency-based pay is a reliable format to use when building legally compliant pay systems. Salaries that are based on employee skills and knowledge necessary to complete job tasks is a nondiscriminatory way to pay employees.

82. B. Pay compression occurs when the pay levels of current employees do not increase at the same pace as the external market. When a similar position opens, the difference between new-hire pay and tenured employee pay is "compressed," or small.

83. D. Pay scales—also called *wage ranges*—offer many benefits to employers. By establishing a baseline for each position and then building in the minimum and maximum pay rates, the employer may discriminate based on differences in labor markets, individual education, work experience, or other competencies related to the job.

84. B. In a quartile compensation strategy system, employers base their pay rates on what other employers in the labor market are doing. By paying less than 75 percent of employers in the area, they are lagging behind the labor market.

85. C. HR professionals have many government resources available to use to make decisions that affect employee pay levels. The Consumer Price Index (CPI) program produces monthly data on changes in the prices paid by consumers that can help employers determine cost-of-living pay increases.

86. D. Pay equity is an important issue for HR to address, but it does not require that employers pay exactly the same rate to all employees with the same or similar job titles. However, employers must be able to demonstrate the nondiscriminatory reasons for pay disparity. This may include different levels of skill, effort, responsibility, and working conditions.

87. A. Variable pay is pay that is not guaranteed but rather contingent upon certain conditions being met. Examples include commissions, piece rate, and bonus systems.

88. B. Total rewards is the term used to categorize the business tools available to attract, motivate, and retain employees. These programs may include a combination of financial and nonfinancial elements.

89. D. Employers with at least 50 full-time or full-time-equivalent employees must comply with the Patient Protection and Affordable Care Act's shared responsibility obligations. This may include employees who work at least 30 hours of service each week in a calendar year, an employee who works at least 130 hours of service each month in a calendar year, or any combination of employees, each of whom individually is not a full-time employee but who, in combination, are equivalent to a full-time employee.

90. C. The Labor Management Relations Act prohibited unions from refusing to hire non-union members. Agency shops in which unions require employees who do not join the union to still pay union dues are allowed in states that do not have right-to-work laws.

91. A. There are three main bargaining subjects as defined by the National Labor Relations Act. Mandatory subjects must be included in the final agreement and include overtime, paid holidays, seniority arrangements, and the grievance resolution process.

92. C. There are degrees of HR's involvement during the collective bargaining process, from gathering data to negotiating terms. HR does not play a role in the union/members communicating or ratifying a vote.

93. D. Section 8 of the National Labor Relations Act defines both employer and union unfair labor practices (ULP). Neither the employer or its representatives nor the union or its representatives may discriminate against individuals for either participating in or declining to participate in union organizing or bargaining activities.

94. C. "Hot cargo" agreements occur when a union and an employer agree to not require union members to handle goods or services that come from a nonunion employer or subcontractor. The National Labor Relations Board does allow union members to refuse to cross picket lines of employers whose workers are on a lawful, primary strike.

95. D. A supervisor must be in a position of responsibility in practice, not just title. This would include the ability to hire, fire, demote, promote, and make decisions about scheduling or pay.

96. B. Bargaining units must be made up of individuals with shared interests concerning wages, working conditions, and hours. The National Labor Relations Board defines employees who meet these conditions as a community of interest, and the community is thus recognized as a lawful bargaining unit.

97. C. While only 30 percent of campaign cards during union organizing will force an election, unions often seek to exceed the 50 percent mark to demand that the employer voluntarily recognize the wishes of its employees by formally recognizing the union without a secret ballot election.

98. B. Picketing occurs when the union and its members gather outside a place of business with signs to draw attention to an issue. It can be done as a political activity or to protest an employer's practices.

99. D. Salting is a union-organizing technique in which the union sends in an individual to apply for jobs for which they are qualified. These "salts" have the intention to attempt to organize a union campaign against your company.

100. A. Bannering is a union-organizing technique in which the union places obvious signs, such as banners or logos, outside your place of business. The technique is designed to advertise a message about your company.

101. B. The Labor-Management Reporting and Disclosure Act (LMRDA) protects the rights of union members. It was in response to many of the corrupt union practices that caused harm to the members and went legislatively unchecked. In this case, the LMRDA protects union member rights to nominate union members for office, to vote, and to attend union meetings.

102. A. The National Labor Relations Act (NLRA) was passed in 1935 to protect the rights of workers to organize a union to bargain collectively.

103. D. HR is often tasked with investigating complaints of employee wrongdoing and thus must be careful to engage in investigative best practices. This includes remaining neutral, seeking data that is legally defensible via documentation, and evaluating when a workplace condition may have contributed to the behavior.

104. C. The National Labor Relations Board grants employees the right to participate in concerted protected activity. This includes the right to discuss wages and working conditions among themselves, face to face or through their social media accounts.

105. D. There are several types of alternative dispute resolution that are nonbinding, meaning the findings are recommendations as opposed to absolute. These nonbinding ADR methods include judicial arbitration, voluntary mediation, and mini-trials.

106. A. The process of employee separation requires a great deal of compliance with various labor laws. The Consolidated Omnibus Budget Reconciliation Act (COBRA) requires that separating employees be notified of their rights to continue health care coverage.

107. A. The Worker Adjustment and Retraining Notification Act (WARN) was designed to help transition employees of large employers when there will be a plant layoff or closing.

108. B. Moonlighting policies in employment handbooks serve to outline employer expectations for employees who have a second job in addition to full-time employment with the organization.

109. D. There are many legal land mines that HR must take care to avoid when drafting a compliant employee handbook. The handbook should be written using language that does not unintentionally create an express or implied contract by diluting or eliminating employment at will.

110. D. Many employee handbooks include a code of conduct that describes some of the more baseline expectations for employee behaviors. More often than not, this includes physical altercations, fighting, theft, and insubordination as prohibited conduct.

111. C. An employee handbook is a manual that helps a company organize and distribute information to employees. In many cases, the policies, procedures, and benefits contained in an employee handbook serve to comply with various labor laws as well.

112. C. HR is often tasked with finding practical strategies to help bridge the gap in communication preferences across age groups in the workplace. In this case, adopting reasonable standards of communication and meeting etiquette by asking employees to refrain from texting is appropriate.

113. B. With up to four generations of employees in the workforce of today, it stands to reason that there will be some generational communication challenges. Because a younger workforce has a communication preference for mobile devices, it may be helpful to train all employees on generational preferences and management expectations.

114. C. A grievance is a formal complaint from an employee, usually to their union. HR is often tasked to work with the union to respond and work toward resolution in accordance with the collective bargaining agreement.

115. A. It is not lawful for an employer or any of their representatives to make decisions about hiring based on protected-class characteristics. This includes both gender and age.

116. D. Many employers and the employee unions have realized that working together produces shared rewards. A labor-management cooperative strategy is one way that these groups can form partnerships that serve all stakeholders as opposed to a single group's interest or agenda.

117. B. Respondeat superior stands for "let the master answer." It is used to hold an employer responsible for the actions of employees that occur within the scope of the assigned duties.

118. A. The Equal Employment Opportunity Commission (EEOC) is responsible for enforcing antidiscrimination laws, including those that protect older workers, such as the Age Discrimination in Employment Act (ADEA) and its amendment, the Older Workers Benefit Protection Act (OWBPA).

119. C. Slight spelling variations are not an automatic Form I-9 error. Employers may accept documents with spelling variations provided they are satisfied that the document otherwise appears genuine and the employee has a reasonable explanation for the difference.

120. C. Task forces are often used in an ad hoc fashion to address specific issues that may or may not have been planned. Task forces are an opportunity to solve critical business problems while giving high-potential employees the opportunity to use their talents in meaningful ways.

121. B. Self-directed work teams can be highly effective as an employee relations strategy. This structure is dependent upon autonomy and the organizational capabilities of team members.

122. C. Any type of intervention strategy should seek to align with organizational strategy, often communicated via the strategic plan. In this way, HR can generate positive employee relations activities that serve culture initiatives, training and development initiatives, business growth initiatives, or any example of what a business may need to steadily focus on for a period of time.

123. A. The term *red flag* is used to describe warning signals that may be tangible or intangible. HR can get ahead of negative employee behaviors when they take heed of red flags and go on a fact-finding mission to prevent a problem from occurring.

124. B. The concept of psychological ownership is one that is represented by how much control (both real and perceived) over their jobs employees have. When employees feel empowered, with some control and perceived rights, they are said to be more committed to the company as a whole.

125. B. A psychological contract exists between employers and employees. While unwritten, it refers to the nature of beliefs that employers and employees have about the relationship.

126. C. A psychological contract exists between the employer and their employees. While unwritten, it can be a powerful force that establishes expectations of behaviors based on both tangible and intangible items.

127. D. Frederick Taylor's study of scientific management focused on how environmental conditions such as job design, lighting, and scheduling of meals and breaks influenced employee productivity and performance.

128. C. Needs theories, such as Maslow's hierarchy, are built on humanistic principles. These include the idea that all employees have needs that either drive or diminish performance.

129. D. Focus groups are an effective tool to gather employee feedback when used under the proper circumstances. Ideally, a focus group will concentrate on narrowly defined issues that affect a group of employees without compromising confidentiality or potential for breaking the law.

130. C. In this example, the HR director is asking you to coordinate skip-level interviews. This occurs when managers meet with employees who are one to two levels below them in the chain of command.

131. D. Gathering employee feedback is an important task of human resource professionals. For that reason, it is useful to have several methods with which to do so. These methods include finding out the reason employees are leaving the organization through meaningful exit interviews, asking what employees need so they don't leave the organization via stay interviews, and conducting narrow focus groups to help inform HR decision-making.

132. B. David McClelland's acquired needs theory is centered on the premise that employee needs are acquired over time, often as the result of life experiences.

133. D. The function of employee relations is heavily focused on the employee experience. Therefore, activities within this domain will build HR skills in effective communication, conflict resolution, and career development.

134. D. Many employers are reaping the benefits of building return-to-work programs for employees suffering from non–work-related injuries. This includes keeping workflow steady while meeting customer demands by reducing the lost time of the person out on leave.

135. B. The experience modifier is used by insurance carriers to calculate premiums. It takes into account both how serious the injuries were and the frequency with which injuries occur. For that reason, Employer B may be expected to have a higher experience rating than Employer A.

136. A. The experience modifier, or *ex mod*, is a factor that is used to price workers' compensation insurance premiums. An employer with a .80 ex mod could expect to pay about 20 percent less than an employer whose ex mod is at the average rate of 1.0. The higher the ex mod, the higher the premium.

137. A. Heat illnesses (including stroke and exhaustion) are a significant risk for workers who perform in extreme temperatures during the summer months. Employees and supervisors should be trained to know the signs, which include nausea, dizziness, cramping, and excessive thirst.

138. A. An IIPP describes not only who will be responsible for implementing safety prevention plans but also what types of activities the employer will engage in to protect their workers.

139. D. Current users of illegal drugs are specifically excluded from protection under the Americans with Disabilities Act. Employers may choose to terminate employment, offer unpaid leave, and/or replace the employee while she seeks treatment on her own.

140. A. It is unlawful to take adverse action against an employee who is taking prescribed medication. This includes prescribed (controlled) medication such as methadone or amphetamines taken under the care and maintenance of a licensed physician.

141. B. Although alcohol is not an illegal substance, employers may prohibit its use on the job as well as prohibit employees from reporting to work under the influence.

142. D. Return-to-work programs are no longer used just as reasonable accommodation for a disabled worker or as a modified duty program for injured employees. Employers are designing programs that can help individuals who are out on non–work-related injuries as well.

143. B. Designing training programs should begin with conducting an assessment. A needs assessment will identify the desired training outcomes to ensure the training will meet the need.

144. A. The Whistleblower Protection Act is enforced through the Occupational Safety and Health Administration (OSHA). It protects employees who report unlawful corporate behavior.

145. D. A written IIPP is a preventive tool used to identify, communicate, and abate hazards in the workplace.

146. C. While many states do require a written injury and illness prevention plan, the primary purpose is to serve as a tool to prevent workplace injuries and accidents. It does so by having employers identify all hazards in the workplace and develop a plan for preventing and controlling those hazards.

147. A. A business continuity plan is designed to recover critical business processes to manage through a disruption. These disruptions are often the result of natural disasters, utility failures, or acts of violence/terrorism in the workplace that prevent business from functioning as usual.

148. A. OSHA has five categories of violations: willful, serious, other than serious, failure to abate, and repeated. The final type of violation (De Minimis) includes those that do not directly endanger worker safety.

149. C. Employers that fail to comply with OSHA citations find themselves in increasing trouble. In the case of Structural Subcontractors Service, LLC, OSHA issued a willful citation and fines of more than $100,000 for knowingly failing to protect their employees from fall hazards.

150. A. According to the Occupational Safety and Health Administration statistics, the construction industry accounts for more than 21 percent of workplace fatalities. The "fatal four" include falls, followed by struck by object, electrocution, and caught in between.

Chapter 7: SPHR Practice Area 1: Leadership and Strategy

1. D. Technology can offer cost control and improve efficiencies in the human resources area by reducing the need for personnel to process HR-related data. Scheduling is an example of an organizational function that makes sure products or services are available upon customer demand.

2. B. Companies in the maturity phase of the organizational life cycle may find themselves captive to their own highly developed policies, procedures, and rules when trying to enhance programs or respond to changing market conditions. Companies in decline are also characterized by bureaucracy but are most likely eliminating programs rather than creating them. Companies in the growth stage of the life cycle are in the process of developing more structure to manage rapid growth factors, and startups are not usually in a financial position to offer enhanced compensation or benefits.

3. C. The strategic role of human resources seeks to achieve company goals by effectively managing the talent of the workforce. Strategy provides the 50,000-foot view of the operational and administrative work necessary to accomplish company goals.

4. B. The strategic planning process consists of a series of activities designed to define needs, assess the internal and external climate, and set goals. The ADDIE model is one method of intervention, particularly when assessing training needs. A risk assessment is used to identify risk and implement activities to reduce or eliminate the risks identified.

5. D. Strategy uses methods such as strengths, weaknesses, opportunities, and threats (SWOT); political, economic, social, and technological (PEST); preplanning; and planning activities to help maximize organizational strengths and mitigate weaknesses. An objective provides a specific description of practical steps used to achieve business goals, and a goal describes the direction the business will take and what it will accomplish.

6. C. A goal describes the direction the business will take and what it will accomplish in specific, measurable terms. Strategy uses the strengths of a business to its competitive advantage, and an objective provides a specific description of practical steps used to achieve business goals.

7. B. An objective is specific and usually identified at the functional level of the organization. Goals may have multiple objectives, and a business strategy may have multiple goals.

8. A. The preplanning element in the strategic planning process sets the stage for success, which includes securing the proper buy-in and commitment from leaders and management. The environmental scan is a functional data-gathering activity used to formulate strategy. Once the strategy has been implemented, an evaluation must occur, and appropriate adjustments must be made.

9. C. Formulating the strategy includes developing the mission, vision, values, and goals of the organization or department. The preplanning element in the strategic planning process sets the stage for success, which includes securing the proper buy-in and commitment from leaders and management. The environmental scan is a functional data-gathering activity used to formulate the mission, vision, values, and goals. Once the strategy has been implemented, an evaluation must occur, and appropriate adjustments must be made.

10. A. Strategy implementation is the stage in which the plan identifies specific action items such as budgets and goals. The environmental scan is a functional data-gathering activity used to formulate strategy. Once the strategy has been implemented, an evaluation must occur, and appropriate adjustments must be made.

11. A. The environmental scan is an activity designed to collect data, not necessarily to take action on the data collected. Information such as internal weaknesses, external threats, internal strengths, and the influence of relevant laws and regulations will be used to help formulate and then implement the strategy.

12. D. The core competencies are the parts of a company's operations that they do best and that set them apart from the competition. The identification of an organization's core competencies is a critical outcome of the strategic planning process, resulting in clear direction of resource allocation, opportunities to outsource non–competency-related activities, and capitalizing on strengths to increase revenue.

13. D. The strategic planning process often results in the identification of seemingly disparate ideas and behaviors, especially with regard to values. It is the purpose of the strategy formulation process to set goals that seek to align company values with the work behaviors of both management and employees.

14. C. SMART goals are an example of how both short- and long-term goals can be written to increase effectiveness. Short-term goals are the result of strategy implementation and define action items that need to occur in the execution of the strategic plan. The action plan breaks down the tactical goals into steps that can be taken by an individual or team to accomplish the goal.

15. B. Once the action plan has been developed, it is possible to identify, quantify, and budget for the necessary resources to take action. It includes activities such as hiring new employees, allocating training dollars, and purchasing new equipment.

16. B. An accrued expense is one that has been incurred and on the books but that is expected to be paid on a future date. Items such as supplies, vendor invoices, and payroll are all typically entered into the books once the expense has occurred and been processed for payment.

17. A. An income statement, or profit and loss statement, is a reflection of the financial results of operations within a reporting period. It includes data on revenue produced from various sources, how much products cost to produce, overhead costs, and what the profit or loss was for the stated period. A statement of cash flow reflects the money that came in and where it was spent. A balance sheet is a picture of the financial condition of a company on a specific day, including assets, liabilities, and equity.

18. A. An income statement is a reflection of the financial results of operations within a specific reporting period. It includes labor costs as part of the overhead calculation. A statement of cash flow reflects the money that came in and where it was spent and how much is available at the time of reporting to pay bills. A balance sheet is a picture of the financial condition of a company on a specific day, including assets, liabilities, and equity.

19. B. A statement of cash flow reflects the money that came in and where it was spent, and it provides a snapshot of the cash available to pay immediate bills. A balance sheet is a picture of the financial condition of a company on a specific day, including assets, liabilities, and equity. An income statement is a reflection of the financial results of operations within a specific reporting period. It includes labor costs as part of the overhead calculation.

20. C. Zero-based budgeting uses real-time operational data to determine how much money will be needed for hiring, outsourcing, equipment, and similar HR expenses. The process also evaluates HR programs for value and return on investment and makes recommendations for changes where necessary. It is not dependent on previous data, nor does it assume that historical information continues to be the correct baseline from which to project. Top-down and bottom-up describe how the budget is created.

21. B. There are two primary methods for building a budget. The first is to base a budget on historical data and make adjustments in areas where the budget was either exceeded or underutilized. Zero-based budgeting assumes nothing, with all programs evaluated for cost and return.

22. C. There are two primary methods for building a budget. The first is to base a budget on historical data and make adjustments in areas where the budget was either exceeded or underutilized. Zero-based budgeting assumes nothing, with all programs evaluated for cost and return.

23. D. The evaluation stage of the strategic planning process must occur over time to ensure that the behaviors of management and the workforce are resulting in desired outcomes. If evaluation occurs only once, a company may miss the opportunity to respond quickly to variables that influence successful execution, as well as miss opportunities to motivate employees through difficult transition periods. For HR, this means communicating and modeling strategic initiatives, including those related to the company's mission, vision, values, and other standards of behavior.

24. B. The HCMP is HR's strategic plan. It is built to align with the corporate strategy and goals by addressing workforce planning needs, risk mitigation, employee development, and other factors related to the functional capabilities of an HR department.

25. D. The human capital management plan accounts for budgetary expenses that come under the control of the HR department. Training and development costs, payroll and associated expenses, and outsourced services are just some examples of items that must be budgeted and planned in advance.

26. B. The human capital management plan is the tool HR uses to communicate direction, desired results, objectives, action plans, and key measurables. It seeks to correlate HR action items with the company's strategic plan.

27. D. Human capital projecting is a budgetary activity that is part of the overall strategic management of the resources necessary to achieve organizational outcomes.

28. B. Human capital projecting seeks to bridge the gap between desired outcomes and existing talent. It includes factors that address the deficiencies, such as the skillset of the existing workforce, cost of implementing development plans, and whether to invest in the existing workforce or purchase the talent from the external labor market.

29. B. Business impact measures are those that are based on how the business was impacted or changed as the result of specific HR efforts. Training initiatives may result in increased revenue or output. Proper hiring may lead to reduced turnover. HR must attempt to quantify the impact of their efforts, particularly because it is not necessarily a revenue-generating department.

30. C. The balanced scorecard seeks to tie the efforts of human resources to defined measurables, usually financial or customer-based. The desired outcomes are typically defined by the strategic plan, and the scorecard measures the achievement of these outcomes across departments.

31. A. A correlation coefficient is a quantitative tool used to capture and analyze factual data to form a conclusion. Qualitative analysis uses facts blended with judgment or other subjective criteria to arrive at conclusions.

32. D. A cost-benefit analysis takes into consideration both objective and subjective costs associated with outcomes. A return-on-investment calculation typically will compare only hard costs to the outcomes. Both calculations seek to measure business impact.

33. C. Outsourcing noncore functions is a useful strategy, provided it results in the desired outcomes. For a service-driven company dependent on sales, reducing training or altering a travel policy may not be the most effective way to align behavior with the corporate objective. Laying off the compensation specialist who calculates incentives, bonuses, and commissions may actually hinder the achievement of the stated outcome. In this scenario, outsourcing the administration of benefits is the best answer.

34. D. The alignment of strategic efforts between stakeholders can be well accomplished through corporate responsibility efforts. Driven by mission, vision, and values; executed by employees and vendors; and responded to by customers are all elements of the purpose of corporate responsibility efforts.

35. D. Managing the due diligence process prior to a merger or an acquisition is the responsibility of HR. It seeks to provide a clear picture of the organizational health of the employment practices of a targeted company.

36. A. A divestiture is a strategy that companies may employ to "divest" themselves of a product line or division to focus more effort on core competencies. It may also be because the divested division or product line is more valuable as a stand-alone entity. A reduction in force is a strategy for reducing the number of individuals in the workforce in response to strategic variables.

37. C. Although offshoring and outsourcing are terms that are often used interchangeably, they are decidedly different activities. Offshoring is the movement of production or services outside of the United States to realize cost savings. Outsourcing is moving a non–core-competency process to a specialized service provider. Both are organizational structure strategies that usually result in layoffs at the location where the services were originally provided.

38. A. Self-service technology is often offered as part of a human resources information system that reduces the need for HR administrative support and increases efficiencies within the department.

39. C. In terms of corporate governance, the regulations are aimed primarily at the relationship between a company's primary stakeholders—shareholders, the board of directors, and management. Other stakeholders—those who have a stake or investment in the outcome of decision-making—include employees, vendors, customers, and lenders.

40. B. Fiduciary responsibility is an obligation of those who are positioned to make top-level decisions that affect company stakeholders. Fiduciary responsibility is a form of risk management in that it protects the interests of all stakeholders while taking into account compliance with corporate governance laws and regulations.

41. C. Section 806 of Sarbanes-Oxley seeks to provide protection to employees who are engaged in a protected activity, such as reporting activities that the employee reasonably believes are in violation of SEC or federal securities laws. It applies to employees of publicly traded companies.

42. B. Porter described five forces that should be considered in strategy development across all industries. They include new competitors, suppliers, buyers, alternative products available to consumers, and the type/level of competition in the industry.

43. C. A PEST analysis involves a review of the political, economic, social, and technological forces affecting businesses at any given time. This analysis can be applied to a specific business function, such as the labor force population, or to the company as a whole. The data derived from this analysis is used to formulate strategy.

44. B. A hiring management system (HMS) uses technology to carry the employer brand all the way through the application process, streamlining and increasing efficiencies as it goes. An applicant tracking system (ATS) is less integrated than an HMS, and a learning management system (LMS) streamlines employee-training data. Employee self-service allows employees—not applicants—to access various bits of their own records.

45. D. A learning management system can track organizational outcomes that are tied to employee training and development. It can track calendars, scores, planning tools, and assessments for managers across all departments to use in reporting development activities and documenting performance. Because it impacts multiple departments, it should be recommended first.

46. D. Reducing the size of the workforce is sometimes an unavoidable strategy used to respond to decreases in sales or production. Publicly traded companies may use this strategy to lower expenses for short-term improvements in net profits to meet earnings targets.

47. A. Reengineering includes changing or eliminating practices to increase customer satisfaction or improve efficiencies. Corporate restructuring focuses on entire departments and their subsequent processes to consider a structural change. Workforce expansions and reductions are strategies that are used to respond to fluctuations in operational needs, such as increased sales or the need to reduce expenses.

48. C. A workforce expansion may be the best solution to accommodate a rapid growth period. Business reengineering or restructuring can be a time-consuming process, which may or may not accomplish the desired customer results. When cost versus time is the focus, reengineering or restructuring may be a better solution.

49. B. Strategic relationships involve careful planning of employee relations activities that meet clearly defined objectives. Responsibilities that are properly communicated, goals that are specific and measurable, and project management skills that are designed to deliver can all enhance internal strategic relationships that get things done.

50. D. The human resource department is considered a staff unit, which means it exists to serve and advise all other departments and line managers. HR credibility is established when they are able to provide solutions to workforce issues for all business units.

51. C. An HR audit is a risk management tool that identifies areas where additional efforts are required. Though not specifically a legal compliance effort, it can serve as a demonstration of good faith intent to comply.

52. D. It is tempting for an HR manager who identifies broad risks to take immediate corrective action. This, however, is not always the most prudent or realistic course of action. The process of applying for EPLI may also be useful to identify risk and set a plan for corrective action.

53. A. Deciding how to structure the organization from a decision-making perspective is a major strategic consideration. Companies that are broadly spread out geographically may benefit from individual cost centers and decision-making authority granted at lower levels in a decentralized organizational structure. Companies that want to have greater control over operational decisions would do best to employ a centralized decision-making structure.

54. D. A cost-benefit analysis considers not only hard factors such as costs or returns. When looking at the benefit of a specific course of action, HR must also consider the impact a strategy will have on the customer and employees.

55. B. HR is responsible for controlling the costs associated with outsourced vendors. Staffing agencies are one example of the types of vendors used to outsource particular HR functions or to meet short-term needs.

56. A. Leading the executive team through the development of a workforce plan will allow them to take into consideration the many factors influencing decisions around downsizing. These decisions include customer impact, legal compliance, and the existing strengths of (or gap in) worker skillsets.

57. C. While all options are attractive, the need at this stage is to first identify and provide the executives with all available solutions to consider. These include severance packages, résumé workshops, and connections with state or local agencies to help with retraining and job placement assistance.

58. D. A functional business structure is one in which company units are sorted by department, with each area reporting directly to the executive director, CEO, or president.

59. C. A product-based organizational structure is most appropriate when a company has multiple brands or products requiring distinctive management. A product-based structure allows businesses to focus on each element of a specific brand, such as R&D or marketing, without having to compete with other outcomes for necessary resources, specifically, talent.

60. B. HR audits may take on many forms, all of which are related to a function of human resources. HR audits include any type of formal review to assess the status of HR activities within the organization including legal compliance, record-keeping, staffing, compensation, and health/safety.

61. C. Divestitures occur when a company decides to sell off assets as opposed to a full shift in business ownership. It may include offloading a product line, a division, or another business unit.

62. A. A balance sheet approach to international compensation addresses issues such as living costs, currency valuations, and tax policies that an expatriate may face while working out of the country. The balance sheet approach seeks to equalize the cost differences between international and home-based assignments. These and other decisions must be addressed when a business strategy moves the company into international territory.

63. D. Companies experiencing loss of revenue may need to find ways to diversify their business offerings. This strategy seeks to capitalize on existing infrastructure and employee skillsets directed toward a similar product or service offering.

64. C. For most employers, salaries and benefits are the largest line items on a company's financial statement, often accounting for more than half a company's overall operating expense.

65. D. As was the case with Canada's largest oil producer, the option of pay decreases allowed employees to share the burden of lost revenue. While not a perfect solution for all companies, larger employers during industry downturns can avoid mass layoffs by using this strategy, thus ensuring availability of personnel when production picks up.

66. B. Human capital represents the knowledge, skills, and abilities of the existing talent with which a company will compete. An HCMP is future-oriented, requiring HR to identify employee skillsets and put resources in place to ensure the talent is aligned with a company's strategic plan.

67. B. A growth plan will require increased marketing and sales activities. A successful growth plan will also require that the company invest in its operations to ensure it has capacity to take on the new business.

68. D. Specific HR strategies will emerge straight from the company's strategic plan. Because of this, the needs of the employees as they relate to company growth will be clearer, as will any compliance factors that will emerge as the result of strategic objectives.

69. B. An environmental scan is an activity that takes place before a global strategy is developed. Analyzing threats and opportunities will help direct decisions about how to best utilize resources to minimize threats and take advantage of opportunities.

70. C. The balanced scorecard is a tool that companies use when they need to report on a diverse set of tangible and intangible performance measures. Traditionally, a balanced scorecard will look not only at financial performance but at business processes, customer feedback, and learning and growth activities as well.

71. B. Key performance indicators are used to determine the current performance of a process when compared to established benchmarks, generally in quantifiable or financial measures.

72. A. Too often, performance standards and benchmarks are established without having a clear idea of what the true results will be. As a result, company leaders and employees may develop unreasonable expectations of the outcomes from a strategic objective. In the development of metrics, companies must be sure to align standards while clearly communicating the expected outcomes, such as improved attendance, increased customer satisfaction, or decreased expenses.

73. D. Forecasting is a critical task during the strategic planning process and involves a variety of tools and activities. These include conducting industry and competitor analysis, building "if this, then that" scenarios, and auditing internal strengths and weaknesses and external threats and opportunities. All data collected are used to help the company predict and prepare for future conditions.

74. A. Successful goals and objectives must be specific, measurable, achievable, relevant (sometimes called realistic), and time-based (SMART). In this way, meeting the hiring and training needs of 12 employees within six months allows for clear expectations and the measurement of success or failure.

75. B. Return on investment is used to determine the value of an investment in a project or program. The formula for calculating ROI must include not only the costs associated with implementation and maintenance but also the value the program will bring to the company. ROI is calculated by dividing the value of gains by the total investment and then multiplying the result by 100 to convert it to a percentage.

76. C. A cost-benefit analysis is used to help companies measure which strategies may be the most economically advantageous by comparing the outcomes of a strategy with the cost of implementation.

77. D. The collection of data related to the workforce is nothing new. But the ability to analyze, interpret, and act on that data to improve HR (and often company) performance is the function of workforce analytics.

78. D. HR has many, many choices when it comes to helping an employer measure progress on strategic outcomes. For a company seeking to increase profits, it is necessary to understand and manage expenses. Therefore, cost per hire is correct.

79. C. Top-down budgets are created by senior leadership. It is a process that allows for expense control and the allocation of resources toward strategic projects in addition to regular operations. The disadvantage to this approach is that budgets are established by staff that may be too far removed from the day-to-day operations to have a clear understanding of the needs.

80. B. The staffing function of human resources includes activities related to recruitment and selection. Staffing projections for use in the formulation of an annual budget must include all costs related to both recruitment and selection, so the cost of recruitment advertising is correct.

81. D. The culture of an organization has the most influence over employees feeling safe in reporting illegal or illegitimate employer behaviors. This is because while many employers have written policies or procedures in place to protect whistleblowers, the company behavior may not support transparency in practice. Factors include the degree to which supervisors encourage speaking up and how employees are treated when they do, as well as the level of confidentiality in other matters, which signals how information is both received and handled.

82. C. For small businesses, any task related to daily operations or responsibilities that could compromise the company's competitive advantage should be kept in house. Additionally, it is unlikely that a small business has in-house resources who are experts in all aspects of the required training topics (safety, harassment prevention, HR policies, labor law). For these reasons, outsourcing training activities is the best choice.

83. D. There are many instances in which HR activities may significantly undermine the strategy and goals of an organization. In some cases, policies that are too restrictive may frustrate management efforts at productivity or limit flexibility with their employees. Performance management systems may not be measuring the proper behavioral targets, rendering them inadequate and demotivating. Compensation practices that are not tied to clear performance outcomes, or that are perceived as unfair, may impede a company's ability to attract and retain talent. For this reason, HR must ensure that their practices are tightly aligned to desired organizational outcomes.

84. B. There are several variables to consider when asked to reduce expenses, so it is important that HR consider company priorities and desired outcomes when making these decisions. In this question, eliminating the company-sponsored daycare center is the best choice because it does not serve the mission of the organization, is not legally required, and eliminating it will result in actual cost savings.

85. A. In a shared services model, HR staff is centralized to streamline department efficiencies; companies are able to service more employees with fewer staff by eliminating HR redundancies. However, removing dedicated HR professionals from local operations often decreases the amount of personal, face-to-face interactions between HR and employees. This can have a chilling effect on the relationship-building nature of much of HR's work.

86. B. Data collected without any interpretation or insight will limit the value of the process. Data that are properly collected and interpreted will aid in decision-making and help HR craft employee services that are meaningful and tied directly to employee needs and wants.

87. D. In offshoring, companies make the decision to move jobs out of the United States to areas where operational costs are significantly lower to save money and increase profits.

88. C. When researching competitive advantage, U.S. employers must consider the quality of educational institutions within the country and the resulting graduates moving into the labor force. Senior HR professionals should take steps to partner with these institutions where relevant to establish a pipeline of future employees. Additionally, the number of non-native graduate students from U.S. universities continues to increase at a pace of about 30 percent per year. HR students take note, however: although the trend overall seems to be holding, applications from foreign-born students applying to U.S. schools to study science, technology, engineering, and math (STEM) are beginning to decrease.

89. B. The processes of HR can be highly administrative, especially in a large company with hundreds of employees. While all of the strategies mentioned have merit, the primary need for this director of HR is to look for ways to reduce the administrative work, particularly for tasks that do not require in-depth, human support.

90. D. Building a business case before engaging in implementation activities is the proper first step in designing a workforce analytics program. A business case will identify planning needs and the necessary resources to both accomplish objectives and properly manage associated risks, both critical pieces of information to help gain executive buy-in and commitment.

91. C. Communicating with all employees regarding the many uncertainties both during and after a merger and acquisition (M&A) is an HR best practice. An effective communication strategy will be built from data (often collected through surveys and metrics) to ensure that the company is communicating the right information, at the right time, to the right people. Components of a strategy should provide opportunities for employee feedback, multiple methods of disseminating data, and highlights of the "new culture" built upon shared rewards and outcomes.

92. D. In this scenario, HR will be called upon to help identify and place critical talent as soon as possible within the new structure. Focusing first on leadership skills and capabilities using confidential interviews, assessments, and company commitment can help reduce the amount of uncertainty (and operational disruption) during the transition period.

93. B. HR has many opportunities to lead before, during, and after an M&A. In this scenario, forming a due diligence team will bring all of the key players together to ensure those who need to be informed are all on the same page.

94. B. Early discussions of M&A require that HR focus on the people issues, specifically factors that may affect the retention of key talent. This is accomplished through observation of the management team as well as the analysis of conditions and data (such as compensation agreements with payout or "golden" clauses) that may incent employees to leave.

95. A. Software-as-a-service (SaaS) is the licensing of software applications by a company that is hosted by an off-site agency. Talent management databases—such as applicant tracking systems—are accessed via the Internet. Depending on the application, an advantage of SaaS is increased efficiency, particularly in areas that are administrative in nature. Senior HR leaders are often tasked with leading the transition into new systems and services, including building a business case that the C-suite (CEO, CFO, COO, etc.) may use to make decisions.

96. D. In this scenario, having an employee acting as the point of contact for the vendor—as well as in-house champion of the program—is most likely to increase success. Most often a member of HR, the liaison is available to help roll out the initiatives, answer employee questions, and manage the details of the relationship with the selected vendor.

97. B. New enterprise software is a type of computer-based information system that is holistic; it stores, organizes, and allows for the manipulation of information related to the organization as a whole as opposed to a single department. Senior human resource professionals are often tasked with helping to understand the strategic application of integrated systems throughout the company.

98. C. While each answer would address the employee concerns, the best answer is to be sure the executive team has allocated the necessary resources to properly train and support employees. The cost of system implementation will need to be addressed early on and include options to utilize both vendor support and employee knowledge in the design and roll-out phases of the project. This strategy may also provide ongoing support as new hires come on board and as current employees continue to learn the new system once live.

99. D. The human resource expense to full-time equivalent (FTE) ratio reflects the total investment of HR dollars spent per FTE. This number generally is smaller in larger organizations because they can spread the total cost of HR services across a greater number of employees.

100. A. Salaries as a percentage of operating expenses reflects the relative amount of compensation cost to the investment in total operating expenses. A high percentage reflects an investment in salaries versus investments in things such as raw materials, tools/equipment, or computers. For service-oriented industries, the benchmark for this number is likely to be higher, as the core competencies are knowledge workers (the people) as opposed to a produced good.

101. C. Many CFOs have been expanding their role in the domain of HR, with varying degrees of success depending largely on the organization's size and capabilities. Shifting the transactional burden of functions such as payroll, benefits administration, and salary deductions is a reasonable compromise, while freeing up HR department resources to focus more on the strategic and people-driven activities that are critical to organizational competitiveness.

102. C. HR technology is rapidly moving beyond what was once only the transactional work of HR. This includes the application of data mining capabilities that serve many HR outcomes. In this case, HR may work with the IT department to build a search based on the behavioral factors of typical rogue employees. This allows for a broad focus with narrowed outcomes that will most likely identify any problem employees.

103. D. There are many reasons why HR professionals must become technologically savvy. These include the need to remain relevant and supportive of the emerging needs of the businesses they serve. During strategic planning, it will be important to understand the technology competitors are using, especially in the search for talent. Finally, HR will be called upon to identify ways in which HR plans may be aligned with business plans, especially those in which knowledge workers are a core competency.

104. A. Environmental scanning involves analyzing internal and external factors that may affect an organization's ability to compete. In this example, reviewing what skills are available in the external labor market and identifying the age of the workforce to anticipate retirements or training needs are both examples of data that may be analyzed during an environmental scan.

105. C. It stands to reason that any workforce planning session likely will identify gaps in worker skillsets. The challenge for HR is to build a business case for senior management that will convince them that certain interventions are necessary to achieve the desired outcomes. Factors to include are the cost of any intervention strategy and the return on investment of actions with a direct link to the bottom line or other meaningful results, as well as the cost/risk of not acting.

106. D. A code of ethics is written from both organizational and employee perspectives. It serves as a guide for behaviors that serve the mission, vision, and especially the values of a company. HR must model these behaviors and coach management (and employees) where necessary.

107. A. The term *span of control* refers to the number of subordinates who directly report to a manager. It is useful in strategy development when there are clearly defined hierarchies. If a company finds the need to eliminate layers of management, HR will have to help restructure the reporting relationships. The term is potentially outdated in describing businesses that are more fluid in reporting and companies that depend on collaboration and cross-functional work teams.

108. B. There are many good reasons to have an anonymous whistleblower hotline but of significant importance is to alert the company to any potential wrongdoing by their employees or managers. It is this fundamental reason that will help employers comply with various labor laws, reduce liabilities, and improve experience modifiers of their insurance plans.

109. C. Corporate governance is a category of HR responsibility that is related to organizational behaviors. These systems and processes seek to do many things, including comply with labor laws, govern ethical behaviors, and act on a company's responsibility to the communities in which they operate.

110. D. Nongovernment organizations (NGOs) provide many strategic benefits to companies wanting to conduct business around the globe. Often, the sustainability and/or infrastructure needs of community far outreach the resources of a single business. Partnerships with NGOs require transparency and a system for governance, which can help improve a company's reputation across multiple borders.

111. A. Sustainable practices are built upon a premise of endurance—that companies use long-term factors such as environmental impact and depletion of resources to make decisions about business practices and strategies.

112. A. More and more companies are responding to social (and in some countries, legal) pressures to help workers de-stress via work-life balance initiatives. This includes crafting policies and practices that allow workers to disconnect from mobile devices and 24/7 access while outside of normal work hours or while on vacation.

113. D. Industrial-organizational psychologists have coined the term *presenteeism for* when employees report to work sick. Scientific research has demonstrated that this behavior has a negative effect on worker productivity and safety, not to mention the risk of infecting many other workers. Offering paid sick leave, having policies instructing people to stay home when ill, training managers on the financial impact of presenteeism, and avoiding disciplinary action when necessary can all have an effect on the negative outcomes of this phenomenon.

114. C. The need for effective decision-making strategies continues to emerge as a critical responsibility in the domain of HR. Training managers to use tools, such as considering a handful of opposite outcomes, can aid in decreasing decision-making bias. Studies are finding that complicated decision-making tools tend to be too narrow and that going deeper into existing hiring practices is not resulting in better-quality decisions—decisions that have a direct influence on organizational performance.

115. B. A major component of building and maintaining an employer brand is company integrity. Integrity revolves around perceptions of what a company values and how it behaves. In the airliner example, the CEO made a very public apology and explained how they would prevent similar instances from occurring in the future.

116. D. The connectivity (or hyper-connectivity) of many individuals today across the globe has impacted nearly all segments of HR programs and organizational competitiveness for talent. This includes an increase in the need for HR programs that support employee social causes, work/life flexibility (such as policies defining "disconnect" time from emails after hours), and the availability of employee training and development activities outside of traditional academic settings.

117. A. The influence of social media and other digital content can change both social skills and a sense of empathy in individuals. Digital devices may facilitate bullying and harassing behavior that eventually finds its way into both personal and professional environments.

118. C. Many studies are emerging that show that the way work gets done in the 21st century is very different from preceding centuries. Specifically, job opportunities in freelance and the rise of the "gig" economy have contributed to much more work being done outside the workplace, either full-time or in a part-time remote capacity. Other studies show that more than 40 percent of companies have a contingent workforce, with talent moving in and out of organizations much more freely than in times past.

119. D. Bureaucratic structures emerged as businesses grew and the need to manage larger work groups and projects developed. These business structures are characterized by narrow spans of control and standard operating procedures to ensure that work gets done and all stakeholders have unity of direction.

120. A. A major disadvantage of bureaucratic structures is that the human aspect of work gets largely ignored. This is because the focus is on human capital as a means to an end as opposed to a resource that can be developed and managed for the benefit of the "whole."

121. B. Open systems explores business structures as complete environments made up of inputs (raw materials, people), throughputs (production/service processes), and outputs (products and services). It is used to apply context to the effects of changing political, economic, or social climates on the fundamental aspects of how business gets done.

122. D. As with any living being, adapting to feedback is a critical element of survival. Open systems theory states that organizations must be vigilant about monitoring feedback from employees, customers, and other stakeholders and then make changes accordingly if they hope to survive.

123. D. The most common management functional models include planning the work, organizing the resources, directing the people, and controlling efforts to achieve outcomes.

124. D. The acronym VUCA describes a business environment that is all at once volatile, uncertain, complex, and ambiguous. These conditions are influenced by globalization, such as changing demographics, rapid change as companies respond to opportunities, and advances in technology, such as digital media and platforms. HR must plan for and be able to operate within a VUCA environment.

125. C. Labor shortages due to changing demographics have placed talent management and mobility at the front of the line for 21st-century HR managers. Shortages are predicted in countries such as the United States and Japan, whereas surpluses are predicted in countries such as India and South Africa.

Chapter 8: SPHR Practice Area 2: Talent Planning and Acquisition

1. B. All three branches of the U.S. government influence the legal and regulatory climate in which HR operates. Congress (legislative branch) may pass or amend a law. The U.S. president (executive branch) may enact an executive order. The courts (judicial branch) may interpret court cases, providing insight into compliance.

2. C. The Office of Federal Contract Compliance (OFCCP) enforces EOs. It is tasked to ensure that equal employment opportunities are afforded by federal agencies and private businesses that contract or subcontract with those agencies.

3. C. An EEO-1 report compiles statistical information related to specific employment data. It must be filed on or before September 30. Employers with operations at a single location or establishment complete a single form. However, those who operate multiple locations may have to complete a headquarters report, an establishment report, an establishment list, a consolidated report, or a combination, depending on specific criteria.

4. B. EO 11246 in 1965 prohibited discrimination on the basis of race, creed, color, and national origin. EO 11375 amended 11246 to prohibit discrimination on the basis of sex.

5. C. A job group analysis is a component of an affirmative action plan (AAP) that places job titles with similar duties and responsibilities into groups for analysis.

6. D. The strategic planning process seeks to identify and plan for changes that will aid in organizational growth. The results of the strategic plan will have an impact on the workforce, such as reengineering work processes, acquiring products through mergers or acquisitions, or outsourcing the non–core-competency functions of the organization.

7. D. Strategic workforce planning includes identifying the skillsets of the existing workforce, matching those skills to the current and forecasted needs, and ensuring that those qualified individuals are available when the company needs them.

8. C. When employees are acquired by an outsourced provider, they're terminated from the organization and hired by the new company. Co- or joint-employment issues are certainly important, and they should be addressed through other HR efforts.

9. B. While all of the answers may come into play in the execution of this strategy, hiring is the best choice in the category of workforce planning.

10. A. Alternative staffing methods include several options to support workforce-planning efforts. They include hiring contract workers, such as a contingent workforce, job sharing, part-time employees, and interns.

11. C. Job sharing is a type of alternative work schedule that allows an employer to reach a broader pool of qualified candidates. It fills a full-time position with two part-time workers.

12. A. Job competencies guide interviewers in formulating questions that elicit information beyond specific tasks and responsibilities assigned to a specific job.

13. C. A job analysis provides the foundation for identifying the knowledge, skills, and abilities (KSAs) needed to achieve specific results in an organization. If the organizational objectives are not being met, a job analysis is a useful tool to begin a needs analysis for proper recruiting and retention of qualified staff. A job analysis includes interviewing other staff and supervisory personnel. Changing recruiting sources may be necessary once a diagnosis has been made.

14. B. Supervisors should sign off on job descriptions to ensure that they are an accurate reflection of the needs of the job. While it is also important to have employees verify the accuracy of the job description, they may inflate the importance of the work or the knowledge necessary to get the job done.

15. C. While EEO laws do not specifically require job descriptions in and of themselves, they do serve to help employers comply. Defining the essential functions of each job helps employers in the recruiting and selection process by identifying the specific knowledge, skills, and abilities required for satisfactory performance of the job.

16. D. Hiring from outside the organization has both advantages and disadvantages. When making the decision to build or buy the talent, HR should consider the time constraints to the hire and whether the internal talent can be developed quickly enough to fill the need. Disadvantages of an external hire include low morale for employees who were passed over for a promotion and the difficulty of predicting how a candidate's skillset and team mind-set will fit in with the position.

17. D. The courts established in *Griggs* that discrimination does not necessarily have to be intentional for it to be unlawful. Because the high school diploma requirement adversely affected a protected-class group, the effects of the seemingly neutral employment test was discriminatory.

18. C. In *Albemarle Paper v. Moody*, the courts established that test validation must be in accordance with the Uniform Guidelines on Employee Selection Procedures (UGESPs). Subjective supervisor rankings aren't sufficient for validation, and the rankings must be tied to job-related criteria.

19. D. According to the UGESPs, reliable tests produce consistent results over time. Validity studies are used to show that pre-employment tests are valid predictors of future success on the job.

20. B. Concurrent validity is similar to predictive validity in that it compares the test scores of a group to their performance on the job. In predictive validity, it is compared at a future time. In concurrent validity, it is compared at the same time as the test is administered.

21. A. When the ability of a multinational organization to maintain close control of its global business units is a priority, companies may use the ethnocentric approach to staffing. Having expatriates who understand the culture and corporate mandates can ensure that those priorities are reflected abroad.

22. D. A geocentric staffing strategy does not make country of origin a priority when making staffing decisions. It focuses on building a management team that is internationally capable. Polycentric strategies focus on hiring citizens of the local country, whereas regio-centric strategies are geared toward hiring within a particular region.

23. B. A time-to-hire calculation is computed based on the date the job was posted and the date a job is accepted by a new employee. In this scenario, the calculation will serve to determine whether the complaint is valid.

24. C. Calculating the turnover rate for a company or a department provides HR with a benchmark. This benchmark allows for company-wide comparisons of turnover by department or by job title, alerting HR to potential intervention needs where applicable.

25. C. The electronic storage of records is becoming a more popular practice in all areas of organizational operations. For HR, this means that preserving the integrity, accessibility, and security of documents, such as Forms I-9 and W-4, must be a top consideration.

26. C. Succession planning is a useful practice in response both to demographic shifts and to organizational growth needs. It is particularly helpful for backfilling critical or difficult-to-fill positions.

27. D. A replacement chart is used as a tool for effective succession planning, broken down within the current organization, usually by department. It allows for a broad view of where the talent is in their stages of professional development.

28. B. Social media is the use of a network of individuals based on shared personal or professional characteristics.

29. D. The use of mobile technology, social media, and videos is growing in popularity because of the ever-changing technological advancement of the workforce. They can be cost-effective methods to mine active job-seekers and attract the interest of those who may not quite yet be looking.

30. B. The UGESPs were jointly developed to help employers comply with EEO laws such as Title VII of the Civil Rights Act and EO 11246. They provide employers with compliance guidelines for the use of selection tests in a nondiscriminatory manner.

31. D. Calculating the percentage of hires is a necessary first step in determining whether adverse impact has occurred. It helps employers evaluate how well or poorly they are doing in meeting their affirmative action goals as well. This percentage is calculated by dividing the number of applicants hired by the total number of applicants. In this scenario, the calculation for the women is 52/395, or 13 percent. For the men, the proper calculation is 48/255, or 19 percent.

32. D. Any pre-employment requirement that a candidate must pass through is considered a test under the Uniform Guidelines on Employee Selection Procedures. For example, paper or digital applications have been identified as tests by the EEOC, subject to requirements that the information collected is both job-related and a valid predictor of future success on the job.

33. B. The Big Five personality factors include traits of openness, conscientiousness, extraversion, agreeableness, and neuroticism (OCEAN). Researchers consistently have found that the trait of conscientiousness is a valid predictor of on-the-job success.

34. B. Employee digital conduct—including posting reviews, complaining about wages, and even having negative things to say about the company—may in fact be protected activity. The case filed by the Equal Employment Opportunity Commission against IXL Learning Inc. is just one example of how a protected-class worker may be the victim of unlawful retaliation based on their digital behavior.

35. D. The rights of employees while online may be protected by many agencies, including the National Labor Relations Board (NLRB) and the Equal Employment Opportunity Commission (EEOC). Under the NLRA, employees must be allowed to engage in protected concerted activity, even when online. However, the NLRB did rule that online posts that are not intended to be read by co-workers are not protected (*Duane vs. IXL Learning*, Case 20-CA-153625, JD(SF)-21-16).

36. C. The similar-to-me error occurs when a rater overlooks negative aspects of a candidate because they share an interest or other characteristic.

37. D. In preparing to build out succession plans, HR must first understand the current state of the factors influencing decision-making. Conducting job analysis with the resulting job descriptions helps to validate the skillsets necessary for the replacement pipeline. A review of the organizational structure also results in information such as leadership span of control to make decisions about the skillsets necessary to lead business units (or in some cases, restructure).

38. C. One of the primary reasons for the shortage of women in technology roles is simply the lack of females in the qualified labor pool. Creating a long-term pipeline by working with state and local agencies and schools to expand the labor pool is the best option from the possible answers.

39. D. There are several reasons beyond patriotism for companies to seek to hire military veterans. These reasons include studies that have shown veterans as having strong leadership and problem-solving skills and other highly valued and transferable skillsets. Additionally, the Department of Labor has established tax credits for unemployed military vets, mainly because this group experiences significant barriers to employment and is thus underemployed.

40. C. Analysis is a significant part of the succession planning process. In a gap analysis, HR will seek to identify potential workers for future roles and design development programs to increase their skills or mitigate their weaknesses to prepare them for the next position.

41. A. While all of the options may improve retention to some degree, the best answer is to ensure that a proper fit is made prior to making an internal transfer—locally or internationally. Retention may be improved when the employee is provided with a realistic view of the job and both the short- and long-term opportunities.

42. A. Succession planning's primary outcome is to fill leadership vacancies, whether because of the achievement of strategic growth targets or simply because of the natural attrition that occurs at all leadership levels.

43. C. Family-related obstacles to international placements remain the primary barrier for employees when considering international assignments. For this reason, it makes sense for HR to help potential placements have a clear idea of what kind of acclimation support will be available both for the candidate and for their partner, and a good sense of education and housing facilities that will be available while overseas.

44. D. International assignments are highly desirable for many reasons, including gaining leadership skills and understanding the global business needs of their company for future application. Because interest in international assignments tends to decline as the workforce ages, it may be beneficial for employers to consider early-career employees as one source for placements. This of course assumes that a nondiscriminatory system is in place to select international assignees and that promotion decisions are based on qualifications and past performance.

45. D. Turnover is costly, and it is important for HR to collect data from multiple sources to ensure any action plans address root cause. In some cases, it may be that the pay rates are not competitive. In other cases, it may be that the company is not measuring the knowledge, skills, and abilities necessary during the selection process. Supervisors may also be a reason for employee turnover, so asking for employee feedback will provide data that HR may use to design solutions.

46. D. While all options have merit, a simple listing of jobs along with a link to apply is *not* the most effective option when it comes to communicating the employer brand. A brand can and should be communicated with the end user in mind, so a Quick Apply button can help reduce the burden on the applicant who is filling out form after form with the same information. A job alert subscription option keeps the job applicant from having to continuously visit the employer's site for regular updates. Video testimonials from current employees give candidates a real view of what it is like to work for the employer and what it takes to be successful.

47. B. While all options to some degree are necessary in establishing the employer brand, defining the employer value proposition is the most important on the list. The value proposition provides individuals with a view of the unique qualities of the employer, attracting like-minded candidates and helping to engage the existing workforce.

48. A. The leadership team can be a powerful source of information as it relates to how they use the company mission, vision, and values (MVV) to shape employee programs. Particularly when building an employer brand, the MVV can guide the direction of the message, helping to attract a qualified workforce and retain qualified workers.

49. C. There are several pre-employment tests that are available for HR practitioners to use; a selection battery includes the set of predictors (tests) that an organization uses to make hiring decisions.

50. A. An in-basket test is a useful tool to assess how a candidate would handle typical tasks associated with the position for which they are applying. It is important that the test have a clear purpose, both so the applicant understands what is being asked of them and to ensure that the test is a valid predictor of successful on-the-job behaviors.

51. C. Gathering historical data on applicants is generally an employer's attempt to predict future behavior. The assumption is that an individual will apply similar skills/ knowledge and perform in the same/similar way in their new role.

52. B. Interview questions are another type of pre-employment test designed to predict future behavior on the job. In this case, the question is asking about a person's power of persuasion, or ability to negotiate for what they need or want.

53. D. There are several types of unlawful questions that should be avoided in an interview. These include questions related to an applicant's protected-class characteristics (age, citizenship, ethnicity) and arrest records where there was no conviction.

54. C. The multiple cutoff approach in an interview is especially useful for critical positions within a company. This approach requires candidates to pass all factors related to job performance; a high score in one area cannot make up for a high score in another area.

55. D. *Utility* is the term used to describe the degree to which a battery of selection tests is useful and cost-efficient.

56. C. "Layoff survivors" are not exempt from the psychological impact that downsizing has on individuals. Research suggests that post-layoff, the remaining employees often are less productive, less trusting of the company, and more likely to report anxiety and job-related stress.

57. A. Managers who perceive that the procedures used to make decisions related to downsizing were unfair and who are unable to express their views on the layoff decisions made are more likely to suffer from a lack of organizational commitment. They are also less effective at managing through the changes that the new structure requires.

58. B. Organizational socialization is both a formal and informal process of helping new hires acclimate to their new work roles and job responsibilities. It includes helping the employee acquire the necessary knowledge, attitudes, and behaviors to be successful.

59. A. Anticipatory socialization occurs outside the context of employment. It occurs most often during the recruiting and selection phase of the employee life cycle, when a candidate is considering how working for an organization may be. It is part of determining fit for both the applicant and the employer.

60. C. The pre-entry stage of organizational socialization/acculturation is when the new hire begins to understand the realities of their new role. The employee begins to get a sense of both the written and unwritten rules at work and undertakes impression management activities to influence how they are seen by others.

61. D. Impression management is a type of self-presentation used by all individuals to control or change how others view them. Impression management behaviors include minimizing poor performance via excuses or blame and maximizing good behaviors through self-promoting behaviors.

62. D. With the growing popularity of social media use, many employers are using cyber-vetting techniques to conduct more thorough searches into an applicant's past. It is important for HR teams to monitor the legal landscape for changes and restrictions to social media use as part of the background process to ensure policies and practices remain compliant.

63. B. With the ever-increasing difficulty of finding certain skillsets, such as marketing and information technology professionals, there has been a surge in "gig" jobs and project work. This strategy is an effective way for HR to help serve critical business needs until a more long-term solution can be found.

64. D. According to the Society for Human Resource Management (SHRM) using data from the Bureau of Labor Statistics, workers older than 65 continue to dominate the applicant pool. In fact, the number of workers age 65 and older who are still working is expected to continue to increase through 2024. For HR, this means ensuring that their employee acquisition practices are not heavily oriented toward younger workers to avoid age discrimination and to not miss out on highly qualified workers.

65. C. Diverse work groups have been shown to increase creativity and innovation on work teams. Improving an employer's recruiting practices may include redesigning jobs so the requirements are not so exclusive and training interviewers to avoid bias in selection procedures.

66. D. The Job Characteristics model by Hackman and Oldham states that changing the way a job is designed can have a motivating effect on employees. These characteristics include skill variety, task identity, task significance, autonomy, and feedback.

67. B. Task significance is the degree to which a person's job has a positive influence on a higher purpose or cause. While some jobs may be inherently difficult and thus demotivating, helping employees relate their position to a purpose can improve job attitudes and outcomes.

68. D. The statistics can be alarming for businesses in all industries: employers worldwide are facing a shortage of skilled workers by 2020. HR must work as strategic business partners to identify internal sources for development and promotion, at the same time partnering with external groups to generate a plan to acquire the necessary talent to compete.

69. B. Cultural compatibility is a major area that HR must manage during mergers and acquisitions. It is important to take an analytical approach to ensure all perspectives and outcomes are being considered, not just the status quo.

70. D. Negotiating job offers requires both talent and technique. In anchoring, a negotiator starts out by fixing a salary amount in the candidate's mind as a starting point. The primacy effect is similar to anchoring in that the candidate has a bias toward the first bit of information they receive. Finally, the exploding offer creates a sense of urgency by asking the candidate to make a decision within a certain period of time, such as within one week.

71. A. Emotional labor occurs when service or other employees are required to mask their true feelings in service of the customer. Studies have found that employees who have heavy loads of emotional labor are more likely to experience feelings of stress and job burnout.

72. B. Emotional contagion occurs when an employee's job attitude "infects" others—in a positive or negative way. By sharing this information with employees, they may experience a stronger degree of control over the attitudes and morale of the people they work with.

73. B. Horizontal loading is a job design technique that adds to existing tasks without a change in title, authority, or decision-making. When used properly, it can increase the motivating potential of a job; otherwise, the enrichment opportunity is perceived more as micro-managing.

74. A. Due diligence is a step in the merger and acquisition process that involves analyzing all aspects of the business being acquired. This includes a review of records related to human resources, operations, finances, sales, and marketing.

75. D. Human resource planning involves analyzing and identifying the "human mix" of talent necessary to meet current and future company goals. The planning process must align with the outcomes from a company's strategic plan and address both surpluses and shortages of talent.

Chapter 9: SPHR Practice Area 3: Learning and Development

1. C. The Copyright Act of 1976 regulates the use of musical, literary, and other works by individuals other than the author. It states that employers who hire employees to create original works as part of their normal job duties are the owners of the copyrights.

2. B. As companies grow and respond to external conditions, it is likely that there will be a need at some point to change direction at a company, department, or individual level. Strategic interventions, such as change management techniques and process reengineering, help the organization align itself with the newly desired state.

3. D. When an organization chooses to implement changes in response to external market conditions, effective management of change must occur for successful implementation. Employees' perceptions, abilities, opinions, and fears should be taken into account in the selection of the appropriate change management or intervention strategy.

4. B. Change management is often necessary as the result of organizational development (OD) interventions. Kurt Lewin's change process theory identified three stages for change: unfreezing, moving, and then refreezing. The moving stage of change management involves aligning (moving) the organization with the new process or behavior. It is at this stage that information is exchanged between the employee and the employer to implement the change.

5. C. Bias is a type of error that may occur at the time of hire, when selecting for training, or during a performance review. It occurs when the rater's beliefs or values shape the way she treats the employee.

6. B. Knowledge management encompasses activities related to the creation, retention, and distribution of the organizational knowledge necessary to get the work done. An effective program will account for backup staff to perform critical or time-sensitive functions such as payroll.

7. B. A learning organization is one in which knowledge is originated, obtained, and freely shared. Peter Senge identified five disciplines that characterize a learning organization. The discipline of personal mastery describes a high level of expertise in an individual's chosen field.

8. A. TQM is a type of OD intervention designed to improve a process, system, or business unit, including the quality of a company's product. Dr. Kaoru Ishikawa is credited with the creation of several TQM tools used to track quality efforts. These include the Pareto chart, check sheet, stratification, and cause-and-effect diagram.

9. A. Of the different analytical tools created by Dr. Ishikawa, the check sheet continues to be the simplest to use. It requires the compilation of a list of items that might be expected to occur, and then it entails data collection to confirm or deny the theory. In this example, a check sheet would be created with the possible reasons employees may be leaving (no advancement, poor supervision, and so on), and then the number of occurrences in each category would be counted.

10. D. Human process interventions are designed to address organizational problems that are the result of individual or team behaviors. Interventions may be designed to include team-building activities, conflict resolution skill-building, management by objective programs, and leadership/management development.

11. C. Human resource management interventions are used when the focus is on individual needs within a traditional function of human resources. This could include business management and strategy needs, workforce-planning needs, HRD needs, compensation/benefits needs, employee/labor relations needs, and risk management needs.

12. C. A complete needs assessment will address the needs at the organizational, individual, and task levels. The organizational level will help determine current and future needs, most likely tied to strategies. The individual level will assess employee competencies when compared to performance standards, and the task level will compare job requirements to employee knowledge.

13. A. When developing and then managing a diversity program, it is important for HR to understand the needs of the employees and the needs of the organization. Offering language training, ensuring that supervisors are capable of managing a diverse workforce, and offering translation services or documents in native languages are all effective ways to build an inclusive company culture where people want to stay.

14. A. The training needs of remote workers are unique and may require HR to be creative when designing programs that serve all stakeholders. In this scenario, taking the technicians out of the field for training is unrealistic and may compromise the service of other customers, not to mention be costly. In this case, a virtual option would be the best approach.

15. C. Executive coaching is an effective tool to use to develop an employee's skillset on a single issue or within a particular area. It includes both work-related and non–work-related deficiencies that are often unique to an executive or management professional.

16. A. Training is an effective tool to use when the performance deficiency is technical or based strictly on the ability to use a specific skill. It is a solution identified as the result of a needs assessment to determine the cause of the deficiency, but it cannot solve every performance issue.

17. B. Training analysis takes place in an effort to design training solutions to meet desired organizational or individual outcomes. It includes identifying the goals, gathering and

analyzing data, identifying performance gaps between desired and actual performance, identifying instructional goals, proposing solutions, and then evaluating options for training as a solution. In this way, HR is more likely to design training content that is effective.

18. B. A positively accelerating learning curve occurs when learning is slow at first but then accelerates as the training continues. This is usually the result of the participant grasping and applying information from previous training sessions to influence learning.

19. A. When more than one trainer will be presenting training sessions, a leader guide helps to ensure consistency in the presentations.

20. B. There are different instructional methods for a variety of circumstances. Passive training, such as lectures and presentations, are useful for large groups. Active training methods are directed more at individual learning needs, and experiential training sessions, such as performance-based training, give participants the opportunity to experience training conditions that are similar to those of the job.

21. C. There are different instructional methods for a variety of circumstances. Passive training, such as lectures and presentations, are useful for large groups. Active training methods are directed more at individual learning needs, and experiential training sessions give participants the opportunity to experience training conditions that are similar to those of the job.

22. C. An electronic performance support system (EPSS) is a training tool integrated into the computer system to be used by employees on the job. It may include access to SOPs, reference guides, field materials, and other tools that will support successful performance on the job.

23. D. Virtual training is a form of e-learning that occurs through the use of digital tools, such as virtual classrooms, discussion and bulletin boards, and self-paced instruction.

24. C. Training evaluations should be completed both before and after the actual training takes place. It is typically accounted for as part of training design. In formative evaluations, the objectives or content is rolled out to a test group to evaluate effectiveness and elicit feedback. In summative evaluations, training participants are asked for their reactions to the training, or they are asked questions designed to evaluate whether learning has occurred.

25. B. Training evaluations should be completed both before and after the actual training takes place. It is typically accounted for as part of training design. In summative evaluations, training participants are asked for their reactions to the training related to the instructor or facilities, or they are asked questions designed to evaluate whether learning has occurred. In formative evaluations, the objectives or content is rolled out to a test group to evaluate effectiveness and elicit feedback.

26. B. Human resources is first and foremost a business partner, so you must consider the input and feedback from all stakeholders. Working with the accounting manager on a needs assessment will identify the gap between the current skills of the employees, the needs of the department, and the strategic needs of the company.

27. A. Leader-member exchange (LMX) theory is dependent upon the quality of the relationship with followers. It views leadership as a reciprocal process, acknowledging that leaders will have different relationships with different followers, as opposed to a trait-based or behavioral theory that is more focused on the leader.

28. B. Research pertaining to the relationship between leadership styles and cultures is growing in popularity as the business world continues to operate within multiple borders. Studies have found that certain leadership styles are more effective than others, depending upon whether a culture is individualistic or collectivist.

29. B. Emotional intelligence is the individual ability to understand and manage emotions, particularly in response to external circumstances. Just as general intelligence may be measured through various tests, so may EI. A positive EI quotient has been correlated with stronger, more effective leaders.

30. D. Transformational leaders have many positive characteristics that affect their ability to influence employee performance. These traits include charisma, courage, self-discipline, integrity, and the ability to inspire others.

31. D. The situational leadership model developed by Hersey-Blanchard describes leadership behaviors that adjust based on employee competency and maturity. For employees who have some competence but variable commitment, a leader may have to direct the employee by "coaching" another way, focusing on the task that needs to be done and developing the relationship the leader has with the employee—thus high task, high relationship. As the employee matures or becomes more capable, the leader should adjust their style to be more relationship-driven than task-driven.

32. A. The Blake-Mouton leadership grid is a tool that uses an axis to describe management behavior. Managers who are most concerned with production over people—such as authoritarian leaders—will scale higher on the concern-for-results (X) axis of the grid.

33. B. There are certain circumstances that require special interventions, either in advance of a situation occurring or as part of a new corporate direction. In this case, the integration of a protected individual through the use of diversity initiatives may help acclimate her to the unfamiliar setting and set the expected standards of behavior for the existing employees.

34. C. Flexible work arrangements are a reasonable response to employees with unique issues who are otherwise qualified to do the work. The graphic designer in this scenario does not necessarily have customer demands requiring the 7:30 a.m. start time, so changing the schedule is a viable option for hiring the talent necessary to get the work done.

35. A. Knowledge management will allow companies to maximize their investment in the development of employees on a global scale. Mining the experience for feedback and adapting similar assignments in the future will aid in successful global placements and repatriation.

36. D. Production measures are those that identify the business impact an HRD intervention may or may not have had on a process. "Production" and "service" can be used interchangeably in this measurement, such as counting the number of dropped calls in customer service.

37. A. Being tactical means implementing small-scale measures that affect larger outcomes. Measuring these small-scale efforts can give HR insight into the big picture, such as the cost of effective training or whether learning is occurring at the training level. Tactical accountability can be measured through all the functions of HRM.

38. D. The impact of HRD activities on a global workforce should not be underestimated. Keeping expatriates updated on training and development opportunities should be one of the goals of an effective expatriate program. Virtual classrooms, e-learning tools, and employee performance support systems are all methods that can be used to communicate equal training and development opportunities to offshore employees.

39. D. A Socratic seminar is named after Socrates, the philosopher who employed a question-and-answer format while teaching to help students work through a problem or idea.

40. B. Simulation training is a type of active training method in which participants are able to try new skills or practice protocols prior to being asked to perform in real life. It is often done away from the location where the actual work will be completed, such as in outer space. This method is beneficial for safety-sensitive jobs or for situations where operator error can have significant negative impact on a process or system.

41. C. Vestibule training is a type of simulation training that occurs at or near the location of the work. It allows for skills practice without the negative impact an inexperienced worker may have on the sales floor or when safety, such as with heavy equipment operators, may be compromised in the absence of competency.

42. A. Socratic seminars combine lectures and demonstrations with opportunities for training participants to ask questions and discuss solutions among themselves.

43. B. A learning circle is generally a facilitated training session in which those with shared needs come together. Often focused on support and professional development, these facilitated sessions allow for shared insights from a group of similarly situated peers.

44. D. Much emphasis on employee engagement has occurred recently, and for good reason. Engaged employees are those who clearly understand their role at work and how it affects achievement of business outcomes. These workers care about the company, their co-workers, and the customer. As a result, they tend to report greater levels of job satisfaction, they are more productive, and turnover rates for these groups are low.

45. C. The key to effective employee engagement programs and tools is understanding what a specific workforce needs and what factors affect engagement levels. Before you can make a recommendation to improve employee engagement, you should invest in a tool that collects information to help the employer make informed, data-driven decisions.

46. A. Because this example of a toxic culture seems to be driven from the top down, HR should work toward creating more effective leaders through coaching. Executive and management coaching can be an effective way to improve leadership skills while focusing on the alignment of people management strategies with company goals.

47. B. Integrating talent acquisition (recruiting and selection) with talent management is essential for several reasons. A true talent strategy will begin with the end goals and create systems throughout the entire employee life cycle to support individual and organizational performance.

48. C. The strategic role of HR in L&D activities begins by hiring talent who are curious and open to employee development activities. If the hiring process is broken, it may compromise your ability to build a talent management program that has meaningful business outcomes. Additionally, a talent management strategy will address the employer brand (career pathing, professional development)—information that is shared with candidates long before they decide to work for a company.

49. B. The U.S. Army has engaged training professionals to design virtual reality (VR) training programs for their soldiers. Modeled after the extreme situations many veterans have described, the VR program gives trainers the opportunity to help soldiers prepare for and address the emotional aspects of war.

50. D. Contingency theories of leadership study the impact of both individual leadership traits and situational or contextual variables. Two of the most well-known include Fiedler's contingency theory and the path-goal theory of leadership.

51. A. Leadership prototypes are characteristics of leaders that followers come to expect. These traits form a mental expectation that followers have of what makes an effective leader. Organizational behavioral scientists have found that these prototypes differ across cultures.

52. B. Any type of organization that has a focus on continuous learning and knowledge management would benefit from a form of "corporate university" such as those implemented by McDonald's and Xerox.

53. C. Donald Kirkpatrick's model for evaluating training focuses on four levels: reaction, learning, behavioral, and results. An expanded version of this from G.M. Alliger and associates further distilled the model into *affective reactions* and *utility reactions*. Affective reactions are those where a training participant had an emotional response to the training, whereas utility reactions are those in which the participant believes that the training will transfer to their job.

54. C. One of the major challenges of the annual performance review is the lack of regular feedback for employees. By developing managers as coaches and teaching them how to provide meaningful feedback via more frequent employee interactions, the employee is more likely to stay on track with their performance goals.

55. A. Studies have shown that the effectiveness of diversity training is mixed. What does seem to be consistent, however, is that participants who receive diversity training report a better understanding of the value of diversity within an organization.

56. D. Many companies such as Disney, GE, and Unilever have recognized the benefits of embedding the customer into their employee development activities. Different from feedback, development activities focus on job activities that help the employee build skills, in this case, skills that are specific to customer needs.

57. A. Many studies have found that in classroom-based training sessions, information is transferred most often through nonverbal means such as tone of voice, facial expression, body language, and hand gestures. This is also one of the many challenges to self-paced, online learning environments.

58. D. Cost reduction as an organizational development activity may be adopted in response to a lost customer or simply because it makes good business sense. Regardless of the impetus, HR must be fully prepared to advocate and support the development of intervention tools that will increase the odds of success. In this case, self-directed teams may need basic financial reporting skills to track financial data that impact success. The teams will also need to have a clear picture of the performance targets against which they will be responsible to measure results. Finally, self-directed work teams are highly dependent upon the performance of their peers, so a 360-degree feedback tool will allow for meaningful performance feedback.

59. B. While all the answer options are significant challenges for multinational employers, the struggle to communicate the company culture across borders is the one related to talent management. HR is tasked with helping their companies build out the employer brand and communicating company values and other cultural factors to all business units and locations.

60. A. Employee involvement strategies focus on empowering employees to make decisions, often on behalf of the customer. By increasing autonomy and trust, employees use their own judgment and critical thinking skills to take action. This approach requires the establishment of performance benchmarks built from standard operating procedures, reference guides, and other training resources.

61. A. Over-reliance on management is often a real obstacle to employee involvement strategies. True employee involvement will require the creation of reference guides for employees so they have access to the information necessary to perform. By doing so, it will be more realistic to reduce middle management so that employees can engage in fast and accurate decision-making when necessary.

62. C. When measuring the efficacy of development activities, it is important to take a look at employee promotions. Promotions usually occur because an employee either has mastered their current job or has been identified as having the necessary skills to move up within an organization.

63. B. For multinational employers, corporate social responsibility (CSR) is often a natural part of doing business within a region. Additionally, social media has made it possible for the employer's efforts (or lack thereof) in this area to be rapidly and widely communicated. CSR initiatives built into a company's talent management program can include the following: establishing the expectation that employees will champion environmental causes, taking on leadership roles in change efforts, providing suggestions and feedback, and elevating emerging issues before they become crises.

64. C. An individual development plan is an excellent tool for employers wanting to have performance conversations with employees on a regular basis, as opposed to the traditional quarterly or once-a-year format. Because it is developmental in nature, there should be an honest review of the employee's strengths and weaknesses, along with a plan to apply the strengths and overcome or minimize the weaknesses.

65. A. An after-action review (AAR) is a process developed by the U.S. Army to build performance strategies out of past mistakes and successes. Informally known as *debriefs* or *postmortems*, AAR is applied by companies after major projects, client meetings, or unplanned events. This discipline and the resulting knowledge can help a company perform in the most effective way possible: by repeating successful behaviors or eliminating/reducing errors. Transparency and trust are necessary cultural components for this OD effort to be successful.

66. D. Conflict and change go hand in hand for many reasons. When employees are expected to engage in constructive conflict, the quality of employer decision-making goes up as they are able to consider all viewpoints. Constructive conflict can also highlight where a course correction may be necessary. A culture of artificial harmony, where conflict is avoided, will not produce the type of problem-solving behaviors that are required of successful organizations.

67. B. The stakeholders of an organization include the employees, customers, vendors, and communities that are affected by an organization's results. More so than individual performance, company performance has a greater impact on all stakeholders and, therefore, is of primary concern.

68. C. The war for talent will not ever truly go away, so it stands to reason that reliance on hiring the best and the brightest will not be feasible for all employers all the time. For that reason, it is important that companies build talent management programs and systems that leverage the performance of all workers together (teams, business units, subject-matter experts, brainstorming sessions) as opposed to focusing on the individual performance of the top percentage of their people.

69. A. A team leader will map high on both axes in concern for people and concern for production. Their Blake-Mouton score would be a 9/9, characterized by encouraging both individual and team development.

70. B. The design stage of the ADDIE model is where a framework for training will be built, based on the needs assessment completed in stage 1. Decisions about course content, delivery methods, and logistics will be made in this stage of the ADDIE model.

71. C. The negative connotation around informal employee communication networks such as a "grapevine" are not necessarily substantiated by organizational research. Leaders should pay attention to what erupts from the grapevine, as even erroneous employee perceptions can be a valuable guide that shapes a leader's message to the group.

72. B. Integrated communications reflect the need for companies to manage information that flows internally among employees and between departments, as well as externally, such as information that is shared with the public or vendors. For this reason, many companies treat communication as a single function to be managed across all departments. HR contributes to this management through policies, modeling, and coaching.

73. A. As a general rule, all organizations have a pattern in which they communicate. This includes communication networks in which most communication flows from the group leader, between co-workers, or along a chain.

74. B. The nominal group technique in decision-making is more structured than traditional brainstorming sessions. It relies, in part, on managing the input from all participants so that a dominating member does not unduly shape a decision. The stepladder technique begins by presenting the task to all team members ahead of the meeting to provide adequate time for reflection. It then puts two members together to discuss the task and draw conclusions and then adds a third to the core group, followed by a fourth, until all ideas have been presented and a decision is made.

75. D. Many decision-making models seek to resolve differences among teams; however, there are challenges to teams that are highly cohesive as well. Groupthink occurs because of several factors, including some team members suppressing their ideas and succumbing to peer pressure out of fear of becoming an out-group member.

76. C. Peter Senge coined the term *learning organization*, which means to identify companies that successfully navigate change through flexibility, innovation, and the acquisition of and response to new information. Learning organizations therefore have become a change management technique used by HR to help their companies evolve in order to compete.

77. C. Whole versus parts training is an important consideration when designing training. Many organizations are turning to micro-learning, where large, complex tasks are broken down into their independent units for ease of training and design. Whole-task training is appropriate for tasks that are highly organized, linear, and dependent upon each other for full completion.

78. B. Active learning is characterized by ensuring that the learner is actively engaged in the material being learned. The old adage "the best way to learn something is to teach it" can be applied to this example, as the new HR generalist will have to develop the process first, learning it as he goes.

79. D. Theories related to organizational development are equally focused on both people and processes. These theories describe different types of interventions aimed to develop people, processes, or sometimes both. OD theories may be applied to individuals, departments, or organizations as a whole.

80. C. A replacement chart is a tool used in succession analysis to predict and plan for personnel changes. It begins by identifying potential employee movement (promotion, transfer, termination, etc.) and then identifies sources for backup should those changes occur. From this, development needs may be identified and a replacement pipeline developed. This process is particularly helpful for critical talent within the organization to ensure business continuity in the event of separation.

Chapter 10: SPHR Practice Area 4: Total Rewards

1. B. In a performance-based culture, line of sight occurs when employees know how their performance affects their compensation.

2. A. A company's compensation strategy is most often in alignment with their stage in the organizational life cycle. Startups usually do not have the capital necessary for a robust

compensation package; they offer the basics, adding stock options and planning for increases and perks as they grow.

3. C. The FLSA allows exemptions from the overtime requirements for workers who meet the salary basis test and who meet the criteria of the categories for exemption. They include executive, administrative, professional, outside sales, and computer employees. In this case, a candidate for the SPHR exam must meet the experience requirements to sit for the test and therefore most likely has a position that directly relates to management or business operations and the use of discretion or independent judgment on significant matters, which are the criteria for an administrative exemption from overtime pay.

4. B. Once the compensable factors have been identified and jobs priced accordingly, range placement can occur. Entry-level workers or those new to the company may be placed on the lower end of the range, whereas longer-term employees or those more proficient at the work may be placed higher on the scale. While compensation discrimination and wage compression certainly do occur, it is reasonable to have different pay rates for different jobs, provided they are based on job-related criteria.

5. B. Deferred compensation plans allow employees to earn a wage but defer payment of that wage to a later time. The wages are not taxed until the employee receives payment. Executive salaries usually have only a portion deferred, which is often designated as retirement funds.

6. C. Perquisites, or "perks," are those compensation components that go above and beyond what is available to the rank and file workers. They often are the least transparent elements of executive compensation and come under scrutiny for being excessive.

7. D. A well-defined compensation philosophy will support multiple outcomes, but the primary need driving this statement is the strategic direction of the business. In many ways, the philosophy and resulting practices will influence hiring, retention, market positioning, budgeting, and which behaviors are rewarded in their company culture.

8. A. A compensation strategy in which a company leads the market for wages will—in theory—attract the most qualified talent. At minimum, leading the market in pay will give an employer access to top-tier talent from which to choose. The location is less important, only in that a lead strategy will be relative to the top pay in each market.

9. A. Business acumen is the ability to understand the nature of a company's operations, including the markets in which a company competes for sales and talent. Acumen is the ability for a seasoned HR professional to use their knowledge to support both strategic and operational business outcomes.

10. C. The most common types of performance-based pay for executives include stock options, profit sharing, and other types of bonuses tied to individual or company performance.

11. D. The portion of executive compensation that is tax deductible for companies is anything that is deemed "performance-related." This includes stock options and bonuses that are above and beyond base wages.

12. A. For international assignees, it may be beneficial for them (or their employer) to litigate wage and other disputes in their home country. While not always enforceable, a choice of law clause will make it more likely for this to occur.

13. C. Restricted stock is a type of incentive with rules about its transfer. Restricted stock is usually issued as part of a salary package and has rules about when it may be paid.

14. B. The purpose of key person insurance is to reimburse a company should the business owner or other key personnel die. It is used to help a company survive should there be a loss of a primary leader.

15. B. There are many considerations when building global compensation plans. These variables include home country and host country laws, along with the individual needs of the expatriates and their families. For these reasons, expatriate compensation can be difficult to standardize.

16. C. Executive stock options come with many tax considerations. In this case, the amount of taxes that would be owed on any gains will most likely be subject to the alternative minimum tax (AMT).

17. C. The primary purpose for adopting a home country–based approach for international assignee compensation is to address employee standard of living. This approach breaks down expatriate compensation into four main categories: taxes, housing, goods and services, and discretionary income.

18. B. The Fair Labor Standards Act defines highly compensated workers as those making more than $100,000. This total "may consist of commissions, nondiscretionary bonuses, and other nondiscretionary compensation earned during a 52-week period, but does not include credit for board or lodging, payments for medical or life insurance, or contributions to retirement plans or other fringe benefits."

19. D. Several types of stock options are available for companies that want to reward employees for company growth but do not want to grant equity ownership. These include a restricted stock grant that is tied to certain conditions being met, phantom stock in which "share" value is mimicked based on actual company performance, and stock that has a vesting schedule to increase retention and loyalty.

20. A. The Consumer Price Index (CPI) is a measurement put out by the Bureau of Labor Statistics. Considered a major economic indicator, it evaluates the average amount paid by consumers for goods and services over time, which in turn identifies increases in the cost of living. Employers may use this number to help calculate cost-of-living adjustments (COLA) for employee pay increases.

21. D. SPHR candidates are expected to have a clear understanding about how external economic factors such as unemployment rates, globalization of the work force, and cost of living affect employee compensation.

22. A. A golden handcuff is a type of employment contract clause made up of short- and long-term incentives designed to entice an employee—usually an executive—to stay at a company.

23. D. There are many factors influencing compensation systems for international assignees. They include international works councils that have built-in employee protections, the differing tax regulations of the home and host country, and the political conditions of the host country that may necessitate hazard pay premiums.

24. D. While many multinational corporations use a blended approach to building international compensation systems, the balance sheet approach focuses on retaining an expatriate once the assignment is complete. It does so by standardizing the elements of expat pay and keeping the person "whole" in terms of compensation, benefits, and opportunities.

25. B. The unemployment rate is an economic factor that influences employer pay ranges. This is because when unemployment rates are low, there is less qualified talent to fill open positions. This means employers may have to pay higher than average pay rates to attract and keep top talent.

26. D. The economies of countries can vary quite significantly, resulting in a higher cost of living for international assignees than for citizens. The Efficient Purchase Index is used by international compensation specialists based on the assumption that an international assignee will eventually calibrate their spending to the local economy. Thus, the assignee may be paid more at the beginning of an international assignment.

27. C. In 2018 the Department of Labor released a new seven-factor test for qualified internships. At the heart of the regulation is that the primary beneficiary of the internship must be the intern themselves. This can be measured by job responsibilities, type of learning occurring on the job, and schedule accommodation for classes.

28. D. While the primary support for an unpaid internship is that it benefits the intern, there are other factors an employer must consider. In this example, it is the extent to which the intern's work complements—rather than displaces or replaces—the work of paid employees while providing significant educational benefits to the intern.

29. B. A hardship premium is used for international assignments—often in developing countries—where the living conditions are below the average living conditions in the expatriate's home country. The hardship premium may also account for other discomforts such as climate, pollution, and isolation.

30. B. A company's compensation philosophy must meet the need of business strategy while remaining legally compliant. It is reasonable to price some jobs differently than others to accommodate hard-to-fill roles, provided it is applied equally to other jobs within the classification and meets other requirements for job relatedness, minimum wage, and exemptions.

31. A. Globalization occurs when higher-paid American jobs are shipped over to countries where the cost of wages is lower. As a result, higher-paid workers in the United States are displaced. This creates a larger supply of talent, allowing employers to consider paying less than they normally would for some positions.

32. C. Areas with higher costs of living will be positively correlated with higher costs of labor. This is so that employers are able to attract and keep qualified talent that can afford to live in the area where they work.

33. A. Efficiency wage has come out of labor economics, occurring when employers use wages to attract, reward, and keep workers; the higher the pay, the more motivating the reward. Empathy wages, however, are emerging as behavioral scientists study the impact of pay as a retention tool; the impact of the efficiency wage is dependent upon other psychological and sociological conditions of work. Some studies have shown that empathy wages (when efficiency pay meets other altruistic employer behaviors) generate feelings of gratitude and, thus, encourage positive worker behaviors.

34. C. An important trend for HR professionals to remain educated on is the emergence of predictive scheduling laws. States such as Washington, New York, and California already have rules on the books that apply to retail, food service, and hospitality workers. These laws seek to limit the unpredictability of schedules that are typical in these industries.

35. A. While tip pooling continues to be an allowable practice, there are many compliance landmines that employers must be aware of, particularly with regard to minimum wage standards. As a general rule, tip credits or adjustments for credit card processing fees may never take tipped employees below the minimum wage established in their wage order. For example, the maximum tip credit that an employer can currently claim under the FLSA is $5.12 per hour (the minimum wage of $7.25 minus the minimum required cash wage of $2.13).

36. C. Statistics show that the number of people ages 65 and older is growing faster than any other age group, and more than 42 million workers in the United States are providing some sort of unpaid care for older and ailing family members. Strategically, this means employers should begin to build benefits programs that will meet the needs of a workforce to take time off to care for their families.

37. D. Many cities in states such as New Jersey and California are adopting employer bans prohibiting them from asking applicants about their salary history. This is because systemic pay disparity occurs when new wages are based on past wages that have been suppressed over time.

38. D. A study by the Society for Human Resource Management found that millennials and baby boomers do actually share some things in common. Both groups frequently cited job security and compensation as being "very important" in terms of job satisfaction, which ultimately leads to retention. Both groups also have silos of traditional hard workers and disrupters to the status quo—just as not all baby boomers were hippies, neither are all millennials hipsters.

39. B. Traditional pension plans are declining in popularity as employers grapple with a workforce demanding flexibility, not only of their schedules but of their benefits. Defined contribution plans, such as the 401(k), have the advantage of being partially funded by an employee's own money and thus goes with them if they change jobs. Traditional pensions that are fully employer funded are not portable.

40. D. The catch-22 of employers needing educated workers and the high cost of education in the United States has left many employees buried in student loans; this type of consumer debt is second only to home mortgages. Employers seeking to retain highly qualified talent (and those who are educated in their respective fields) are starting to build benefits programs that include student loan payoffs.

41. B. As a health care provider, it would stand to reason that your organization is committed to offering employees and their families benefits to maximize their own health. Offering benefits to adult children who are beyond the legal cutoff age for mandatory benefits can serve the company mission while offering something different from their competitors that attracts and retains talent.

42. D. The need for HR to manage diversity can declare itself in all aspects of human resource management. The Department of Labor has issued somewhat conflicting guidelines under Presidents Obama and Trump. For now, plan fiduciaries—including HR—are directed to "...always put first the economic interest of the plan..." while also minimizing plan costs to participants.

43. B. When it comes to diversity, supervisors are the front line to managing employee needs and expectations. This situation is a good opportunity to provide additional training to supervisors, while also educating them on what information was used to make the decision.

44. C. The Securities and Exchange Commission requires that employees be given written notice if they will be unable to access their investment funds for more than 3 but less than 60 days. Blackout periods usually occur when a major structural plan change is being made. It may also occur, such as with Enron, when accounting fraud has been revealed or once a merger is underway and new employees are being added to the plan.

45. D. While all of the options are correct as they relate to the overall strategy, only option D is related to the internal total compensation function of HR. By offering staffed clinics, Walmart can better control the cost of point-of-care services for employees.

46. B. Bonuses that are truly discretionary—management decides the amount of the bonus, recipients of the bonus, and the bonus is not guaranteed—are not required to be included in overtime calculations. With these types of situations, however, it is always wise to seek counsel to make sure HR is able to clearly communicate associated risks.

47. B. The rise of telework continues to have a positive financial impact for many companies. In this example, much of the work done for an engineering/construction firm is already done at sites other than a traditional office setting, so designing telework programs would be a good starting point. This type of program could also increase retention in an industry that is beginning to experience a shortage of skilled workers.

48. D. Senior leader total rewards packages have many variables that must be considered. Depending on the need of the organization, it is prudent to explore a hybrid of options.

49. A. Higher deductibles, switching plans, and the general uncertainty of the health benefit market makes factoring in benefits increases a regular part of the annual budgeting process. As a general guideline, employers should expect between a 4 percent and 6 percent increase each year in their health insurance spend. Note that this does not include age band or package changes, both of which may adjust the total increase upwards.

50. C. Compensation committees are used to help establish executive compensation packages. They serve in an advisory role, independently reporting to a board of directors.

Chapter 11: SPHR Practice Area 5: Employee Relations and Engagement

1. C. There are many tools HR may use to build an effective alternative dispute resolution (ADR) process. A peer review panel may be an effective way to fairly hear the grievances of employees, reducing the likelihood of lawsuits.

2. A. Distributive justice addresses employees' perceptions of fairness in the distribution of outcomes. In this case, the production manager does not believe that the punishment is appropriate for the offense.

3. A. Contractual rights granted to employees can be entered into formally in writing using tools such as employment contracts, separation agreements, and collective bargaining agreements. However, courts have ruled that employee contractual rights may also be implied in employee handbooks and policies that create an expectation of continued employment or termination only for cause.

4. D. A separation agreement is a type of employment contract that spells out the terms and conditions related to employee or executive termination or separation. More often than not, it includes some type of severance pay and, by signing the employee, exchanges the right to sue the employer for a grievance.

5. C. Federal and state laws regarding workplace privacy concerns can vary significantly. For this reason, HR should write clear policies that have been reviewed by the company attorney prior to engaging in any workplace monitoring efforts.

6. C. The practice of caucusing by union representatives can be used for several reasons. This includes when there may be a disagreement between the union members that needs to be resolved outside of the presence of the employer negotiator. It is also an effective tool to control the pace of negotiations or to take a break if emotions begin to run high at the bargaining table.

7. D. Senior HR professionals must build effective attendance strategies that meet the needs of both the employer and the employee. Efforts such as tracking attendance, understanding the cause of absenteeism, and quantifying the costs of absenteeism can help HR build response plans to the underlying reasons for attendance issues in the workplace.

8. A. When it comes to the evaluation of employee experiences at work, HR should look for consistency across all employee demographics. Employees should not be having different experiences in an organization with effective performance and behavioral standards.

9. C. Positive employee relations strategies are organizational efforts that focus first on the people. This focus allows for greater engagement and trust, which in turn fosters productivity and customer service quality.

10. D. The National Labor Relations Board has ruled that prohibiting all video recordings or photography at work may violate an employee's right to engage in protected concerted

activity. For example, a reasonable employee may construe that taking a picture of a wage schedule on a bulletin board is prohibited.

11. B. A combination of issues such as the ones described illuminates the need for a company culture that is driven by company strategy that includes creation and support of a positive, inclusive company culture. This includes defining the proper way for both managers and employees to behave.

12. A. The first step toward establishing an affirmative defense against a charge of sexual harassment is to write a zero tolerance policy for unlawful behaviors.

13. A. Strategic HR in the area of employee and labor relations are broad—not narrow—in scope. Embedding corporate culture initiatives into all HR systems requires a top-level view along with the marshaling and management of the resources necessary to execute.

14. D. An arbitration agreement is an effective tool employers may use to help resolve grievances outside of the justice system. For an agreement to be enforceable, current employees must receive (and return a signed copy of) the agreement when the policy is developed and at the time of hire for new employees.

15. B. Works councils are most often found in European countries. They function like trade unions in that they are designed to represent the rights of workers through collective action and agreements (such as work agreements or covenants).

16. D. HR must be prepared with data to counterbalance demands from the union that the company does not want to meet. Using in-house, real-time information can help persuade a union that their demands are unreasonable or unnecessary.

17. A. Ultimately, the collective bargaining process is supposed to improve the working environment or benefits of the employees. For this reason, HR should seek to build a positive relationship with the union representative to ensure the collective bargaining process achieves what it needs to achieve without acrimony from either side.

18. C. Policies that prohibit political activity at work are often designed to be part of a larger union avoidance strategy. The National Labor Relations Board prohibits overly broad policies, so HR must be sure that this and other types of policies do not unintentionally violate the law.

19. D. The Department of Labor (DOL) states in its "persuader" rule that employers and labor consultants/lawyers must report to the DOL the scope and cost of their union avoidance efforts.

20. A. Employers are not permitted during a union campaign to threaten employees to persuade them to not vote for a union.

21. D. Happy employees rarely unionize, so adopting and promoting a culture of transparency and respect can go a long way toward preventing union activity from starting. This includes clearly explaining how decisions to make changes are made, reminding employees of how competitive the company is, and treating all employees with courtesy and respect.

22. B. Many union-organizing campaigns begin long before the employer knows they are underway. One organizing tactic is the placement of "salts"—new hires whose intention is to organize employees who often begin to speak out on behalf of a group or groups.

23. A. Rapid changes, especially those such as layoffs or work furloughs, cause many employees to fear for their job security. Employers and supervisors who fail to effectively manage these changes often find themselves facing a union-organizing campaign.

24. C. While overall union membership has been considered to be on the decline for the last several years, union-organizing efforts are actually increasing. This is primarily the result of unions targeting non-manufacturing employers, specifically those in service industries.

25. C. While there are many ways to negotiate on specific issues, negotiation experts recommend waiting to see the full list of demands before committing the company. In this example, while agreeing to one additional paid holiday seems innocuous, the union may also plan to ask for double-time pay for all company holidays. In that context, the true cost of agreement is higher.

26. D. The central tendency error occurs when managers rate all employees as average.

27. D. Management coaching is often the responsibility of human resources, especially when the performance is related to an HR function. Some managers rate all employees as average because they are fearful of conflict, so training her on how to offer constructive feedback will develop her management skills. Teaching her about the types of rater bias will help her avoid the errors in the future. Helping her complete the appraisal will improve the odds of getting them delivered to the employees in a timely manner while ensuring that the feedback is meaningful.

28. B. It is possible to make intangible performance measures such as cultural behaviors and strategic initiatives measurable. An effective solution requires both clarity and specificity, so HR should work with all involved to have a solid understanding of what success factors in these areas look like. From there, tools and training for raters can be established.

29. A. A performance measurement system begins by developing performance metrics and ends by giving employees feedback.

30. D. One of the major challenges for organizations is that their performance appraisals focus more on individual behaviors that are quantifiable, as opposed to business or cultural behaviors that are less tangible. If employees are measured only on their individual behaviors, they are more likely to focus their development efforts in that area, often at the expense of organizational cohesiveness.

31. A. While the talent cycle must align to the employee life cycle, the performance management activities begin with an accurate review of performance measurements. From these benchmarks, other talent management activities may be built.

32. A. Executive teams are designed to drive organizational effectiveness through group effort. Consequently, transparent, lateral feedback that is given as needed is a benchmark of this management structure.

33. C. Union security agreements are clauses in a collective bargaining agreement. They require that employees make payments to the union to remain employed. While these agreements cannot require employees to join the union, they can compel the employees to exist as dues-paying non-members. Note that the 2018 Janus ruling no longer allows this for public unions.

34. B. HR often plays the role of providing relevant data for the collective bargaining process. In this case, knowing the total number of current union members will help you estimate on the high end what that benefit would cost. This is accomplished by using current shoe pricing and projected purchases in the new contract period.

35. A. Any situation that occurs as the result of a working relationship has the potential to cause issues for employers. Additionally, employers are extremely limited on regulating any type of social media behaviors of their employees. For these reasons, HR should address the work-related behaviors that were the result of the situation and remind them of professional workplace standards.

36. C. Ultra-concession bargaining is a strategy used most often by management to pressure unions into making concessions they otherwise may not have made. This is often accomplished using aggressive techniques such as rescinding what was originally negotiated and threatening shut-down or sale.

37. D. Union-management cooperatives, or co-ops, are growing in popularity. This is because unions and employers recognize that the acrimony reflected in history does not serve employee needs. Granting decision-making authority and access to company financial records builds trust and increases the likelihood that the business will survive in a difficult economy.

38. D. A lump-sum pay increase occurs when employers pay a single, annual bonus in lieu of an hourly pay raise. Because this payment is not added to base pay, it helps mitigate increases to overtime and pension plans. Union contracts often build upon each other, so maintaining a lower hourly rate can also chill the effect of compounding over several contract years. And finally, a lump-sum payment can be negotiated to account for any cost-of-living increase expectations on the part of employees.

39. B. Two-tier pay systems are characterized by new hires being paid less for the same/similar jobs than incumbents. In retailing, where turnover is traditionally high, most workers will soon be in a lower tier, having the effect of cutting wages overall.

40. A. Voluntary employee benefit agreements and associations (VEBA) transfer the obligation of providing retiree health benefits from the employer to the union. This decreases the company's liabilities on the company balance sheet.

41. C. When a union takes on the responsibility for retiree benefits through a VEBA, they become part of separate financials from the employer. This keeps the benefits protected from creditors should the company declare bankruptcy or from being viewed as negotiable under future contracts.

42. B. There are several areas up for negotiation, and they include work rules. Employers seek to renegotiate work rules to improve productivity and/or reduce cost. This may include redesigning jobs, using performance-rather than seniority-based systems, and/or being allowed to use contract workers when necessary.

43. D. The National Labor Relations Board in 2015 granted unions the right to hold expedited elections. This change severely diminished the ability of employers to respond once a union campaign is underway. For this reason, HR must help their employers build and maintain perpetual avoidance strategies such as positive employee relations, open-door policies, in-house grievance procedures, and transparent communications.

44. A. The National Labor Relations Board has made it clear that employee statements about work and working conditions are a "protected concerted activity." In this example, the NLRB found this policy to be over-broad when Chipotle Restaurant fired an employee for negative tweets and other behaviors regarding low wages.

45. A. Psychological empowerment is a motivational construct that may be used by employers to understand and, therefore, improve job satisfaction. Specifically, meaning indicates person-to-job fit (values-based), competence is an individual's belief in their abilities and skills, self-determination is related to autonomy, and impact is the degree to which an employee has influence and control over job outcomes.

46. B. Employee engagement, job satisfaction, and organizational commitment are the three main types of job attitudes. Organizational commitment is the degree to which an employee is attached to an organization and is influenced by the degree of overall job satisfaction.

47. C. There has been some confusion, and thus misapplication, of the definition of employee engagement. What is understood to be true, however, is that having high levels of employee engagement increases employee job satisfaction and thus their performance. Employee engagement differs from other job attitudes in that it refers to the investment of multiple resources (psychological, emotional, physical, etc.) into the work tasks, as opposed to in the company as a whole.

48. A. Many experts agree that the study of organizational behavior started with the Hawthorne studies. From these studies, the phenomenon called the Hawthorne effect emerged, which noted that paying attention to employee behaviors and needs will result in improved productivity and more positive job attitudes.

49. C. Too often, managers and employers assume that the only way to increase employee motivation is to increase their pay. In many cases, organizations may use extrinsic rewards (other than money) in service of intrinsic motivators. Intrinsic motivators are tasks employees enjoy completing because they find them interesting and satisfying. In this example, a graphic designer may find it rewarding to work on more open-ended, creative projects as opposed to the more systematic tasks that are the "necessary evils" of these types of roles.

50. D. The implications from the high-profile harassment claims in the news and the resulting #metoo movement are many. The expectation is that there will be an increase in complaints of harassment, both to internal sources and to external agencies. Companies will need to look at their use of nondisclosure agreements—and subsequent payments—to ensure they are not violating employee rights. Employers will also need to take steps to reduce claims of favoritism in the workplace, such as those that may arise if supervisors are allowed to manage or otherwise make decisions about employment benefits of someone they have a romantic interest in.

51. B. Beginning in 2018, companies are restricted on the types of settlement claims they may deduct from their corporate taxes. Section 162(q) of the act disallows "i) any settlement or payment related to sexual harassment or sexual abuse, if the settlement or payment is subject to a nondisclosure agreement; or (ii) attorneys' fees related to the settlement or payment" to be used as a tax deduction.

52. D. The term *diversity* refers to individual differences among employees. There are two types of diversity—surface level and deep level. Surface level includes the observable traits such as age, gender, and ethnicity. Deep level includes employee job attitudes, values, personality traits, and beliefs.

53. D. There are several biological factors that are being studied in the field of organizational behavior. In addition to the study of genetics is the study of organizational neuroscience. Advancements in this field have implications for the work application of creating sustainable change, awareness, and thus mitigation of unconscious bias and how to work with a diverse group of people and across cultures.

54. C. Diversity councils are formed to help embed diversity initiatives throughout the company operations. They accomplish this by having a diverse group of individuals meet and work on diversity-related initiatives and solve problems. It is imperative for the head of the council to have a solid understanding of business operations while also having enough authority to be credible and enough authority to approve initiatives. For these reasons, the VP of operations is the best choice.

55. D. An effective system for managing employee performance reaches beyond the operational task of performance appraisal. While performance feedback is important, so also are the developmentally focused activities of goal-setting and coaching.

56. A. Multisource feedback, also known as 360-degree feedback and upward appraisals, involves multiple raters at various levels within the organization. They are useful tools to get a clear picture of how an employee is performing while at the same time reducing rater bias and involving subordinates in the feedback process.

57. B. Face time is a term coined to describe the physical presence of an employee at a job site. Dynamic face time occurs with in-person interactions, such as meeting attendance, whereas passive face time occurs through simple observation, such as seeing a person working at her desk. Studies have shown that face time can influence how co-workers and managers perceive an employee. Thus, unintentional bias can occur when a telecommuting employee's commitment or dependability is questioned because of a lack of face time.

58. D. Behaviorally anchored rating scales (BARS) are characterized by degrees of employee performance expressed as behavioral descriptions.

59. B. Critical incidents are behavioral descriptions of important behaviors for job performance. In developing a behaviorally anchored rating scale, writers must develop critical incidents at high, medium, and low effectiveness.

60. D. Range restriction occurs when only a small part of a rating scale is used when giving performance appraisals. Employee morale can be affected when this occurs; employees who believe they are top performers will feel as though their contributions aren't distinguished from those of the more lackluster performers in the department.

61. B. Forced distribution requires that raters place a percentage of their employees in each category of high, medium, and low. Similar to grading on a curve, supervisors categorize all employees using a predetermined formula, such as 20 percent high, 10 percent low, and 70 percent in the middle.

62. C. Stress is a form of system arousal that can help employees focus attention on certain tasks, but only up to a point, or optimal level. Once that level has been reached, employee performance becomes more randomized and, as a result, declines. Employers can help increase awareness of this by education and training initiatives while also providing challenging work and environments that reward learning.

63. D. Too much stress—both personal and professional—has a negative influence on all job attitudes and performance. Negative outcomes may include turnover, withdrawal behaviors (such as absenteeism), lower levels of organizational commitment, illness, use of sick time, health care benefits, and workplace accidents. With some studies noting that more than 60 percent of Americans say that managing stress is important but only 35 percent think they are doing a good job at it, this is a significant area where HR can contribute.

64. B. There are many benefits to return-to-work (RTW) programs, but one of the greatest benefits is that a well-crafted RTW program can serve those who have been injured at work and those who have a non–work-related injury or illness. RTWs can help offset the financial impact of an employee reliant upon state disability programs and help employers keep talented employees at work.

65. A. Response planning is a critical element in any type of employer risk management practice. Proper planning includes conducting assessments, identifying resources, building response plans, and then training the workforce on each plan.

66. C. There are many types of crises a company may be called upon to respond to. This includes workforce planning issues such as the loss of critical personnel, a pandemic event such as the swine flu, and recovering/responding to both natural and manmade disasters. All three have a component of the continuation of business so that all stakeholders are protected.

67. A. To be approved to participate in an OSHA co-op or partnership, employers must set goals related to reducing workplace hazards. In this case, tower owners in Nebraska worked with OSHA to get approval to participate in a partnership program designed to make the workplace safer for all employees in the industry.

68. D. The science of ergonomics involves studying the way the physical work environment stresses various body parts. Poor ergonomic design or behaviors can result in musculoskeletal diseases. While there is no specific OSHA standard that addresses how to prevent these types of injuries in the workplace, employers are obligated to do so under the general duty standard.

69. D. Because of the unique needs and nature of IPV in the workplace, a domestic violence policy should be written separately from other policies (such as workplace violence). An IPV policy should include language that addresses how a restraining or other protective order will be handled, how a security or potential security threat will be addressed, and what type of leave may be available to employees who are victims of domestic violence.

70. C. Many forms of bullying and harassment are the result of the escalation of workplace incivility such as rudeness or disrespect. While the other elements speak to compliance with unlawful harassment laws, workplace civility initiatives are embedded within the culture. This approach serves as a first line of defense against micro behaviors escalating into violent or unlawful bullying or harassing events.

71. A. Behavioral benchmarking is a talent management technique used to identify gaps in leadership competencies. This is often used in response to major changes in the workplace that may require OD interventions at the leadership level or a refocus of organizational resources to fill gaps.

72. C. Talent management programs and processes are being designed using applied theories from the domains of business (industry best practices), human resources (360-degree feedback), and psychology (self-awareness tools such as personality profiling and emotional intelligence).

73. C. One of the main inhibitors to talent management system sustainability is the lack of action planning for follow-up. Too often, employers utilize their resources designing and implementing a system and not enough resources maintaining and evaluating the program.

74. B. A company's compensation philosophy and the resulting system for measuring and rewarding executives would have to consider internal and external equity factors. Examples of these factors include ratio of CEO pay to individual contributor pay and labor market rates.

75. D. For publicly traded companies, it is important to understand the requirements for CEO and NEO performance evaluations. Because there is lack of consistency regarding this issue, many companies choose to design systems for executive performance appraisals as part of best practices in corporate governance.

Chapter 12: Practice Exam

1. B. Transactional leaders are characterized by a "this for that" style. These leaders use both rewards and discipline when necessary to accomplish organizational and departmental objectives.

2. C. Relationships at work, even those that are consensual, have the potential for issues in which HR will have to intervene. This includes the risk of sexual harassment should the relationship become unwanted by either party.

3. B. In this high-risk industry, it would be prudent for human resources to begin building a safety program for those workers who are most at risk. This effort may include data collection, incentives, and compliance efforts as part of the overall intervention strategy.

4. C. Any time there is an increase in injuries and accidents, HR should take the time to analyze for root causes. From this, hazard abatement strategies may be developed and could include new personal protective equipment requirements or worker training.

5. D. When a data breach of this magnitude occurs, it is important for HR to help the company respond in accordance with governing agencies but also in a manner that protects the interests of both the company and the affected individuals.

6. C. Physical assets such as workstations and servers can be tracked and monitored as part of a company's efforts to prevent cyberattacks on sensitive company and customer data.

7. A. Establishing a hierarchy of assets helps a company craft an effective data security program. Building controls for these assets may include policies, practices, and the deployment of internal and external resources, but it will be difficult to know where to deploy the resources without understanding what is most at risk/important.

8. B. In this case, a team approach may work to help minimize an act of workplace violence. Security cameras can act as a deterrent to crime. Having the cameras internally monitored increases the ability for a quick response should an event occur.

9. C. The Fair Labor Standards Act addresses more than just legal compensation; it also limits the type of work that may be done by minors. In this example, a meat slicer is considered a hazardous job and is therefore prohibited for workers between the ages of 14 and 15.

10. A. Mental illnesses are generally covered under the Americans with Disabilities Act and apply to employers with 15 or more employees. This employee may need to be reasonably accommodated as a result of her disability.

11. D. Both the host company and the staffing agency have responsibilities to ensure the safety of individuals who will be working with hazardous materials. Communicating with the agency allows for a coordination of effort, including the need for protection, training, and verifying that the workers are going to a safe workplace.

12. C. There are several different ways information can be collected, stored, and eventually utilized in a 21st-century workplace. In this example, the company is using microchips to identify employees.

13. D. With implantable technology, there are several types of risk that an employer may need to take steps to minimize. The capabilities and design of the microchip must be reviewed to ensure it does not send information about an employee, unlawfully track employee movements, or cause infection or other health issues.

14. C. In risk management, employers may seek to eliminate, mitigate, or transfer the risk. An example of a mitigation effort is one that reduces—but does not eliminate—the likelihood of a data breach. For that reason, an employer policy that prohibits the sharing of employee passwords is the best answer.

15. B. A written incident response plan can be a critical part of a company's response system should an incident of workplace violence occur. An effective plan should identify manager and employee responsibilities, first responder resources, evacuation and head count procedures, and how to coordinate any media response.

16. A. A business continuity plan will most likely detail an information technology (IT) response to the enterprise system of a company. This is needed to get critical business processes that are based on technology back up and running as soon as possible after an incident.

17. C. The SEC adopted new executive pay ratio rules that went into effect in 2017. The rules require a public company to disclose the ratio of the median of the annual total compensation of all employees to the annual total compensation of the CEO.

18. A. OSHA's voluntary Strategic Partnership Program (SPP) brings together unions and employers to adopt a cohesive set of safety standards that address safety hazards in the workplace.

19. C. A safety program without the support of top management has an increased chance of failing to address the unique needs of the organization. For example, if the director of HR does not wear her safety glasses in the warehouse, it is unlikely that others will follow the rules either.

20. C. Safety incentive programs that reward employees who do not get injured may inadvertently retaliate against those who do get hurt. Additionally, incentive programs that are too generous may discourage reporting of injuries.

21. A. OSHA's Voluntary Protection Program (VPP) is open to employers that have an effective, well-established safety program. If the employer is accepted into the program, the employer may be removed from routine, scheduled inspection lists.

22. B. Employers have a global duty of care to keep international assignees safe. This obligation may take on many forms, but it generally must account for the unique needs of employees that travel or live abroad as part of their work responsibilities.

23. D. An employer may decide to purchase additional types of insurance to accommodate the unique needs of international employees. Brokers who provide these types of policies often have resources far beyond the administrative, including navigating the need to negotiate should an event occur and medical or emergency travel services for the employee and family members should the need arise.

24. D. A return-to-work program is one that returns an injured worker back to the job in a modified capacity. Once the injured employee is working modified duty, his pay comes from payroll as opposed to his wages being part of the overall compensation claim.

25. D. There are some cases where it is entirely reasonable for an employer to pay a temporarily injured worker a lower wage while on a modified duty assignment. Employers that adopt this strategy must take care that no retaliation is occurring and that they are not violating the laws of the states in which the employee was injured.

26. B. An independent medical exam (IME) is a useful tool when there is a dispute about an injured worker's abilities. Often binding, it is conducted by a neutral, third-party physician.

27. D. The process of collective bargaining and the resulting agreement is a right granted to employees by way of specific law. In this example, the National Labor Relations Act granted individuals the right to organize and bargain collectively through a union.

28. B. Employee rights can be granted by both federal and state laws. These rights are considered to be absolute and cannot be compromised by employers without penalty or bargained away in an employment contract including a collective bargaining agreement.

29. D. Noncompete agreements are clauses or documents that prohibit a separating employee from competing with the employer in the same line of business for a specified period of time. If these agreements are overly restrictive or in a state that does not allow an employer to prevent an employee from making a living, they may prove difficult to enforce.

30. A. Nonpiracy agreements, in which separating employees agree to not to recruit a company's talent, can be beneficial under the right conditions. As with any of these types of agreements, however, it is best to have them reviewed by legal counsel prior to implementation.

31. B. Wrongful discharge—also called *wrongful termination*—occurs when an employer terminates an employee for an unlawful reason such as discrimination, failing to break the law on behalf of an employer, or exercising their rights granted by law (right to vote, whistleblowing, etc.).

32. D. The concept of "just cause" is that employees may expect that employment at will does not apply to them. This condition may be met only when there is an employment contract (written or implied) or when the employee is covered by a collective bargaining agreement.

33. B. "Just cause" is a concept that describes an employer's justification for taking employment action. It cannot be used as a reason for termination if the employee refused to break the law or exercised a statutory right.

34. B. An employee's perception of fair treatment is influenced by many factors. In this scenario, Augustine believes that the outcome (pay increases) was unfair.

35. D. Employers may choose to adopt arbitration practices for many reasons. One is the rising cost of legal fees associated with fighting employment-related disputes. Another is to ensure employees receive due process. Regardless of the reasons, arbitration best practices include a waiver of employee right to sue after an agreement has been settled; the use of a professional, neutral arbitrator; and a signed, written agreement that has been approved by counsel.

36. C. Companies must take steps to address employee privacy concerns in all HR practices. This includes properly storing records that have information related to an employee's medical condition or history.

37. C. Employee recognition practices are similar to pay practices in that they can be entitlement-oriented or performance-based. Recognition for sales efforts (quotas, new customers, account retention) is based on employee performance.

38. A. Diversity programs have many components that, when combined, make them an effective tool used to promote a positive organizational culture. These components can include committees, work teams, training, mentoring, and the evaluation of results for reporting and refinement.

39. D. What starts out as mere lack of etiquette or discourteous behavior can quickly escalate if left unchecked. For this reason, it is imperative that HR address expected standards of behavior in an employee handbook as well as in practice.

40. C. Employee recognition programs can be individually based or company-wide. They can be especially effective when employees understand how their behaviors contributed to the company's success.

41. D. The best defense against a claim of defamation is to be truthful, clear, and unequivocal when providing an employment reference. Many employers are also able to avoid a charge of defamation by only giving out information that is factual, such as dates of employment or a job title. In some cases, former employees will provide written authorization for a previous employer to share information from their personnel record, providing some management of risk against a defamation charge.

42. B. A grievance is a formal written complaint filed when an employee has moved beyond simply feeling dissatisfied. In a union environment, HR and the union will most likely have a formal grievance procedure.

43. C. Named after the court case that established them, Weingarten rights grant covered employees the right to have representation in disciplinary meetings.

44. D. If an employee is dismissed or otherwise harmed by a decision that violated his rights to representation in disciplinary meetings, he may be entitled to back pay and reinstatement.

45. D. Grievance arbitration involves a neutral third party to settle disputes that are rooted in different interpretations of a labor contract. This process is different from *issues* arbitration, which utilizes a neutral third party to settle disputes regarding how a contract will be written.

46. B. As a result of the general decline in union membership over the years, unions have targeted specific industries and types of workers. The unionization of professional workers such as nurses and engineers are examples of this.

47. A. Unions have successfully organized low-skilled workers mainly because of the hard work, low pay, and difficult working conditions characterized by these types of jobs.

48. C. The growing percentage of women in the workforce has forced unions to alter their focus on issues that matter to this demographic. These issues include child, paid family leave, maternity leave, pay equity, and flexible work arrangements, just to name a few.

49. B. Progressive discipline policies involve the establishment of a series of steps. These steps often include some variation of a series of verbal, written, and final written warnings that, if unmet, will eventually result in termination.

50. D. Gathering feedback is an important element of employee relations systems. It is the only way HR may design or recommend changes that will truly influence employee satisfaction. Common ways to obtain feedback include suggestion boxes, focus groups, and employee surveys.

51. B. The rise of technology has opened up many digital options for HR seeking to obtain employee feedback. Teleconferencing involves satellite technology that is designed to link facilities and groups for the purpose of exchanging feedback, information, and ideas.

52. D. Organizations have many internal options to choose from when needing to communicate with their talent. These methods include employee newsletters, videos, and postings on company intranets, memos, and staff meetings.

53. D. At the center of taking any action against a worker is the need to consider employee rights. In this scenario, there are several labor laws that may be applicable for Taylor's case. At this stage, HR's best role is to help the supervisor gather and review as much relevant information as possible before making a decision to proceed with the discipline.

54. A. HR often serves in an advisory capacity when the need for discipline arises. Generally, it is up to the direct supervisor or manager to ultimately make the decision to discipline their employee.

55. B. Most employees genuinely want to succeed in their work environment. When they clearly understand the behavioral expectations and outcomes, most will apply the proper levels of self-discipline to be successful in their jobs.

56. C. Positive discipline approaches are characterized by constructive partnerships between the employee, manager, and human resources. The goal is to clearly communicate the expectations for behavior and engage in joint problem-solving.

57. D. The positive approach to discipline focuses on joint problem-solving as opposed to a series of progressive consequences of employee behavioral issues. It requires extensive training for managers and supervisors to both understand and apply behavioral science theories such motivation and performance coaching.

58. A. Progressive discipline policies include a series of steps (verbal, written, final written, etc.) to address employee performance deficiencies. There are certain egregious offenses, however, in which an employee may be immediately discharged. These include falsifying an employment application, theft, and alcohol or drug use at work.

59. D. There are many reasons managers may hesitate to discipline their employees. Some supervisors are not effective conflict managers, while others may know that they (and others) are guilty of similar offenses. The fear of the company or they themselves being sued may also influence a manager's decision to take corrective action to resolve negative employee behaviors.

60. A. Notification requirements at the time of employee separation can vary greatly between federal and state regulations as well as between individual employer practices. Of the options, only the COBRA notification for continuation of health benefits is federally mandated for covered employers.

61. D. Written policies for the sake of having policies can cause employers all sorts of problems, from implementation to managing risk. It is important that human resources evaluate all current and potential policies to ensure that they are relevant, effective, and legal.

62. C. HR is often called in to help with investigations of employee wrongdoing. Of the options presented, confronting the employee and showing the proof of the theft should be enough to either get the employee to confess or to terminate the employee for cause.

63. C. Policies are general guidelines for both company and employee behaviors. Procedures, on the other hand, are more specific practices of how processes should be completed or systems should be implemented.

64. C. A rule is a specific guideline that serves to restrict certain employee behaviors. Often found in the handbook under "Code of Conduct," rules are written so there is very little interpretation needed as to their meaning.

65. D. There are many risks that can be created simply by the language used in a company handbook. The term *permanent employee* dilutes employment at will, and a probationary period—as opposed to an introductory period—does the same. Prohibiting social media use completely can erode an employee's right to engage in protected concerted activity under the National Labor Relations Act.

66. C. Disclaimers such as the one in the question are used to preserve the nature of at-will employment between the employer and employee.

67. B. Downward communication flows from executives, managers, and supervisors down to the employees.

68. C. Any type of suggestion system allows an upward flow of communication from employees to management.

69. D. Gathering feedback from both internal and external sources is a critical task for human resources. Feedback can be used to recognize, reward, and discipline employees but also to inform organizational decision-making to improve procedures.

70. C. The General Duty standard emphasizes the need for employers to protect employees from hazards, even in the absence of a specific directive (standard) to do so. In addition, they have a general duty to comply with all applicable standards that pertain to their workplace.

71. A. Security risks are those that affect the financial, physical, informational, or human assets of an organization.

72. C. Security risks are associated with financial operations and practices in addition to securing the physical assets of a business.

73. A. Employee embezzlement or theft is a type of fraud committed against the employer and is subject to prosecution.

74. D. Incidents such as natural disasters, terrorism, workplace violence, and loss of utilities are threats to more than just employee safety. These events may disrupt services from resources such as police and fire, as well as impact a business's ability to continue offering services or shipping products.

75. B. A human resource audit is a type of assessment used to gather information about an organization that can be used in decision-making. Evaluating the HCMP is useful to gather data about employee skillsets and future plans to make decisions about current and future staffing levels.

76. B. Any time there is an uptick in near misses, a company should take notice. Encouraging employees to speak up will help identify potential hazards and allow for a preventive response. Site walk-throughs can help identify hazards, as well as give HR the opportunity to talk with employees about what might help to keep a near miss from becoming an injury.

77. B. Management by objectives (MBO) is characterized by an agreement between a manager and employee that ideally cascades down from a company's strategic plan.

78. D. Employers often hesitate to even mention the word *union* for fear that it will give the employees ideas. However, a nonunion philosophy serves to communicate to employees the employer's desire to hear their grievances directly and provides the employer with the opportunity to respond before they are required to do so under strict regulations.

79. B. In personality theory, conscientiousness has been linked to successful employee outcomes. This trait is characterized by employees who follow all rules and procedures and have a general sense of care about the well-being of others.

80. C. Organizational citizenship behaviors have been linked to individual traits including conscientiousness, courtesy, altruism, sportsmanship, and civic virtue.

81. A. Employee engagement is a term that has lacked coherent application in many organizations. Organizational scientists have found some agreement, however, in that engagement behaviors include the investment of personal energies such as physical, emotional, and cognitive into the work tasks themselves.

82. D. A bureaucratic organization is one that is characterized by administrative workflow, rigid policies, and procedures. These types of structures evolved from the shift of small family-owned farms and businesses to organizations that employed hundreds of people as the result of the Industrial Revolution.

83. C. The focus of the humanistic theories of motivation is on the psychological conditions under which people work. According to these theories, the psychological conditions under which employees work are just as important as the environmental conditions.

84. A. Systems theories view organizations as a "whole" entity as opposed to focusing on a single part. These theories consider the inputs, the throughputs, and the outputs of a company along with the context (political, economic) in which they perform.

85. B. Traditional application of many motivation theories is based on increasing rewards or punishment. Studies have found that this does not work when it comes to improving creativity; in fact, it actually narrows the focus to simply getting the reward. Increasing diversity has been shown to open up creative processes by gaining multiple perspectives and different ways of thinking.

86. D. Intrinsic rewards are those that come from within. Employees who perform because they like the work or take pride in their effort are said to be intrinsically motivated.

87. D. Management as a practice has had to evolve as the nature of business has evolved. Traditional forms of management made up of hierarchies, policies, and rules are most effective in environments where high degrees of compliance are necessary or desired.

88. B. Emotional labor is the degree of effort it takes to manage emotions at work. In customer service settings, for example, an employee may get frustrated with an angry customer but must mask their true feelings to meet customer demands.

89. D. The fundamental attribution error states that people have a tendency to attribute other people's negative behavior to an internal character flaw and their own negative behaviors to a cause of the situation.

90. B. A gainsharing plan is a type of compensation that is tied to performance. It can be the result of either increased revenue or cost-saving activities.

91. A. Equity theories of motivation pivot on the idea that employees are motivated most by when their inputs (what they put into the job) are equal to the rewards (what they receive in return).

92. C. Change uncertainty is a source of stress for employees that is directly tied to changes in the workplace. It occurs in the context of employees being uncertain as to how a change will affect them personally, their department, or the company as a whole.

93. D. Organizational development consists of a series of interventions that may address strategic, operational, or human resource–style challenges. As a result, OD consists of scientific theories designed to improve organizational effectiveness and employee well-being, all of which must be applied in a workplace setting.

94. B. Nominal groups and the Delphi technique are often confused with one another. A nominal group can meet face to face, but the discussions are more tightly controlled/facilitated than in the Delphi approach. Both are used to reach consensus in decision-making.

95. D. Franchising is a business structure in which one company licenses the rights to another business to use their brand, supply chain, and workflow practices. Ownership remains separate in this type of structure.

96. C. Zero-based budgets are not built upon the previous year's spending. This approach allows departments to build budgets that are more in line with a company's strategic plan and business objectives.

97. A. Co-sourcing is an alternative staffing strategy that can lend itself to several positive outcomes. Often used when talent is scarce or for project-based work, co-sourcing can result in cost savings when leveraged properly.

98. D. Business operating expenses such as salaries, rent, equipment, technology, benefits, and more all make up a company's overhead. For HR purposes, labor is often the largest expense, followed closely by employee benefits.

99. C. Division of labor is a term that identifies the responsibilities of each individual within a department or company.

100. A. The key distinction between line and staff management is revenue generation. Line managers are those who are responsible for processes and people who generate revenue for a business. Staff managers are those who support line managers such as accounting, IT, and HR.

101. B. There are many external sources of information related to how HR makes decisions. In terms of credibility, HR should rely on evidence-based tools such as governmental, academic, or scientific resources that have been proven valid and reliable.

102. C. Anchoring bias in negotiations occurs when an individual starts with a higher dollar amount, thus anchoring that amount in your mind as a starting point. In this case, you did not plan to pay on the high end of the range, but the candidate starting point was high enough to get you to change your behavior and offer more than intended.

103. A. Employee knowledge, talents, and skills that add value to an organization all make up what is called human capital. The availability of future skillsets for which an employer may compete is included in this category; for this reason, human capital management plans focus on both acquiring and retaining a qualified workforce.

104. B. VUCA conditions are the "new normal" for business and HR. The best answer then is to plan for multiple scenarios and outcomes, including both best- and worst-case situations.

105. A. While all the conditions in the options contribute to high turnover, lack of non-legally required time-off flexibility for employees is the most contradictory to a company that states that serving employees is their highest value.

106. D. Transactional orientation and onboarding practices include automating processes such as Form I-9 and W-4 processing. Transactional practices increase efficiencies through automation while at the same time helping employers manage the risks associated with processing errors.

107. D. As McDonald's Corporation discovered, certain practices with its franchisees led to a charge that the corporation indirectly controlled the conditions of employees, causing them to "ostensibly" believe that they were employees of McDonald's Corporation, not only of the franchise. For this reason, the National Labor Relations Board revised their definition of joint employment, and franchise employees were allowed to sue the corporation and franchisee in a class action wage and hour lawsuit.

108. B. Malcolm Knowles conducted foundational research in andragogy—how adults learn. One finding was that adults orient toward learning that is focused on practical problem-solving or immediate use. Children, however, are taught to orient more toward general knowledge to be used at a future date.

109. A. A quartile compensation strategy seeks to align wage bands to the relevant labor market. It relies on valid market data to properly build wage ranges, from which employee pay decisions are made.

110. B. Entitlement forms of pay are those that reward employees for years of service or for loyalty. A cost-of-living adjustment is not given based on any particular performance criteria; therefore, it is a form of entitlement pay.

111. C. The Department of Justice (DOJ) is responsible for litigation related to violations of the Sherman Antitrust act. This act prohibits price fixing of any sort, including market-based pay.

112. D. A foreign subsidiary is a legal term defining ownership. A company that is more than 50 percent owned or controlled by a parent company in another country is a foreign subsidiary.

113. D. Fiduciary responsibility applies to many individuals with positions of authority within an organization. Fiduciary responsibility requires that these individuals act without self-interest, making quality decisions that serve all company stakeholders.

114. B. Nongovernment organizations are gaining in popularity as a tool to help global and multinational businesses engage in social responsibility initiatives. NGOs are typically nonprofit, voluntary, and independent of any particular government.

115. D. Many experts believe that the use of self-funded health insurance "captives" will only continue to grow. This is because businesses are finding that they can more effectively control the cost of benefits plans through the use of data to shape benefits offerings to employees and predict exposure. It also allows employers to purchase stop-loss insurance, which can be used to cover the costs of catastrophic years.

116. D. Human resource professionals have high ethical standards that must be adhered to. This includes not using their decision-making authority to meet personal needs or commitments.

117. A. Many HR practitioners and businesses use the terms *work engagement* and *job satisfaction* interchangeably. Organizational science has found that work engagement refers to how employees feel about the job tasks, whereas organizational commitment refers to how employees feel about the company as a whole.

118. D. Job analysis is the process used to define a job in terms of its component tasks from which all other HR practices and strategies may be built.

119. C. A rolling average—sometimes called a moving average—is used to calculate an average for a specific period of time. In this scenario, as a new month is added, the oldest number is dropped.

120. A. When considering the implementation of any new technology, HR must consider the needs that the company is seeking to meet. A needs analysis will provide information to help calculate the return on the investment, as well as identify what information suppliers should include in a request for proposal.

121. C. The main purpose of building a business case is to help an employer make a decision on a particular course of action. This includes a description of the potential risks of taking—or in some cases, not taking—action.

122. B. The Department of Labor allows private employers to commission polygraph tests for employees under certain conditions, including when an employee is suspected of theft or embezzlement. The administration of the test, however, must be done by a licensed professional, with the results kept confidential.

123. A. High-involvement organizations are those that seek to give authority to all levels of employees. These organizations are defined by flat-line structures, transparency, and pay for performance compensation programs.

124. B. The job characteristics model describes the influence of job design on worker engagement and ownership. Specifically, research has found that allowing employees to control their work (autonomy) and providing them with meaningful feedback increases a sense of responsibility and ownership of their jobs.

125. D. A negatively accelerating learning curve is characterized by rapid learning at the beginning of training, with a tapering off as the skills are mastered.

126. B. Learning circles are called many things (Socratic circles, quality circles, etc.), but all have a similar purpose. Learning circles are generally organized around a theme or purpose and are characterized by diversity, respect, and collaboration toward success in specific outcomes or targets.

127. C. Pay equity laws are trending more and more in the United States. In this case, pay history bans are designed to reduce the systemic pay disparities between men and women—if women are paid unequally and employers pay based on salary history, it stands to reason then that asking about salary history will perpetuate the disparities.

128. C. Organizational justice issues around compensation have an absolute impact on the nonmonetary value of total rewards. Justice issues include the manner in which rewards are allocated; employee behavior will be altered to the extent that rewards are earned and that rewards are discretionary.

129. A. Emotional intelligence is considered to have three aspects: self-awareness, other awareness, and emotional regulation. Emotional regulation is the ability of individuals to recover rapidly from an experienced emotion.

130. D. Organizational science has spent a lot of time trying to understand the impact that emotional intelligence has on individual employee performance. A review of the studies found that there was only a modest correlation between EI levels and employee performance. Studies have found, however, that EI can be learned; it varies from individual to individual; and it is distinct from but positively related to other types of intelligence, such as IQ.

131. B. With multiple generations in the workplace, it can be difficult to balance the different priorities for career development. Boomers generally are seeking monetary gains and stability along with flexibility. Immediate rewards and career portability are valued by generation Xers, and millennials gravitate toward parallel careers and choice.

132. B. Surface-level diversity is what many think of when they hear the term *diversity*, mainly because they are observable. Surface-level diversity includes traits such as sex, race, and age.

133. A. Deep-level diversity includes the attitudes and beliefs of each individual. Studies have shown that when measured and understood, deep-level diversity factors may contribute more to individual and organizational performance than its counterpart, surface-level diversity.

134. B. One main consideration for an employer seeking to adopt an alternative overtime pay calculation of the fluctuating workweek is whether the employee's schedule actually fluctuates on a week-to-week basis.

135. D. Teams often take on a single personality made up of the job attitudes of its members. Social pressure from teammates can strengthen either a positive or negative team attitude. Emotional contagion occurs when a negative (or positive) mood infects the attitudes of a team.

136. C. Of the "golden" category of executive benefits, a lifejacket is used to ensure an executive remains with a company after an event such as a merger or acquisition.

137. B. Phantom stock is one way to pay employees for company performance without having to grant actual shares.

138. A. Risk mitigation techniques are focused on minimizing the risk, which in this case is losing good employees to competitors and being unable to satisfy their book of business.

139. D. Implied contracts can be established if HR does not take care to word information properly. A best practice is to use statements of at-will employment on documents such as job offers and job descriptions. It is also important that supervisors and other performance raters are trained to avoid making performance statements such as "you'll have a job here for life if you keep performing this way" to avoid claims of an implied contract.

140. C. Assessing the business impact of any type of operational disruption (natural or manmade) is the focus of a business impact analysis (BIA). HR should consider lost or delayed sales or income, increased expenses (overtime, outsourcing), potential regulatory fines, and other impacts that may be the result of a business disruption.

141. B. Controls that are introduced to reduce workplace hazards may be administrative, engineering, or the requirement of personal protective equipment. In this example, a process was changed to reduce hazard exposure, which is a type of engineering control as defined by OSHA.

142. A. OSHA recommends that employers both inspect and respond to employee safety hazards that may exist due to poor lighting at workstations. This includes assessing the type and intensity of station lighting along with the presence (or lack of) glare/shadow controls that can contribute to eye strain.

143. B. A global pandemic of the flu (such as H1N1 in 2009) is a threat that occurs when a new strain of the virus emerges. New strain pandemics are resistant to seasonal vaccines and can spread quickly. For that reason, employers should have flexible attendance policies that encourage workers to stay home when sick to avoid the spread of the disease.

144. C. The high-profile nature of the multitude of 2017 and 2018 sexual harassment claims in the workplace is bound to change the organizational climate in some way.

Anti-harassment and training responsibilities have been around for a long time, but the employer culture of retaliation seemed to discourage reporting in many of the cases. While difficult to predict, it seems that the stigma of reporting and increased credibility of worker charges forecasts an increase in harassment claims that HR departments should be prepared to investigate.

145. D. Stress due to work or non–work-related circumstances is a real issue that employer safety programs may need to address. According to the CDC, symptoms may include tension headaches, excessive absenteeism, unusual or out-of-character behaviors, crying, and difficulty making decisions.

146. B. There are many methods employers may choose to conduct an assessment of the specific types of risks associated with sending expatriates to various parts of the world. In this case, the assessment may be begin by accessing the United States' Centers for Disease Control's global health website, which includes up-to-date information on the global health risks in various countries.

147. D. The European Agency for Safety and Health at Work (EU-OSHA), trade unions, and works councils all have taken some measure of responsibility for designing and enforcing safety standards that protect workers.

148. A. Job analysis serves as the fundamental starting point for many HR processes, both operationally and strategically. When done properly, job analysis both defines the work but also identifies the relevant criteria that are important for success. From that criteria, employment tests designed to predict performance can be selected.

149. C. Cyber-vetting is the process of using the Internet to determine an applicant's qualifications for a job. Some studies estimate that more than 70 percent of employers use social media to screen candidates before hiring.

150. C. Studies have found that by allowing individuals with non–work-related injuries to participate in return to work programs, these individuals feel more in control of their responsibilities at work. Helping individuals struggling with disabilities through RTW programs changes their focus from what is a "problem" to the tools they may use for effective management related to their work, attendance, and other outcomes.

Index

C

X

Z

Comprehensive Online Learning Environment

Register to gain one year of FREE access to the online interactive learning environment and test bank to help you study for your PHR and SPHR certification exams—included with your purchase of this book!

The online test bank includes the following:

- **Practice Test Questions** to reinforce what you've learned
- **Bonus Practice Exams** to test your knowledge of the material

Go to http://www.wiley.com/go/sybextestprep to register and gain access to this comprehensive study tool package.

Register and Access the Online Test Bank

To register your book and get access to the online test bank, follow these steps:

1. Go to bit.ly/SybexTest.
2. Select your book from the list.
3. Complete the required registration information, including answering the security verification to prove book ownership. You will be emailed a PIN code.
4. Follow the directions in the email or go to https://www.wiley.com/go/sybextestprep.
5. Enter the PIN code you received and click the "Activate PIN" button.
6. On the Create an Account or Login page, enter your username and password, and click Login. A "Thank you for activating your PIN!" message will appear. If you don't have an account already, create a new account.
7. Click the "Go to My Account" button to add your new book to the My Products page.